The challenge for the comprehensive school

By the same author

Social relations in a secondary school
Interpersonal relations and education

The challenge for the comprehensive school

Culture, curriculum and community

David H. Hargreaves

First published 1982
by Routledge & Kegan Paul Ltd
Reprinted 1982, 1983, 1984, 1986 and 1988

Reprinted 1990 by Routledge
11 New Fetter Lane, London EC4P 4EE

© *1982 David H. Hargreaves*

Set in IBM Baskerville 11/12 by
Academic Typing Service, Gerrards Cross, Bucks
and printed in Great Britain by
St Edmundsbury Press Ltd, Bury St Edmunds, Suffolk

ISBN 0-415-05899-6

Contents

For Harry Rée
another educator extraordinary

The conception of education as a social process and function
has no definite meaning until we define the kind of society
we have in mind.
John Dewey, *Democracy and Education*, 1916

One other field in which the growth of democracy seems
urgently necessary is the ordinary process of decision about
the development of our communities.
Raymond Williams, *The Long Revolution*, 1961

The general purpose of education is to foster the growth
of what is individual in each human being, at the same time
harmonizing the individuality thus educed with the organic
unity of the social group to which the individual belongs . . .
in this process aesthetic education is fundamental.
Herbert Read, *Education through Art*, 1943

Preface

An academic working in the field of educational studies has two principal audiences. First, there is the population of his own students, whether they are young teachers in initial training or highly experienced teachers following advanced courses and higher degrees; second, there are his professional colleagues, fellow academics. But there is a third audience, that which I have come to think of as the 'real teachers' or those teachers in schools who are neither students nor academics but who are kind enough to invite me to speak at their school or their conferences.

Of the three audiences it is the last which tends to be most fiercely critical of an academic educationist, and over the years I have learnt much from them and their skill in posing blunt and penetrating questions. Left to themselves, academics spend most of their time trading alternative diagnoses of education in relation to various theories and to research evidence; the policy implications are often of secondary importance. Practising teachers expect the social scientist to reverse this priority, at least from time to time; a diagnosis is 'academic' in the pejorative sense unless it is a backcloth to a specification of how the education system could be improved. In this book I have drawn upon a range of sociological ideas and concepts. Yet I am aware that practising teachers are impatient with the technical vocabulary (jargon) of sociologists and find recent writing by sociologists of education rather difficult to follow. This is not surprising; whilst I have no wish to defend sociological obscurantism or shoddy writing, I accept that sociologists will often need to write primarily for one another rather than for the general reader. Because this book is directed to the third audience of practising teachers rather than to my academic colleagues, I refer to recent sociological writing in less detail (and sometimes with fewer criticisms) than I would wish, and spend more time than is customary on directions for educational change. I hope, however, that the book will encourage the reader to follow up some of the sociological references and through them be able to tune into some of the issues with which sociologists of education are currently concerned.

Like many of my colleagues, I am convinced that there should be more dialogue between academics and teachers; this book is no more than the opening statement – if a rather lengthy one – of what is intended to be a conversation between academics and teachers. So if these opening remarks are phrased simply and without too much detail or qualification, then that is surely appropriate. Both parties will have much more to say to one another.

I am greatly indebted to Connie Kelland, a truly professional secretary, for typing the manuscript.

1 The two curricula of schooling

I had acquired the one faculty with which every school
infallibly endows its pupils, that of being bored. It is very
important, of course, that every child should in the course
of time become fitted up with this negative capability. If
they didn't have it, they'd never put up with the jobs they
are going to get, most of them, on leaving school. Boredom, or the ability to endure it, is the hub on which the
whole universe of work turns. The genius and the chimpanzee are impatient of it, and here and there in a civilised
society occur individuals who hark back to these ancestral
types and are resistant to scholarship. Their subsequent
careers vary. They may be kicked about and generally
deplored like the genius, put behind bars like the ape, or
supposing they manage to combine the two acts and show
the public chimpanzee playing genius, or genius playing
chimp, then they get applauded as Great Personalities.
Most of us, however, are unable to survive being educated.
We learn reading and boredom, writing and boredom,
arithmetic and boredom, and so on according to the
curriculum, till in the end it is quite certain you can put us
to the most boring job there is and we'll endure it.[1]

This is Jack Common's description of his working-class
education in Northumbria at the beginning of this century.
He realizes, with the hindsight of an adult's reflections on
childhood, that the school teaches not one curriculum, as
we usually think, but two. The first or formal curriculum
consists of the 'subjects' that the teachers intentionally plan
and teach in lessons with their familiar and distinctive subject

1

labels. The second curriculum, now often called the 'hidden' curriculum, is not intended or planned by teachers and so tends to remain unnoticed. Like the official one, the hidden curriculum has its own special subjects and pedagogy; and for Jack Common the main subject is boredom and the capacity to endure it. For working-class pupils in particular it is these hidden lessons that must be learned in school; it is the hidden, not the formal, curriculum which most effectively prepares the young for the world beyond school.

Despite the massive reforms in curriculum and pedagogy since those days, there are still many bored pupils in contemporary British secondary schools. In a recent national survey of Britain's sixteen-year-olds,[2] almost a third did not like school and just over a third liked it very much. Over half these pupils thought homework boring. Most adults think of childhood and school days as a happy and carefree time – the happiest days of one's life, it is said. But for most adults, I suspect, these happy memories are not strongly associated with school lessons, but rather with the freedom and leisure of youth and the joys and despair of youthful friendships. To the visiting adult, with vivid memories of his or her own schooldays, life in school today seems very much happier and more interesting. But pupils themselves can make no such comparisons, and like young people in every age are reluctant to profit vicariously from the experience of their parents. To many pupils today school is as boring as it was for Jack Common's contemporaries, notwithstanding the objective improvements that have been made over the last half-century.

As part of my work I sometimes follow a class or group of pupils for a whole day – a privilege sadly denied to most teachers – to try to capture how the school day appears to pupils. It is, for most of them, a curiously fragmented experience. The day is broken into blocks, punctuated by bells every forty minutes or so, when pupils must move from classroom to classroom, with a change of teacher and subject. Not long ago I followed two girls, of average intellectual capacity in the teachers' view and with the general indifference to school that characterizes many fifteen-year-old girls. Though not particularly naughty or stupid, they did occasionally come into conflict with their teachers. The school operated a most elaborate system of 'setting' and options. With considerable ingenuity these two girls had manipulated the system so that they always went to the same classes together. At the end of the day I tried to summarize their response to their schooling. There had been no hostile rebellion from them, though they had been rebuked many times for 'talking' and for not paying attention. School lessons for them appeared to be like seven very dull television programmes, which could not be switched off. They did not want to watch and made little effort to do so; occasionally the volume rose to a very high level, so they listened; occasionally the programme became sufficiently interesting to command their attention, but it was never more than a momentary diversion from the general monotony. Part of the problem appeared to be that they were not, in fact, seven new independent programmes. All of them were serials, which demanded some knowledge of earlier episodes. Indeed, most of the teachers generously provided a recapitulation of earlier episodes at the beginning of every lesson. But the girls had lost track of the story long ago. Two of the programmes were, in fact, repeats; since their first broadcast had aroused no interest in the girls, it is not surprising that the repeat evoked no new response. So these two girls responded as most of us do when faced with broadcasts of low quality that we cannot switch off: they talked through the broadcast whenever they could. The easiest form of resistance was to treat the lessons as background noise which from time to time interrupted their utterly absorbing sisterly gossip. And of course they made the most of the commercial breaks, as it were: they were the first to leave each lesson and the last to arrive at the next one. In many respects it is a marvellous anticipation of their adult roles, where these features of school will be replaced by the noise of a factory, the intrusions of the supervisor's exhortations, the monotony of unwanted routine jobs. It is not yet fully appreciated by these two girls, who dream of the joys of leaving school and going to work for money. They may, like Jack Common, see the parallel later.

Although Jack Common's account is neat, the insight into

3

the existence of the hidden curriculum is not unique to him. One of its most perceptive investigators is John Holt, a teacher. That a pupil-turned-adult, like Jack Common, should recognize it is not perhaps surprising, for many pupils retain their capacities to 'see through' teachers' pretensions; but that a *teacher* should look behind the opacity of his own intentions and actions is remarkable. In fact it was the achievement of several years' hard work and sustained self-analysis. John Holt kept a diary. And he learned how to watch his pupils, especially when they did not think they were under observation. In the diary Holt explored, painfully and slowly, what he saw, what he did, what he felt.[3]

3 December 1958

We had been chatting about something or other and everyone seemed in a relaxed frame of mind, so I said, 'You know, there's something I'm curious about and I wonder if you'd tell me.' They said, 'What?' I said, 'What do you think, what goes through your mind, when the teacher asks you a question and you don't know the answer?'

It was a bombshell. Instantly a paralysed silence fell on the room. Everyone stared at me with what I've learned to recognise as a tense expression. For a long time there wasn't a sound. Finally Ben, who is bolder than most, broke the tension, and also answered my question, by saying in a loud voice, 'Gulp!'

He spoke for everyone. They all began to clamour and all said the same thing, that when the teacher asked them a question and they didn't know the answer they were scared half to death. I was flabbergasted . . . I asked them why they felt gulpish. They said they were afraid of failing, afraid of being kept back, afraid of being called stupid, afraid of feeling themselves stupid.

What is most surprising of all is how much fear there is in school. . . . Most children in school are very scared. Like good soldiers, they control their fears, live with them, and adjust to them. But the trouble is, and here is a vital difference between school and war, the adjustments children make to their fears are almost wholly bad, destructive of their intelligence and capacity.

4

For John Holt the main subject of the hidden curriculum is not boredom but fear. But the fear is not very obvious to teachers, for it is carefully controlled, even by young children. One of the basic lessons of the hidden curriculum of fear is that the pupil must learn not to betray his fear to the teacher, who will be upset at the idea that a pupil should be afraid; part of the fear that must be controlled is the fear of upsetting the teacher. Even when the official curriculum is directed to the 'fun' of playing a 'game', the hidden curriculum of fear can be effectively taught:

16 June 1959

A year ago I was wondering how a child's fears might influence his strategies. This year's work has told me. The strategies of most of these kids have been consistently self-centred, self-protective, aimed above all else at avoiding trouble, embarrassment, punishment, disapproval, or loss of status. This is particularly true of the ones who have had a tough time in school. When they get a problem, I can read their thoughts on their faces. 'Am I going to get this right? Probably not; what'll happen to me when I get it wrong? Will the teacher get mad? Will the other kids laugh at me? Will my mother and father hear about it? Will they keep me back this year? Why am I so dumb?' And so on.

Even . . . when I did all I could to make the work non-threatening, I was continually amazed and appalled to see the children hedging their bets, covering their losses in advance, trying to fix things so that whatever happened they could feel they had been right or, if wrong, no more wrong than anyone else. . . . They are fence-straddlers, afraid ever to commit themselves – and at the age of ten. Playing games like Twenty Questions, which one might have expected them to play for fun, many of them were concerned only to put up a good front, to look as if they knew what they were doing, whether they did or not.

These self-limiting and self-defeating strategies are dictated above all else by fear. For many years I have been asking myself why intelligent children act unintelligently at school.

5

The two curricula of schooling

To succeed, perhaps even to survive, in school a pupil must, in response to this alleged curriculum of fear, acquire the complex strategic skills which constitute the art of pleasing the teacher and satisfying his demands. Teachers are, of course, aware of many of these strategies; they do not need Holt to tell them that they undermine the objectives of the official curriculum, destroy intelligence and negate true learning. Teachers recognize the strategies, but often mistake their source, for they put them down to 'childish silliness'. In fact, they are a highly rational and intelligent adaptation to the hidden curriculum of fear which passes unnoticed by the teacher.

It is not that pupils are insufficiently articulate to explain the hidden curricula of boredom or fear to their teachers; the problem is that they lack the power to define what should count as the reality of schooling. Their legitimate criticism is so easily discounted by teachers who reformulate it as 'insolence'. From time to time pupils betray their defensive strategies, sometimes because they lack the social skills needed to hide them and sometimes because they find a sufficiently trusting teacher to acknowledge them openly. Anita Halliday tells the story of a pupil whom she questioned for exceptionally poor handwriting. 'Well,' replied the pupil, 'I have to write like that so you can't see how many mistakes I've made.' Occasionally pupils express their point of view more systematically, as in the famous *Letter to a Teacher* by the children of the School of Barbiana in Italy. Like Holt, they began by keeping little note-books from which they patiently and slowly created one of the most trenchant attacks on school ever published. They knew the fear that Holt discovered:[4]

> During the oral exams my heart would stop beating. I found that I was wishing on others what I did not want done to myself. I stopped listening to the lessons. I would think only about the oral exams coming up in the next hour. . . . During those oral exams the whole class sinks either into laziness or terror. Even the boy being questioned wastes his time. He keeps taking cover, avoids what he understands least, keeps stressing the things he knows

6

well. To make you happy we need know only how to sell our goods. And how to fill empty spaces with empty words.

Teachers and adults become blind to the hidden curriculum because that is not what schooling is officially supposed to be about. We believe our own grown-up propaganda. One needs the eyes of a child or a stranger to see. It makes sense, then, that perhaps the greatest exponent of the hidden curriculum is Jules Henry, an American anthropologist who treated his own culture as if he were an anthropologist coming from another, quite different culture to study his native land. Fortunately for us among the institutions he chose to investigate was the school. Like Holt's work, Henry's account is based on meticulous observation of classroom life. Here is one of the many incidents recorded by him:[5]

> Boris had trouble reducing 12/16 to the lowest terms and could only get as far as 6/8. The teacher asked him quietly if that was as far as he could reduce it. She suggested he 'think'. Much heaving up and down and waving of hands by the other children, all frantic to correct him. Boris pretty unhappy, probably mentally paralysed. The teacher quiet, patient, ignores the others and concentrates with look and voice on Boris. She says, 'Is there a bigger number than two that you can divide into the two parts of the fraction?' After a minute or two she becomes more urgent, but there is no response from Boris. She then turns to the class and says, 'Well, who can tell Boris what the number is?' A forest of hands appears, and the teacher calls Peggy, who says that four may be divided into the numerator and the denominator.

Here is a mundane little scene, at first sight quite unworthy of comment. It is an event with which we are all, as teacher or pupil, very familiar; it happens all the time and so hardly merits examination. Armed with Holt's insights, we can see here a classic illustration of the hidden curriculum of fear of failure. But Henry is not an educationist who detects here an adaptation to school alone and who seeks to tell teachers about the unintended effects they have on children's learning capacities. Henry is an anthropologist and for him it is through the hidden curriculum that the most basic and powerful cultural lessons of Western society are taught. Here is part of his commentary:

> Thus Boris's failure has made it possible for Peggy to succeed; his depression is the price of her exhilaration; his misery the occasion for her rejoicing. This is the standard condition of the American elementary school . . . so often somebody's success has been bought at the cost of someone's failure. To a Zuni, Hopi, or Dakota Indian, Peggy's performance would seem cruel beyond belief, for competition, the wringing of success from somebody's failure, is a form of torture foreign to those non-competitive redskins. Yet Peggy's action seems natural to us; and so it is. How else would you run our world? And since all but the brightest children have the constant experience that others succeed at their expense they cannot but develop an inherent tendency to hate – to hate the success of others, to hate others who are successful, and to be determined to prevent it. Along with this, naturally, goes the hope that others will fail. . . .
>
> Looked at from Boris's point of view, the nightmare at the blackboard was, perhaps, a lesson in controlling himself. . . . Such experiences imprint on the mind of every man in our culture the *Dream of Failure*, so that over and over again, night in, night out, even at the pinnacle of success, a man will dream not of success, but failure.
>
> The external nightmare is internalized for life. It is this dream that, above all other things, provides the fierce human energy required by technological drivenness. It is not so much that Boris was learning arithmetic, but that he was learning the essential nightmare. *To be successful in our culture one must learn to dream of failure.*

For Henry the school is the heartbeat of our culture and its drilling of cultural lessons into pupils is the primary, if nevertheless largely hidden, curriculum of schooling. In Holt's analysis the hidden curriculum is destructive of the official curriculum and so makes 'bad' pupils; in Henry's more radical analysis, as in Jack Common's, the hidden curriculum overwhelms the official curriculum and makes 'good' citizens who can fit into what they call their 'civilization'.

That the school through its hidden curriculum transmits cultural lessons is one of the themes of Ivan Illich in his well-known book, *Deschooling Society*, which proposed the abolition of schools and professional teachers. Illich begins with a relatively simple and reasonable proposition, that we have come to confuse education with schooling to the point where they have become synonymous. A major achievement of the hidden curriculum is that pupils are taught that learning can only occur in schools, and that learning is the result of teaching by a professional, qualified teacher. As with all the claims made for the hidden curriculum, it is difficult to provide *evidence* that this is what is taught; but if this is indeed one of the lessons of the hidden curriculum, we know that it is a false one. Perhaps the greatest learning achievement of man is the acquisition of language. Yet it is acquired very fully before the child enters school and the major 'teacher' is the mother. As yet the monopoly over teaching of the teaching profession does not extend to the requirement that mothers should be 'qualified' to teach their children their native language. For Illich this lesson of the hidden curriculum has profound effects, for schooling turns the formal curriculum into packages of knowledge, into commodities which must be passively consumed, or acquired like wealth in the form of examination certificates. It is the hidden curriculum, not the formal one, which educates modern man into his distinctive form, and the hidden curriculum transmits the same basic lesson wherever there are institutionalized schools, whatever the variation in the formal curriculum:[6]

> Other basic institutions might differ from one country to another: family, party, church or press. But everywhere the school system has the same structure, and everywhere its hidden curriculum has the same effect. Invariably, it shapes the consumer who values institutional commodities above the nonprofessional ministration of a neighbour.

9

Everywhere the hidden curriculum of schooling initiates the citizen to the myth that bureaucracies guided by scientific knowledge are efficient and benevolent. Everywhere this same curriculum instills in the pupil the myth that increased production will provide a better life. And everywhere it develops the habit of self-defeating consumption of services and alienating production, the tolerance for institutional dependence, and the recognition of institutional rankings. The hidden curriculum of school does all this *in spite of contrary efforts undertaken by teachers* and no matter what ideology prevails. [Italics added]

What teachers intend to do, especially through the formal curriculum, is much less successfully transmitted, according to Illich, than the contrary lesson of the hidden curriculum which teachers generally disregard.

Although many of the writers we have discussed so far differ over the main 'subjects' taught in the hidden curriculum, there seems to be a common assumption that the hidden curriculum is broadly the same for all pupils and affects them all in the same way. In contrast, some sociologists argue that the hidden curriculum varies in content according to the *social class* of the pupils and/or that the same elements of the hidden curriculum have a different impact on pupils of different social-class backgrounds. Most British teachers view sociological discussions of social class with some scepticism. 'Why', they ask the sociologist, 'do you always see *educational* issues in class terms?' There seem to be two related objections; the first is that social class is unduly emphasized in sociological accounts, and the second is that in contemporary society the significance of class has greatly declined.

There is no doubt that social class is amongst the most slippery and ambiguous concepts in the sociological vocabulary.[7] For most sociologists, social class is about the social structure of society and the differences between individuals and groups in occupation, social position, income, property and power. One aspect of the issue concerns the differential allocation and distribution of these valued goods, and another issue is the differential opportunities of access to these valued goods. Whether or not these social differences are merely differences or unjustifiable inequalities is naturally a matter of deep debate, both for sociologists and for members of society. In many surveys class is often measured by the simple fivefold Registrar General's scheme, which ranges from Class I professionals, managers and executives to Class V unskilled manual workers. This is then often reduced to a twofold scheme of non-manual 'middle classes' and manual 'working classes'. All sociologists recognize – though they do not always say so – that this is a considerable oversimplification. To call both an office clerk (whose father was an unskilled manual worker) and a High Court judge (whose father was a landed aristocrat) 'middle-class' is to display the bluntness of the classification. The same objection can be made when we lump together as 'working-class' the highly skilled craftsman in industry with the casual labourer. Among the working classes there is a long history of the 'labour aristocracy' and most observers recognize the difference between the 'rough' and the 'respectable' among the working class. Even the class loyalty and solidarity which is commonly attributed to the working class can probably be applied only to particular sections of the working class in particular areas, and in any case is mirrored in the social relations between certain sections of the upper middle classes. We must remember, however, that the Registrar General's scheme is merely a convenient, if very crude, index of social class; but this is not in itself an adequate argument that the phenomenon of social class which it seeks to measure does not have a very real existence. In any event it cannot be denied that many studies which have investigated the relationship between various educational phenomena and these admittedly crude indices of social class have shown clear and marked differences by social class. It is well known that the children of parents in manual occupations are, in comparison with the children of parents in non-manual occupations, likely to be in lower streams at school, to achieve less well in 'objective tests' and public examinations, to show less favourable attitudes to school and weaker aspirations, to be underestimated by their teachers, to leave school early and 'drop out' of further or higher education, and so on. Social class has proved itself to be a powerful tool for uncovering important individual differences among pupils, and represents the major academic contribution to understanding education from sociologists over the last thirty years. And these social-class effects persist in spite of many social and educational reforms.

At the same time sociological writing often seems to take little account of the very real changes that have taken place in the class structure over the last hundred years and in people's conceptions and experience of social class. It is patently true that for most people today the class hierarchy seems much less clear and rigid than it was in Victorian England; we are today much less aware of having a distinct station in life to which we must keep. To the modern eye even the novels or films of the 1930s and 1940s portray a vanishing class structure which seems quaint. Social hierarchy may still exist, but there has been considerable blurring of barriers within it. At the time of my writing, for instance, dustmen, who are traditionally near the bottom of the hierarchy, earn 12 per cent *more* than a civil-service clerical officer, traditionally a very respectable white-collar job. At the same time we have to remember that the clerk has better conditions of work, and probably better promotion prospects, greater access to important goods and services, and a better pension. For many people society seems much more 'open' than it was and the differences between people much less accentuated. Some sociologists would not deny that there have been changes, but would argue that the changes have been relatively slight and that the 'decline in deference' in class relations since the Second World War have created an illusion that class is disappearing. They can point to the facts, for example, that most of the economic resources in our society are still concentrated in very few hands or that the proportion of working-class students in university has hardly changed this century. Our conceptions of class may be changing, and many people, including teachers, may feel very unsure to which class they belong, but social hierarchy is certainly not dead. A salutary reminder of class differences is the half-hour journey from the 'stockbroker belt' suburbs of a city to the poor inner-city districts. The transition from the large detached houses in extensive, pleasant grounds to the tightly packed treeless streets of 'Coronation Street' terraces betrays the marked discrepancies in wealth and living conditions that still exist.

Such a journey would give a portrait of social class that is much closer to the sociologist's conception of social class than the desiccated groupings of the Registrar General's classification. For class is a complex social and cultural formation and each man can make sense of himself only in relation to his family, his kin and their forebears and the social and cultural worlds in which they lived, *and* in his relation to other people with different families, histories and cultures. Whenever in this book I speak of 'working-class' people, I am using a shorthand form; but I am thinking less of the analytical categories of social surveys and much more in terms of the complex communities that live in inner-city terraced cottages, in high-rise flats and in council estates. It should be easy for a teacher, especially, to bear this in mind, for anyone who has taught in a school serving such an area knows how different it is from the school which contains children from owner-occupied semi-detached and detached houses of a pleasant suburb.

The question is: do children experience a different hidden curriculum of schooling according to their social class? Bowles and Gintis in their influential book, *Schooling in Capitalist America* – the title informs us that the perspective is a Marxist one – answer boldly in the affirmative. Their claim, elaborating a theme implicit in Jack Common and partially argued by Illich, is that schools through the hidden curriculum achieve *social control*; that is, schools maintain and render legitimate (as a fair and natural process) a stratified or class-based society that is, in fact, profoundly unequal and unfair. The argument is complex and long; and it is controversial, as is the evidence they adduce to buttress the thesis. To comprehend it fully requires some understanding of the Marxist approach to political economy. Here, I shall approach it through two very simple ideas. The first is the fact, well known to everyone, that the school plays an important role in the allocation of the young to their subsequent

13

occupations. What and how well pupils do in school often affects the jobs pupils can and do choose to enter. It is one of the functions of the school to prepare the young for their place in the work-force. The second idea is what sociologists refer to as a 'conflict model' of schooling; that is, there is a fundamental conflict between what teachers and pupils want and expect from schooling. This conception was most pithily expressed by Willard Waller over fifty years ago when he described the school as:[8]

> a despotism in a perilous state of equilibrium . . . The teacher–pupil relationship is a form of institutionalized dominance and subordination. Teacher and pupil confront each other in the school with an original conflict of desires, and however much that conflict may be reduced in amount, or however much it may be hidden, it still remains. . . . Dominance and subordination in the schools are usually discussed as 'discipline'. On the objective side, discipline is a social arrangement whereby one person is able consistently to exert control over the action of others.

In the work of Bowles and Gintis these two ideas are skilfully brought together. Just as schools are hierarchical organizations with dominant teachers over subordinate pupils, so also are industrial and commercial organizations, with dominant managers over subordinate workers. There is a close parallel or correspondence between the social relations of schooling and those in the world of work; it is this which constitutes the hidden curriculum of schooling. Pupils are not slotted into the occupational structure in a random manner. The school system, though allegedly fair and meritocratic, helps to ensure that some pupils (mainly middle-class) move into occupations of dominance and others (mainly working-class) into positions of subordination. In this way the educational system helps the class structure to be maintained and reproduced from generation to generation:[9]

> The educational system operates in this manner *not so much through the conscious intentions of teachers* and

administrators in their day-to-day activities but through a close correspondence between the social relationships which govern personal interaction in the work place and the social relationships of the educational system. Specifically, the relationships of authority and control . . . replicate the hierarchical division of labour which dominates the work place. [Italics added]

Pupils who are destined for higher education, and thus for professional and managerial roles, are, as they progress through the educational system, subjected to social relations with their teachers which emphasize autonomy, independence and creativity. At the other end of the scale, those pupils (mainly working-class) who are destined for low-level manual occupations are subjected to custodial regimes which emphasize obedience to rules and passivity; it is they who are to become the docile work-force:

> The correspondence between the social relations of schooling and work accounts for the ability of the educational system to produce an amenable and fragmented labour force. The *experience of schooling, not merely the content of formal learning*, is central to this process. . . . The educational system, through the pattern of status distinction it fosters, reinforces the stratified consciousness on which the fragmentation of subordinate classes of production, the educational system must teach people to be properly subordinate and render them sufficiently fragmented in consciousness to preclude their getting together to shape their own material existence. . . . The perpetuation of the class structure requires that the hierarchical division of labour be reproduced in the consciousness of its participants. The educational system is one of the several reproduction mechanisms through which dominant elites seek to achieve this objective.

Bowles and Gintis's book was read by an unusually large number of practising teachers, since it was adopted as the main course text on an Open University sociology of education course followed by many teachers. Their reactions to the book varied considerably; some saw it merely as Marxist propaganda to be rejected, but for others the book came as a startling and unnerving revelation of the hidden functions of schooling. Certainly some of the claims in the book seem exaggerated. To anyone who lived through the winter of 1978–9 in Britain, the working-class labour force did not seem to be the docile and subservient workers described by Bowles and Gintis; if the educational system is seeking to promote this, it is apparently failing rather badly to do so. The correspondence between schooling and the class structure was much more apparent during the nineteenth century and the first two decades of the twentieth. It is significant that the Marxists frequently cite material from the last century, where the analysis is much more persuasive. It can be argued that writers such as Bowles and Gintis take too little account of the changes that have taken place in the class structure and in schooling since the last century. On the other hand, it can be argued that we understand the past so well because we are distanced from it and that our insight into the present is clouded by our belief that our present society is more just and equal. Patterns established in the last century may be attenuated today but it can be argued that they have by no means disappeared. Most teachers sense that Bowles and Gintis have captured an important truth, even though they may have exaggerated it. There is indeed a noticeable difference in the hidden curriculum of the social relations between teachers and pupils in a sixth form as contrasted with those in a low stream of fifteen-year-olds in an inner-city comprehensive school. It is difficult not to connect this with the occupational structure and the reproduction of the class structure. The correspondence may not be very strong, and one may be suspicious of any purported causal connection between the two, but the fit is, for teachers, uncomfortably close.

From this brief review of some of the major exponents of the hidden curriculum of school a rather confused picture emerges. Apparently it contains several 'subjects' and is taught by a variety of mechanisms; there is, however, general agreement that it is not intended by teachers, and so tends to pass unnoticed by them. In my analysis I wish to take some

ideas from them all: from John Holt, the anti-educational
nature of the hidden curriculum; from Jules Henry and Ivan
Illich, the argument that the hidden curriculum works
against the promotion of active, creative individuals and a
harmonious community; from Jack Common and Bowles
and Gintis, the negative impact of the hidden curriculum
on working-class pupils in particular and the idea of the
perpetuation of social injustice through schooling.

My argument is that our present secondary-school system,
largely through the hidden curriculum, exerts on many
pupils, particularly but by no means exclusively from the
working-class, a destruction of their dignity which is so
massive and pervasive that few subsequently recover from it.
To have dignity means to have a sense of being worthy, of
possessing creative, inventive and critical capacities, of having
the power to achieve personal and social change. When
dignity is damaged, one's deepest experience is of being
inferior, unable, and powerless. My argument is that our
secondary schools inflict such damage, in varying degrees,
on many of their pupils. It is not intended by the teachers,
the vast majority of whom seek and strive hard to give their
pupils dignity as I have defined it.

To find convincing evidence for this argument will be
difficult. Most of the hidden-curriculum literature offers two
related propositions: that the hidden curriculum makes a
greater impact on pupils than does the formal curriculum,
and that this is true for most, if not all, pupils. It is not at
all clear what should or could count as evidence to verify
or refute that argument. Over the years it has proved to be
extremely difficult to evaluate the effectiveness with which
the formal curriculum is taught and learned; these problems
are greatly magnified with the much more nebulous concept
of the hidden curriculum. So it must be conceded that we
are very far from being able to make comparisons between
the two in terms of their relative impact on pupils. Hitherto
the propositions have been furthered by persuasive argument
which introduces new and indirect evidence, usually in a
rather weak form, or by interpreting established evidence in
a new way.

For a few, the arguments presented so far will be sufficiently

17

persuasive, but there is much more relevant material to be discussed, and not merely to strengthen the argument, necessary though that is. The literature on the hidden curriculum draws attention to some of the unnoticed and unintended consequences of schooling; it tells us one part, a neglected part to be sure, but only one part of a complex educational story. Yet it gives surprisingly few indications of how we might change schools for the better. I shall take it that Illich's radical cure for the ills that schools induce, the 'de-schooling of society', is either mistaken or not a feasible reform. We must therefore give ourselves wider terms of reference in the hope that, through a close look at British secondary education, we can specify more precisely the undesirable aspects of schooling *and* the ways in which schools might be reformed. Reform is not just a negative process of discarding those elements of which we disapprove; we might then too readily throw out the baby with the bath-water, as does Illich. We must also detect what schools could and should do and explore how such tasks can be grafted onto the best of what schools currently achieve.

The work on the hidden curriculum makes depressing reading because it concentrates so heavily on the undesirable features and functions of school. Though you would not know it from much of the sociological literature, schools consistently yield the most astonishing achievements. They, too, often pass unnoticed and uncelebrated, but they must not be forgotten, even though they are not 'news'. Bearing this in mind, we must continue for a while to scrutinize the darker side of schooling.

We can begin where all analysis begins, with a common-sense objection to my argument about the destruction of pupil dignity. Most pupils in school simply do not give the impression of lacking dignity. In most secondary schools today, even with the most difficult of classes, teachers' relationships with their pupils are frequently characterized by friendliness and good humour, a remarkable tolerance and patience, and a genuine concern to get the best out of pupils. There has been a marked change in teacher–pupil relationships over the last twenty years. The humourless, army-sergeant authoritarian is fast disappearing. Teachers,

it can be argued, have never in the history of British education been more concerned with the promotion of pupil
dignity. Certainly it would be very rare for a pupil to protest
overtly that school is damaging his dignity. This is, however,
the subtlety (and difficulty) of the hidden-curriculum argument: that it can be effective only as long as it remains
hidden and unintended and the fact that it is for the most
part hidden blinds us all, including most pupils, to its existence and power. Most pupils accept school with varying
degrees of resignation as their lot; there is very little they can
do about it. But there is a distinct minority which reacts with
overt bitterness and hostility and the issue at stake is how we
interpret that reaction.

In school this minority comprises those pupils who turn
against school in explicit opposition. This group is predomi-
nantly but not exclusively urban working class in composition.
It is also largely male, though the number of girls in this
category is rising rapidly. In 1967, when I was earning my
academic 'colours' by coining sociological neologisms, I
called it the 'delinquescent subculture' of the school – a
group with delinquent-prone values and attitudes.[10] In the
conventional language of teachers they are the 'awkward
squad', the 'trouble-makers'. Their opposition to schooling
expresses itself in an aversion to school-work and lack of
co-operation with teachers. This is the immediate and 'obvious'
way to interpret such conduct, and it is an interpretation that
anyone who tries to teach such a class of pupils will find
difficult to deny. I shall argue, however, that these pupils'
protest is only incidentally against learning, against the
formal curriculum, against the teachers as persons – though
ironically teachers have tried to defuse the opposition by
revamping the formal curriculum and cultivating more
informal social relations as well as by, in other cases, becoming
more authoritarian. The argument is that the opposition
can be interpreted as an attempt to remove and negate the
indignities meted out to them by the hidden curriculum.
No writers have expressed this contention more succinctly
than Sennett and Cobb:[11]

There is a counterculture of dignity that springs up among

these ordinary working-class boys, a culture that seeks in male solidarity what cannot be found in the suspended time that comprises classroom experience. This solidarity also sets them off from 'suck-ups'. Hanging around together, the boys share their incipient sexual exploits, real and imagined; sex becomes a way to compete in the group. What most cements them as a group, however, is the breaking of rules – smoking, drinking, or taking drugs together, cutting classes. Breaking the rules is an act 'nobodies' can share with each other. This counter-culture does not come to grips with the labels their teachers have imposed on these kids; it is rather an attempt to create among themselves badges of dignity that those in authority can't destroy.

This argument is a fairly simple one: that this pupil opposition is a rejection of school because schooling destroys their dignity. In response, the pupils set up an *alternative* means of achieving dignity and status by turning the school's dignity system upside down. In the opposition's counter-culture dignity and status are earned by active hostility to school and teachers, whenever this is possible. The teachers contribute to this alternative system, paradoxically, by trying to subvert it, for whenever a teacher seeks to undermine it, he provides the opposition with yet a further opportunity of achieving status in the alternative system. The counter-culture requires and depends for its existence upon teachers' attempts to eradicate it. As a solution to the dignity problem it is exceedingly clever, for the harder teachers try to make these pupils conform, the more the counter-culture thrives. On this interpretation we must recognize that the counter-culture is strongly *rational* in its own terms and sophisticated. From the teachers' point of view, however, the opposition seems irrational, since teachers are operating quite different criteria of what constitutes rationality. Because teachers often do not recognize this rationality, the opposition is genuinely puzzling: it seems pointless. It must therefore be explained, and the explanations preferred by teachers are ones which are heavily deterministic, that is to say, ones in which the oppositional pupils do not *choose* to behave in this way but are driven and constrained into opposition. Common sense and some social science conjoin to provide excellent rationales: oppositional pupils may be driven by psychological forces ('He's seriously disturbed and in need of psychological help – a good case of maladjustment') or by sociological forces ('What can you expect of a girl who comes from a home like that?'). There is, of course, some truth in these explanations; they would not appear so frequently in teachers' and social scientific explanations if they were patently false.

My argument is not that they are entirely mistaken, but that a partial explanation is being taken to be the whole explanation. I am not, of course, suggesting that pupil misconduct in the classroom is somehow not really misconduct at all, but a kind of political protest which teachers simply repress. These pupils can be very naughty, and intentionally so, sometimes showing themselves to be shockingly cruel and vindictive to teachers and to other pupils. And often the pupils will (at least privately) condemn their own behaviour as heartily as do their teachers. We have to be careful, on the one hand, that we do not 'read' too much into pupil opposition and, on the other hand, that we do not interpret it in too narrow and simplistic a fashion. Counter-cultural opposition has some highly specific features: misconduct is not simply directed against the teacher but also towards the audience of counter-cultural peers, because it represents a social solution to a personal problem. Whilst it is true that social scientists have been prominent in offering these interpretations, they are by no means incompatible with teachers' own experiences. Many teachers can readily recognize the difference between individual misconduct and counter-cultural opposition, and they often have ambivalent feelings towards the latter, having a partial sympathy with it.

Neat psychological or sociological explanations, of defective personality or defective home background, nevertheless remain popular as explanations. There are two main faults to this approach. The first is that such explanations attribute the blame for pupil opposition to forces in the pupil, (psychological) or in the home or social background (sociological) and distract attention away from any part the school may play in the generation of the opposition. In so averting criticism from themselves, teachers sustain their own interests and avoid the need for any self-analysis. That such explanations support teachers' self-interest is not in itself sufficient to demonstrate that the theories on which they draw are false; but it alerts a suspicion in us. The second fault by the argument is that in every school there are many pupils have similar family and social backgrounds to those of oppositional pupils but who do not join the counter-culture. If the teachers' explanations were sound, many more pupils would be in opposition than is in fact the case. These two faults suggest that the explanation lies in some complex *interaction* between, on the one hand, certain psychological and sociological forces affecting the pupils and, on the other hand, certain processes occurring within the school itself. Both are necessary conditions to the emergence of the counter-culture of opposition, but neither is sufficient in isolation from the other.

Oppositional pupils do not *appear* to lack dignity because their conduct is so often not merely rebellious, but also precocious, self-confident, arrogant. So it is. At other times teachers catch a glimpse of the carefully hidden low level of self-esteem, when the mask of adult self-assurance looks like a paper-thin veneer. Behind the assertive toughness stands a pathetic little boy lost. But the abrasiveness of the counter-culture understandably irritates many teachers more often than it arouses their pity. In consequence, we often fail to see it as the very tentative, vulnerable and only partially successful attempt to restore dignity that is its true nature. The counter-culture is heavily dependent on teachers' opposition to it for much of its life-blood; it is a symbiotic relationship in which the counter-culture rarely evolves above the level of a lowly parasite which irritates its host but yet cannot break free into an independent cultural system. In the end it is the teachers' version of a culture of dignity which prevails because theirs mirrors society at large. However big and powerful the counter-culture becomes in some schools, it can never lose its essentially parasitic qualities.

That the counter-culture has no more than limited success

in creating an alternative means of conferring dignity is not, however, its most startling characteristic. The wonder is that it exists at all. Pupils who create the counter-culture of dignity must find that their dignity is damaged in school and elsewhere to generate the need for the counter-culture. But the destruction of dignity cannot be so severe that the urge to promote an alternative system is itself damaged. The counter-culture can flourish among pupils who retain some *sense of dignity* on which to build; and the pupils must somewhere find the resources with which to build a new system. If it is the hidden curriculum of schooling which largely per-petrates the damage to dignity – a thesis still not adequately documented – then it is only partially successful in its un-intended effects; the pupils can defend themselves against the force of the hidden curriculum sufficiently to offer an alternative which will then act as a barrier of resistance against further effects of the hidden curriculum. Perhaps the hidden curriculum is not as pervasive or overwhelming at least with oppositional pupils, as some of the writers allege. With deviant pupils, the hidden curriculum, like the formal curriculum, is partially inculcated and partially rejected.

To the teacher who has the persistent, daily task of coping with difficult pupils it is very natural to live a kind of double life. The first, in the classroom at the front-line of the battle, is organized around the immediate tasks of discipline and control and of seeking to educate these pupils as best one can in the circumstances. The second life is one in which the teacher reflects upon these events and seeks explanations for them. It is natural that many teachers should resort to relatively simple and deterministic explanations in terms of constraining psychological and sociological forces. And it is not merely that they wish to deflect criticism and blame from themselves. Rather it is difficult to see and integrate the many different layers of interpretation by which the counter-culture is more adequately understood.

In a brilliant study of these working-class boys in a Mid-lands school, Paul Willis has carefully unravelled some of the strands of this alternative culture of dignity.[12] More success-fully than any other writer he shows that it is not, as some sociological accounts suggest, that lower working-class boys become oppositional *because* they come from a certain kind of home and social background. Rather we can interpret the 'class values' of these boys as an important *resource* on which they can creatively draw to erect the counter-culture as a means of salvaging their dignity which is diminished in school. Pupils in British schools are judged against a measuring rod in which mental qualities are regarded as superior to manual qualities. Schooling may not ignore the physical, but it is the mind and intellect which are cultivated most carefully; for most people that is what education is self-evidently about. Willis shows, as earlier studies have also shown, that by this measuring rod some pupils are relative failures. These are the pupils in the lowest streams in the third–fifth years at secondary school, where the counter-culture normally emerges. The counter-culture inverts this measuring rod by which they are judged failures: the physical is now held to be superior to the intellectual. It has been argued for many years by sociologists that among 'working-class values' there is an emphasis on aggressiveness and masculinity. Such values provide a resource to pupils with damaged dignity, for they can draw upon the culture of masculinity to sustain their inversion of the mental–manual distinction which their teachers operate. Status within the counter-culture is achieved through an aggressive and 'hard' masculinity, which is now associated with adulthood and maturity. Mental labour and all that is theoretical, all that is so highly valued to be successful in school, is associated with femininity and the effeminate. It is no accident that these pupils commonly refer to the 'bright' boys in school as 'poufs'. And Willis goes on to show how this has important consequences in the preparation of these boys for shop-floor culture, for the maintenance of working-class sexism, and for the encouragement of fascist attitudes to the new underclass of immigrants, especially Asians who are seen as 'soft'. Willis writes:

> The particular excitement and kudos of belonging to
> [the counter-culture] comes from more antisocial
> practices. . . . It is these more extreme activities which
> mark them off almost completely, both from the

[conformists] , and from the school. There is a positive
joy in fighting, in causing fights through intimidation,
in talking about fighting, and about the tactics of the
whole fight situation. Many important cultural values are
expressed through fighting. Masculine hubris, dramatic
display, the solidarity of the group, the importance of
quick, clear and not over-moral thought, comes out time
and again. Attitudes to [the conformists] are also expressed
clearly and with a surprising degree of precision through
physical aggression. Violence and the judgement of violence
is the most basic axis of the [counter-culture members']
ascendance over the conformists, almost in the way that
knowledge is for teachers. In violence there is the fullest
if unspecified commitment to a blind distorted revolt. It
breaks the conventional tyranny of 'the rule'. It opposes it
with machismo. It is the ultimate way of breaking a flow
of meanings which are unsatisfactory, imposed from
above, or limited by circumstances. It is one way to make
the mundane suddenly *matter*. . . . Fights, as accidents
and other crises, strand you painfully in the 'now'. Boredom and petty detail suddenly disappear. It really does
matter how the next seconds pass. And once experienced,
the fear of the fight and the ensuing high . . . are addictive.
They become permanent possibilities for the alleviation of
boredom, and pervasive elements of a masculine style and
presence.

We can see in this account a clear reflection of what
Miller[13] has defined as the 'focal concerns' or values of the
lower working class. These are: *trouble* and *toughness*, which
offer an obvious model for the male as a 'tough guy' who is
hard, fearless, emotionally undemonstrative, and skilled in
physical fights, as portrayed in the cinema by Clint Eastwood;
smartness, or a shrewdness shown in a capacity for quick
repartee and the ability to outsmart, 'con' or dupe the
stranger or outsider who is a 'sucker'; *excitement*, which
breeds a constant search for immediate thrills or 'kicks' and
the taking of risks; *fate*, or the attribution of the causality of
events to good or bad luck; and *freedom* and *independence*,
the deep resistance to those in authority, accompanied by

assertions such as 'Nobody pushes me around' or 'I know how to take care of myself'. It may well be, of course, that such values are rational adaptations of the lower working class to their lot in life. The suggestion is that they form a cultural heritage available to young people brought up in certain inner-city environments.

The problem is how we interpret the clear parallel between such working-class values and the expression of them by certain pupils in school. We may take an 'input' view which argues that pupils simply import such values into school because lower working-class pupils are so heavily imbued with them that they cannot leave them at home as they pass through the school gates. Or we take a 'process' view which suggests that these values are expressed in a strong form in school only when they are activated by certain conditions which arise within the school itself; that is, under normal conditions these values would appear in no more than a weak form in school, since they are highly incongruent with the values of teachers and are usually suppressed by teachers. The classical or 'input' view argues that working-class boys do badly at school and join the counter-culture because their values (for example, the emphasis on aggressiveness) make them resistant to schooling. An alternative or 'process' interpretation argues that, of the boys who fail in school, those with a working-class background have at their disposal a latent set of values to which they can and do turn when they need to find an alternative source of dignity. Neither view is probably adequate in itself; the generation of the counter-culture requires us to make both arguments, though exactly how the two should be combined is still far from clear. But even a limited acceptance of the second view greatly undermines the neat deterministic sociological accounts that are associated with the first view, which so often reduce to the simplistic proposition that these pupils fail *and* become difficult in school because they come from deprived, working-class homes.

Moreover, if we combine the two views, some interesting possibilities and problems emerge. Does the counter-culture rely on the pupils coming from homes where the traditional working-class values appear in a strong form? Some of

Willis's material, in which he makes a parallel between the experiences of the boys in school with that of their fathers at work, is consonant with such a view. If that is so, then when a group of pupils all experience the same assault on their dignity in school, and when all or most of the group members have, through their family and community, a common pool of working-class values on which they can draw, the counter-culture of dignity will emerge in its classic and most success-ful form. This is a possibility which could be investigated. But there is also the problem: what happens to pupils who experience an assault on their dignity but *lack* the resources or working-class values that are important to the creation of a counter-culture? How do they respond? Are these the boys and girls who hang around the fringes of counter-culture groups, struggling to tune into the culture of aggressive masculinity? Such boys – and girls – are familiar in many classrooms; their conduct strikes the observer as an exaggerated imitation of some of the group's leaders, a desperate attempt to find acceptance. In practice, they are often not accepted, but are seen as a source of amusement, for after all they add to the fun by disrupting the lessons. Frequently their frenetic displays merely confirm their status, to teachers and oppos-itional pupils alike, as 'nutters' for whom teachers can provide complex psychological explanations as 'maladjusted'. It is possible that they are pupils who simply lack the requisite working-class values and so do not understand the complex rules of the games in the counter-culture, thus lacking the qualifications for admission to the counter-culture. If this is so, then such pupils would find their dignity more profoundly threatened, since they can participate in neither the official status system of the school nor the alternative counter-culture. Are these the pupils who withdraw psychologically, because they dare not run away physically? Is it they, rather than the members of the counter-culture, who are truly deprived of dignity?

It has been known for many years that teachers, in contrast to psychiatrists, see withdrawn children as a much less serious cause for concern than aggressive, noisy pupils, for the obvious reason that oppositionals disrupt the lesson and require immediate attention from the teacher. Is it the

27

'silent opposition', so easily escaping the teacher's attention, who are the most important problem? Because such pupils who withdraw are so silent, their objections to schooling are unvoiced; it is the oppositionals who make the angry objections and endless complaints. In this they are aided and abetted by their friends; the counter-culture has a collective strength from which oppositionals derive the courage and social support that is needed to rebel. In this do they speak only for themselves, or are they the spokesmen for other pupils too?

These are bold questions to which we have no clear answers; at present we lack the evidence to say. But, if there is *some* truth in the argument that the counter-culture represents not merely an expression in school of attitudes originating in defective or 'culturally deprived' homes but rather a creative opposition to school with its own sources of dignity, yet open only to those who possess the admission price of relevant cultural resources, then we have some grounds for at least listening to the criticism they may make of school. When teachers and pupils give us conflicting accounts of schooling, it is the teachers' voices which are usually granted credibility. When the pupils are defined as deviants, their accounts are double suspect. There are always at least two sides to every story; we know, understand and often rightly sympathize with the teachers' story. If we are to understand schools, we must listen to some of the other accounts, albeit with a proper scepticism. But before looking at school from their point of view, our most difficult task, we must consider some more of the ingredients that comprise the perspective on school on those who join the counter-culture.

2   The decline of community

In the last chapter, four propositions were argued, but not (as yet) convincingly demonstrated: that there is a hidden curriculum of schooling; that the effect of the hidden curriculum on many pupils can be understood as an assault on their dignity; that working-class pupils in particular are the victims of the hidden curriculum; that the school's counter-culture can be interpreted as a form of resistance to the assaults on dignity. In respect of the last proposition it was claimed that 'working-class values' cannot be treated simplistically as the cause of the counter-culture but should be seen as a resource on which some pupils draw to withstand the hidden effects of schooling. In this chapter I want to argue that some important recent changes within working-class communities have helped to create among young people from the working classes an urgent need for a dignity system of the kind created in the school's counter-culture. The thesis is contrary to the popular theory that the school counter-culture is automatically produced by the importation into school of certain working-class values as an expression of 'culturally deprived' backgrounds. I will argue that the destruction of dignity has two sources, one in the school in the form of the hidden curriculum, and one in the world inhabited by pupils at home. These two forces pressure some young people in the same direction, towards the creation of a counter-culture.

My argument will follow very closely the work of Philip Cohen,[1] whose own analysis rests heavily on the extensive sociological investigation of the East End of London carried out by others over the last hundred years. The main theme is the slow but continual erosion of working-class community. The East End has long been a differentiated world, rather than a neat, homogeneous community; yet it nevertheless showed a high degree of social integration. This was ensured by three main factors.

The first element is the pattern of the extended family. Traditionally, when a daughter married, she lived close to her mother and her new husband if necessary moved to the district. The new 'nuclear' family was located within a stone's throw of a large family network of several generations. When a girl married, it could be truly said that her mother did not lose a daughter, but gained a son. One's relatives were always 'round the corner' or 'along the street'. To be working-class was to be enmeshed (and perhaps trapped) in a tight web of family, friends, neighbours and workmates; it was a familiar, fairly stable social world. Such continuity would bring its own tensions and restrictions; family members and neighbours acted as powerful and conservative forces of social control. But it also brought continuity, the transmission of values and practices, and considerable mutual help and support. Mum could teach her daughter the skills of being a housewife and mother, and looked after the children as well as keeping a close eye on the progress of the marriage. Secrets were hard to keep and privacy difficult to guard, but the compensation was often a protection against loneliness, isolation and deprivation.

In the closely packed streets, with overlooking neighbours at the front and the back and overhearing ones at each side, we note the second element, the particular ecology of working-class life. Everyone belonged to a *street*; when asked where one lived, one would simply name the street, for the street identified one and displayed one's social location. The street was where one played, gossiped, sat on the step to watch the world go by and call across to neighbours. The women patronized the 'corner shop'; the men drank in the local pub; the children formed street gangs. At times of celebration – a coronation, the end of the war – the street members co-operated in decorating the street with flags and bunting strung between the houses, and tables and chairs would be brought out for a street party.

The third element is the local economy. In the East End this was organized around the dockland, certain craft industries (such as tailoring and furniture-making) and the markets. Most people worked locally; there was neither the need nor the money to travel far to work. Sons naturally followed fathers into the same or into an allied job; occupational skills and traditions were transmitted within the family to sons as readily as were domestic skills to daughters.

Cohen argues that in the East End this social structure remained relatively stable until the 1950s. Robert Roberts,[2] describing a similar working-class community in Salford, dates the beginning of the breakdown at the end of the Great War. Throughout the country these communities were subjected to further massive changes in the later years of the twentieth century. Among the most important everywhere were 'slum clearance' and 'area re-development'. Large numbers, especially young couples, were rehoused in new council-house estates, often at the edge of towns and cities a long way away from 'home'. New immigrants, especially from the Commonwealth, moved in, as did speculators and new Rachman-type landlords. Larger old houses were 'gentrified' by a new middle class seeking homes in the inner city. Neighbouring, the extended-family network, the street community, all declined rapidly. Supermarkets challenged the corner shop. High-rise flats which replaced many slums in inner-city locations did not replicate the social structure or the physical structure of the streets which they supplanted. Young mothers and old people became socially dislocated and isolated, 'flat-bound' and so physically and socially separated. Children no longer played outside the open front door or round the corner, but in new public spaces where they were not known by passing adults and not seen by anxious parents. Daughters moved to the other side of town, as did many sons who were no longer following in father's occupational footsteps. Jobs began to change, with a decline in traditional crafts and skills; many had to commute to work. The decline in manual occupations did not, surprisingly, generate a new wave of Luddite-style 'computer-breakers'.

In material terms there was a distinct advance for many, even though some new council housing is proving to have a remarkably short life and many working-class people continue to live in homes that are technically unfit for human habitation. But the cost in other terms has been high. The acute social dislocation which once occurred in the rush from rural areas into the towns at the beginning of the industrial revolution reappears in a new diaspora from the inner-city slums to high-rise flats, suburban council estates and new towns. The elaborate working-class culture which developed in the interim is being rapidly diluted or eroded. The transmission of that culture from one generation to the next is interrupted: vital chains of cultural communication are severed.

One thinks, for example, of such extreme cases as Kirkby, to the north-east of Liverpool, made famous as the model for 'Newtown' of the television 'Z Cars' series and as one of the most vandalized housing estates in Britain. Some 10,000 homes were built here in nine years and the population grew to over 60,000. As part of the slum clearance drive in Liverpool, families were wrenched from the old inner-city working-class communities in Scotland Road and deposited in new estates some miles from the city. Kirkby was given the nickname of 'Bunnytown' since at one stage nearly half the population was under fifteen years of age, giving it the highest child population in Europe. It is a telling index of the place's distorted social constitution. The old extended families had been broken beyond repair; many men were unemployed or had to commute to Liverpool for work. Vandalism was not confined to the young: some council tenants began to damage their own accommodation in the hope that they could force the council to find them alternative housing. No doubt the local politicians and planners had the highest ameliorative motives, but their ignorance of, or disregard for, the sociological realities of social structure and culture had disastrous consequences. As one observer[3] expressed it, 'Over a hundred years of cultural tradition was dismissed without apparent thought.' Some urban sociologists of the 1930s considered inner-city slums to be exemplars of 'social disorganization'. Here, in Kirkby, was a new and sudden social disorganization on an unimagined scale.

There is, of course, a real danger of romanticizing the working-class communities of the past. It is very easy to slide into an idealized nostalgia for the past, especially among those who were brought up in a traditional working-class environment but who have now become middle-class. It is easy to forget the horrors and conflicts that existed in working-class communities, their conservatism, their xeno-phobia, their sexism in which so many women were im-prisoned. Robert Roberts's *The Classic Slum*, itself a classic, is an acid antidote to these romantic tendencies. Here we have a more balanced view: images of homogeneous, interdependent communities with strong collective identities give way to a less rosy reality of subtle social hierarchies. There was, it seems, no social snobbery like working-class snobbery:

> In general, slum life was far from the jolly hive of com-munal activity that some romantics have claimed. . . . Richard Hoggart's personal intimacy with the working class in its more 'respectable' reaches during the '20s and '30s of this century leads him into praising family units and 'cosiness'. These qualities, however, do not, I think, appear either so evident or so laudable if one examines the working class at more levels and over a wider range of time. Certain nineteenth-century traits, of course, ran far into the twentieth and affected longest the ultra-conservative lower working class – among them, the gulf that stood between parents and children. From family to family there were naturally many variations in its importance, yet this division, I feel, made a profound impression on the minds and social attitudes of millions of manual workers. To ignore its influence is to distort any picture of working-class relationships in the first half of the twentieth century.

In his documentary-cum-autobiographical writing Roberts

eschews the highly selective portrait of working-class life of some influential, popular writing.

We must accept these strictures on our understanding of the history of the working class, yet that fundamental changes occurred cannot be denied. The break in cultural transmission in working-class communities, which was by no means so sharp amongst the middle-classes, coincided with a general decline in deference to those in authority. Working-class people began to taste the relative prosperity of escaping the degrading poverty of the past; the status of women was changed; the power of the unions grew in strength; the awe in which the propertied classes, politicians, clergy – and teachers – were held began to fade. As Roberts notes:

> Old deference died; no longer did the lower orders believe
> *en masse* that 'class' came as natural 'as knots in wood'. . . .
> Socially the barriers of caste that had previously existed
> between the skilled worker and his family and the lower
> industrial grades were permanently lowered; the artisan
> felt less superiority, the labourer and the semi-skilled man
> more self-assurance. . . . When unemployment struck,
> with a new authority, men no longer begged, as their
> elders had done, for the 'right to work'; they insisted on
> the right to be maintained with a voice and vigour unheard
> of before, the maintenance of a sort the State grudgingly
> allowed. The children of the undermass were mute no
> more.

And the impact of these social changes was to be felt in the schools, though sociologists have made little record of it. One Salford teacher on the edge of retirement who had spent his life in inner-city working-class schools observed to me:

> The school's not like it was. We used to be like a family,
> because you see all the kids came from a real community,
> the old style working-class community. We didn't have to
> do anything special: we just drew on what was there in
> the home background. But it's not like that any more. And
> there's not much we can do about it. How can you make a

community in a school when there's no community
out there? And the rewards aren't what they were. When
I began teaching most of the kids were grateful. They're
more likely to tell you to eff off these days, than say
thank you. And teaching's much harder than it used to
be. In the good old days you could rely on the cane.
You didn't actually use it much, but it was always there.
Now they'll have you in court for assault. They know
their rights, their mothers and fathers do. They talk
about it at home and the kids hear about it and follow
suit at home. In the old days the parents were by and
large on your side. If a kid went home and complained
that he'd been wallopped at school, he'd get another
clip round the ear from dad as well. It's different now:
you can't be sure of any support from home. Punishment
gets you nowhere. You have to cajole, reward, praise,
threaten, bluff, all in the right proportions at the right
moment, that's what it's all about.

Philip Cohen, writing about a later period than Roberts,
and about the East End of London rather than Salford,
sounds a different note. Referring to the major planning
changes affecting the East End he says:[4]

The situation facing East-Enders at present, then, is not
new. When the first tenements went up in the 19th century
they raised the same objections from local people, and for
the same very good reasons, as their modern counterparts
– the tower blocks. What *is* new is that in the 19th century
the voice of the community was vigorous and articulate
on these issues, whereas today, just when it needs it most,
the community is faced with a crisis of indigenous leadership. . . . The labour aristocracy, traditional source of
leadership, has virtually disappeared along with the artisan
mode of production. . . . More and more East-Enders are
forced to work outside the area; young people especially
are less likely to follow family traditions in this respect.
As a result, the issues of the workplace are no longer
experienced as directly linked to community issues.
Of course there has always been a 'brain-drain' of the

35

most articulate, due to social mobility. But not only has this been intensified by the introduction of comprehensive schools, but the recruitment of fresh talent from the stratum below – i.e. from the ranks of the respectable working class – has also dried up.

The two views are not contradictory. The working class were indeed to be mute no longer, but they could speak in certain channels only, the most important of which was in the workplace, the unions. It is significant that the Labour Party pays careful attention to the unions as the spokesman of the working class, perhaps because there is nowhere else to listen. At the level of the residential community, however, there were now only individual and unorganized spokesmen rather than a collective voice. The struggle for a new dignity was, for very good reasons, concentrated at the workplace because it was there that demands for better pay and better conditions of work could be realized. The carefully tended alliance between the unions and the Labour Party stilled many other voices on many other issues among ordinary working-class families.

Meanwhile, back in the home, working-class parents faced new problems, especially with their children. On the one hand, as we have noted, cultural transmission and controls were impeded, and probably made less effective by the rapid rise in the numbers of mothers going out to work. On the other hand, by the late 1950s, the dawn of the permissive society was breaking. A new, liberated and affluent generation was launched into 'teenage culture', whilst their slightly older and university-educated peers were satirizing Conservative ministers to the delight of many (and horror of some) on newly acquired television sets. Social and sexual taboos were enthusiastically broken, in some ways mirroring the experience of the 1920s after the First World War. Such changes would have been a massive challenge for the traditional working-class community; but the working class was becoming fractured into isolated 'nuclear' families of two parents and their children and the sharp increase in the number of 'one-parent families'. The tensions and problems of working-class parents increased dramatically, and the preaching of the middle classes about 'the abdication of parental authority' was of little practical help. It is at this point that we see the emergence of the new youth subcultures – the Teddy boys, the mods, the rockers, the skinheads and 'punk'.

It is not, according to Philip Cohen, a coincidence. In his view the tensions in the family, especially among the parents, were expressed in and produced:

> a generational specific symbolic system so the tension is taken out of the interpersonal context (of the family) and placed in a collective context, and mediated through various stereotypes which have the function of defusing the anxiety that interpersonal tension generates.
>
> It seems to me that the latent function of this subculture is this – to express and resolve, albeit 'magically', the contradictions which remain hidden and unresolved in the parent culture. The succession of subcultures which this parent culture generated can thus all be considered as so many variations on a central theme – the contradiction, at an ideological level, between traditional working class puritanism and the new hedonism of consumption; at an economic level between the future as part of a socially mobile elite, or as part of a new lumpen. Mods, Parkers, Skinheads, Crombies, all represent, in their different ways, *an attempt to retrieve some part of the socially cohesive elements destroyed in their parent culture*, and to combine these with elements selected from other class fractions, symbolising one or other of the options confronting it. [Italics added]

The argument is not an easy one, but it is a most sophisticated and persuasive attempt to explain the different working-class youth subcultures in Britain. Against it, explanations in terms of American influence, commercial exploitation, parental failure, and so on, seem jejune and trivial in comparison. (We know, for example, that commercial exploitation followed, not created, the various subcultural styles.) The main idea I want to take from Cohen is that the youth subcultures, despite variations in form, all represented a kind of magical attempt to recover community. Before so doing, however, it is right to follow his thesis a little further. We can illustrate the argument with two examples, the mods and the skinheads.

The mods, Cohen suggests, explored and attempted to realize the conditions of the white-collar worker who is socially mobile. Their dress and music reflect the image of the hedonistic and affluent consumer. In contrast, the skinheads represent a symbolic inversion of the mods and explored the traditional lower working-class option:

> Music and dress again became the central focus of the style; the introduction of reggae (the protest music of the West Indian poor) and the 'uniform' (of which more in a moment) signified a reaction against the contamination of the parent culture by middle-class values, and a reassertion of the integral values of working-class culture – through its most recessive traits – its puritanism and chauvinism. This double movement gave rise to a phenomenon sometimes called 'machismo' – the unconscious dynamics of the work ethic translated into the out-of-work situation; the most dramatic example of this was the epidemic of 'queer-bashing' around the country in 1969–70. The Skinhead uniform itself could be interpreted as a kind of caricature of the model worker – the self-image of the working-class distorted through middle-class perceptions; a meta-statement about the whole process of social mobility. . . . I believe that it is through the function of *territoriality* that subculture becomes anchored in the collective reality of the kids who are its bearer, and who in this way become not just its passive support but its conscious agents. Territoriality is the process through which environmental boundaries (and foci) are used to signify group boundaries (and foci) and become invested with a subcultural value. This is the function of football teams for the Skinheads, for example. Territoriality is thus not only a way in which kids live subculture as a collective behaviour, but the way in which the subcultural group becomes rooted in the situation of its community. In the context of the East End it is a way of retrieving the solidarities of the traditional neighbourhood, which

have been destroyed by redevelopment. The existence of
communal space is reasserted as the common pledge of
group unity – you belong to the Mile End mob in so far
as the Mile End mob belongs to you. Territoriality appears
as a magical way of expressing owner-ship; for the Mile
End Road is owned not by the people but by the property
developers.

Now what is the relation of these various youth cultures
to the experience of young people in school, especially the
oppositional counter-culture? The youth cultures rapidly
began to influence young people in their middle teens at the
very point when, because of the raising of the school-leaving
age, the young were staying at school longer. A longer
education, it was assumed (though not by many teachers),
would be valuable for all pupils. And we know that those
youth cultures, such as the mods, which appealed to the
socially mobile, tended to concentrate on pupils in the
highest streams; those which were oriented to the lower
working class, such as the rockers and the skinheads, found
a more natural home in the lower streams, consisting of
'early leavers', 'non-examinees' and the so-called 'Newsom
children'. The cultures of the rockers and skinheads fused
into the school's counter-culture, and provided it, in the form
of very long or very short hair and various dress styles, with
a distinctive uniform, with a symbol of rebellion against the
teachers if not – as was true in many schools for long periods
– a target for very real conflict between teachers and pupils.
Contemporary battles over ear-rings for boys or the sporting
of safety-pins in the form of jewellery are the natural heir to
the battles in the early 1960s over long hair – now sported
by the younger male staff.
  My argument is that parts of the counter-culture in school
represent that aspect of youth cultures which, according to
Cohen's thesis, reflect an attempt to recover a sense of
solidarity and community which was now lacking in the
home environment. The school, through its hidden curriculum,
threatened their dignity; but whereas formerly it had been
easy for the working-class pupil to treat school as an inescap-
able if rather unrewarding necessity, an unfortunate intrusion

39

into childhood and adolescence, it was now becoming difficult to maintain this attitude of indifference. The reason is simple: traditionally the working-class pupil's identity was strongly rooted in home life, in the extended family, in his clear occupational future in father's footsteps or in her anticipated marriage in a home not far from mother. To be born working-class was for most people to inherit a clear past, a stable present and a predictable future, even though that future might appear bleak and financially insecure. Nurtured in such a culture and social structure, the school could be treated as an alien institution staffed by distant and alien teachers. As Robert Roberts commented on his teachers in the early part of the century:[5]

> Still hardly accepted as members of a profession, teachers in Church and State schools fought respectfully for social recognition. Sons and daughters very often from top working-class families, they felt the need to conform as closely as possible to what they knew of middle-class standards. Disseminators among the poor of bourgeois morals, culture and learning, they remained economically tied to the lower orders, living in genteel poverty with an income little higher than that of the skilled manual worker. . . . As the century grew older both the economic and social gap between teachers and the skilled manual workers widened: teaching became a 'profession' and its members establishment figures in the lower middle class.

In such circumstances the working-class pupil could treat the teacher as one of 'them' rather than 'us'; school had to be tolerated, as it had been tolerated by their parents, and up to relatively recent times, many working-class parents waited as anxiously as their children for the day that schooling ended, for then (for parents) a wage could be earned and (for the youngster) adult status could be achieved. In short, working-class pupils could simply *dissociate* themselves from schooling.

As I have sought to show, the traditional culture and structure of working-class life is now being slowly but surely fragmented. When we read Robert Roberts today, we can still detect the continuities that reach to our own time; and we recognize what we had almost forgotten; but he evokes a world which is almost lost. The pupil from the working classes cannot put school aside as his forebears did because there is no clear and stable working-class world he can fully inhabit and from which he can derive a clear identity. The school pupil, like the member of the youth cultures, must *create* some community if he is to find one, even if he had to do so, as Cohen says, 'magically' and in some primitive form. Enough residues of traditional working-class culture survive to provide some guidelines, as in the cult of masculinity and aggression. They appear now in an unorganized and distorted form, in counter-cultural classrooms and on football terraces.

Not all cultural transmission has ceased, of course. Sons still learn from their fathers about the kinds of community and solidarity that can be achieved. Willis's book shows the close parallel between the experiences and activities of working-class men at work and the conduct of their sons in school. Observable in industrial work, says Willis:[6]

> is the massive attempt to gain informal control of the work process. Limitation of output or 'systematic soldiering' and 'gold bricking' have been observed . . . [in sociological studies of work], but there is evidence now of a much more concerted – though still informal – attempt to gain control. It sometimes happens now that the men themselves to all intents and purposes actually control at least manning and the speed of production. Again this is effectively mirrored for us by working class kids' attempts, with the aid of the resources of their culture, to take control of classes, substitute their own unofficial time-tables, and control their own routines and life spaces. Of course the limit to this similarity is that where the [oppositional pupils] can escape entirely, 'work' is done in the factory – at least to the extent of the production of the cost of subsistence of the worker – and a certain level of activity is seen as necessary and justified. . . . Shopfloor culture rests on the same fundamental organizational unit as counter-school culture. The informal group locates and makes possible all its other elements. It is the zone where

strategies for wresting control of symbolic and real space from official authority are generated and disseminated.

Men at work, often in monotonous tasks repeated every few seconds or minutes, are bored and sometimes create a solidary community of workmates, united against the bosses and their machines, a community in which some autonomy and dignity can be restored. Pupils in schools are bored, often despite the teachers' efforts to make school-work interesting, and create their own solidary community, united against the teachers and educational work. Fathers and sons could be said to fight in a similar struggle for dignity.

Even more important, teachers, like most middle-class people, have little or no direct experience of manual occupations in industry and so cannot see the parallel. Huw Beynon's *Working for Ford*, which should be compulsory reading for any secondary-school teacher (and perhaps would be so if teacher-training institutions could break free of their narrow and myopic definitions of education), captures the experience of working on the assembly line and displays the links between the nature of factory life, the collective opposition of workers and working-class values:[7]

This is the world of the operator. In and out of cars, up and over the line, check the line speed and the model mix. Your mind restlessly alert, because there's no guarantee that the next car will be the same as the last, that a Thames van won't suddenly appear. But still a blank – you keep trying to blot out what's happening. 'When I'm here my mind's a blank. I *make* it go blank!' They all say that. They all tell the story about the man who left Ford to work in a sweet-factory where he had to divide the reds from the blues, but left because he couldn't take the decision-making. . . . If you stand on the catwork at the end of the plant you can look down over the whole of the assembly floor. Few people do, for to stand there and look at the endless perpetual tedium of it all is to be threatened by the overwhelming insanity of it.

Beynon found men articulate:

You don't achieve anything here. A robot could do it. The line here is made for morons. It doesn't need any thought. They tell you that. 'We don't pay you for thinking', they say. Everyone comes to realise that they're not doing a worthwhile job. They're just on the line for the money.

The men naturally saw their jobs as dull and monotonous and would have preferred jobs where they could have more autonomy and be 'their own boss' – driving a lorry or back in the services. The shop stewards, by contrast, would have preferred jobs in which they had scope to help people, as in a hospital or educational establishment. But, for one reason or another, most had little choice but to stay at Ford's; like children at school, they had to put up with what they could not escape. It is hardly surprising that many men felt intense release when they were 'off the line', and made use of opportunities to be so when they could, by accident, luck or design. There is no moral commitment to the firm, no identification with the job which diminished rather than enhanced their humanity or their pride in achievement and the exercise of skill. So the major consolation was friends. In the words of one worker:

I wouldn't miss this firm at all. It's the worst firm I've heard of for scandalizing people. When I started I never thought I'd last three weeks. I'd only miss the lads. I've got some good mates here in the union. We're all together. If Mick's in lumber, we're all in lumber. It's a good feeling. The organization here union-wise is pretty good. It gives you peace of mind to be able to speak your mind. That's what I'd miss if I left here. Being in the union with the lads. I'd feel I'd let everyone down if I just left.

Another worker argues that it is the ineluctable horrors of work which drive men to the companionship afforded by the union; with a few changes in words it could be a school-boy's account of why he joins the counter-culture:

The point about this place is that the work destroys you. It destroys you physically and mentally. The biggest problem is getting people to accept it, to accept being

43

here day in and day out. So you've got low morale from every point of view. You're inflicted with a place of work and you've got to adapt because it won't adapt to you. So morale is terribly low. But you can build on this you see. You can't get much lower than hell and so you can increase morale through the union. Pull together sort of thing rather than dog eat dog. That's how I've found it on the trim. We're all in hell and you can get a bond out of that. We're all in it together like. That's where the union comes in.

What Beynon calls the factory consciousness of the shop stewards and workers is generated by the particular experience, of factory work and the attitudes of management, which takes a specific form when combined with some latent working-class values, especially collective values:

The stewards were held together by the stewards' organization and by a common ideology. Jointly they provided each other with guidelines on how to act in specific situations. They also jointly moulded the way in which they came to understand their collective position within the plant – as the leadership of the shop floor. To take first things first. A central principle which underlies 'us' is that of the collectivity. The whole basis of trade unionism is collectivism of one kind or another – 'united we stand, divided we fall' – and this doesn't end with the collective bargain and the strike. Collectivism permeates the very fabric of relationships within the union and is imprinted upon the position of shop steward. . . . The dominant culture of our society is basically individualistic. It is enshrined in ideas about best men winning and the like. This way of seeing things doesn't fit the shop floor very well.

The familiar commentators who tell us that British industry must give up 'out-dated' class attitudes, 'restrictive practices', and 'us and them' dichotomies make too simple an analysis; they do not recognize that these attitudes cannot be shaken off like purposeless superstitions, because they are constantly reactivated and reinforced by the very way we structure and organize our industrial organizations *and* the educational institutions in which the young are prepared for work. Yet can it not be said that the parallels between school and work are being pressed too far? The casual visitor to Ford's Halewood plant can readily imagine the destructive effects of shop-floor work and can soon come to understand why the workers respond as they do – and Beynon's work shows that this is not all like the popular, mass-media stereotypes of the car worker. But the same casual visitor in the schoolroom would probably find the conduct of oppositional pupils much more difficult to comprehend, for the parallel between management and teachers is less telling than that between workers and pupils and the nature of school-work seems much less boring and inhuman than work on the shop floor. The analogy seems strained, if not misleading.

As some of the most valuable elements in working-class culture have been disturbed or destroyed in the wake of various social changes, schools have surely become happier places in which to be educated. It is undeniable that teachers have become friendlier and more tolerant; that they often care profoundly about their pupils and seek to empathize with their condition, especially when they come from 'a bad background' and 'a broken home'; that teachers have established systems of pastoral care in an attempt to compensate for such deficiencies; that they have developed new curricula with the specific intention that they should be more interesting, relevant and useful to pupils; that teachers constantly strive to make positive links with parents – all this happens in most good schools, which includes many working-class schools. How, then, can it be argued that schools tend to damage pupils' dignity when in so many ways the school appears to be going in the *opposite* direction to that taken by working-class communities and the organization of industrial work? Is it not closer to the truth to argue that the school is the one major agency which is actively concerned with the promotion of dignity in pupils, since teachers have the sure knowledge that in so many cases the home, the neighbourhood and work so signally fail to achieve this? Is not the basic argument about the destruction of dignity in school seriously jeopardized by these facts?

45

Or have teachers mistakenly tried to solve the more fundamental social structural and cultural problems by superficial solutions grounded in improvements in curriculum content and personal relationships? Is the hope that more interesting lessons and warm, caring relationships with pupils can mitigate the effects of social change a misguided one? Have teachers tried to act as surrogate good parents in a way that fails to influence the more fundamental social experience of young people? Have teachers been too afraid to enter the taboo 'political' arena and so have shied away from the challenge of attempting to give youngsters an insight into their condition, as well as the inspiration and skills to improve that condition? Have teachers really thought through the problems of preparing children for adult status in a changed modern world? Are the fashionable concerns with improved standards and better links with industry the key educational problems of our age? Are our schools travelling in the right direction, but merely lack the financial resources to do their job properly? Are those teachers, who believe that a truly socialist government, which implemented a more equitable distribution of material rewards, would automatically solve most of the social problems currently masquerading as educational problems, right in that optimistic conviction?

Have the schools, in short, changed enough and in the right ways? Can we honestly explain – and justify – how it is that at the age of eleven years when pupils enter their secondary schools almost all of them enjoy school, but five years later a third of them actively dislike school and in effect are inoculated against any further doses of formal education? Even to begin to address these important questions – most of which were studiously kept off the agenda of the Great Education Debate initiated by Prime Minister James Callaghan in 1976 – we must return to the contrast between what teachers intend and how pupils actually experience their schooling, namely the hidden curriculum and its relation both to the formal curriculum and to the school organization of British secondary schools.

3 Examinations and the curriculum

The hidden curriculum refers, as we have seen, to all that pupils learn in school which is not intentionally taught or communicated by the teachers and the school system. It thus stands in contrast to the formal or official curriculum of school subjects and to the extra-curriculum of clubs and activities offered to pupils outside school lessons. Although the contents of the two curricula are very different, they can be taught simultaneously: in a lesson the surface message of an activity is concerned with the formal curriculum, but at the same time a latent lesson of the hidden curriculum can be taught. Jules Henry points out that man has a remarkable capacity for polyphasic learning, or learning more than one thing at the same time. He takes the simple illustration of a pupil who has been called by the teacher to the front of the class to spell the word 'August' on the blackboard for all to see. Such a pupil, Henry points out:[1]

> is not only learning the word 'August' but also how to hold the chalk without making it squeak, how to write clearly, how to keep going even though the class is tittering at his slowness, how to appraise the glances of the children in order to know whether he is doing it right or wrong, etc. If the spelling, arithmetic or music lesson were only what it appeared to be, the education of the . . . child would be much simpler, but it is all the things that the child learns *along with* his subject-matter that really constitute the drag on the educational process as it applies to the curriculum.

The hidden curriculum, in Jules Henry's terms, can be most

easily understood by analogy with a communication system such as a telephone. The system can carry an overt and formal message, what the callers say to each other, but it also generates random fluctuations that cannot be controlled and are not part of the message, namely the background *noise*, which the callers soon learn to ignore and discount. The hidden curriculum is like the background noise on the telephone:

> It is this inability to avoid *learning the noise with the subject-matter* that constitutes one of the greatest hazards for an organism so prone to polyphasic learning as man. It is this that brings it about that an objective observer cannot tell which is being learned in any lesson, the *noise* or the subject-matter. But – and mark this well – it is *not* primarily the message (let us say the arithmetic or the spelling) that constitutes the most important subject-matter to be learned, but the noise! The most significant cultural learnings . . . are communicated as *noise*.

Bowles and Gintis take a similar *contrastive* approach to the hidden and formal curricula in their argument that the social-class structure is reproduced through the mechanism of the hidden curriculum. They note that 'the heart of the process is to be found not in the content of the educational encounter – or the process of information transfer – but in the form: the social relations of the encounter'.[2] Now it is unquestionable that considerable understanding has been achieved by this contrastive definition of the hidden curriculum, but there is a danger that it may lead us to neglect that there is an important hidden curriculum *of* the formal curriculum. The subjects of the formal curriculum can carry multiple messages, some of which are relatively hidden. A few simple examples will suffice. The allocation of girls to domestic-science lessons may carry a message that only girls should be knowledgeable about home economics; the teaching of history and geography from the older British textbooks may carry a latent message to immigrant pupils that their own cultures are inferior; the teaching of political

48

history with an emphasis on the activities of kings, queens and statesmen may convey a hidden message that history is not about ordinary men and women and the labour movement. Teachers are becoming aware of, and are correcting, such sexist, racist and social-class biases in the subject-matter of lessons.

In looking at the hidden curriculum *of* the formal curriculum, however, I want to consider aspects which have been of particular interest to sociologists of education: the hidden-curricular messages communicated by the ways in which we *select* and *organize* and *evaluate* the official curriculum.[3] For most people the major change in British secondary education over the last twenty years has been comprehensive re-organization. It has been a highly controversial development, in both national and local politics. For many, and for teachers in particular, it has been a painful as well as challenging experience. The merits and demerits of comprehensive schools will continue to be debated for many years. In this same period there has been another major development, which has aroused very little controversy and almost no public discussion, namely, the rapid growth of public examinations for the adolescent. At one period approximately a quarter of the secondary-school population, largely in grammar schools took the 'O'-level General Certificate of Education. Soon the examination became open to pupils from the higher streams of secondary-modern schools, partly from the pressure of parents who wanted an opportunity for the children who had 'failed' the eleven-plus selection test, to take the grammar-school examinations. After the Beloe Report of 1960 the new Certificate of Secondary Education was introduced, and today most pupils in secondary schools will be entered for one (or both) of these public examinations. In the official view there remains a substantial minority of some 30 to 40 per cent of pupils for whom these public examinations are not suitable. In practice, however, many schools allow almost all pupils to enter for at least one or two subjects in the CSE.

What were the grounds for this proliferation of public examinations? There was, as noted, considerable pressure from parents, who recognized that success in a national examination could be of considerable help to young people in getting a 'good' job. Many teachers, too, have come to welcome the examinations with some enthusiasm. It is said that the justification for more public examinations rests in the need to open opportunities more widely, to end the restriction of entry to such examinations to an elite, grammar-school type pupil, to reduce any sense of failure among those pupils lacking the capacities to take 'O' level. No doubt to some extent those ideals have been realized. Some pupils who would have been denied entry to a grammar school under the 'tripartite' system or who in grammar schools found themselves consigned to the lowest streams may now, in the comprehensive school, be given greater opportunity and encouragement to enter for public examinations. And it may be that considerable benefits have been given to some working-class pupils through these reforms. But I suspect there are other, additional motives for teachers' espousal of public examinations, ones which were not announced to or debated with parents and public. One motive – and we shall examine another much later – is that examinations provided a powerful incentive to pupils to work. It is precisely at this period that pupils were becoming older (because of the raising of the school-leaving age), bigger (because of the effects of improved post-war nutrition) and more resistant to discipline (because of the changes in authority relations throughout society). Adolescents were, in short, becoming more difficult to teach and control. Examinations offered a buttress to these failing powers. Their most important advantage was that they transformed an inter-personal problem, of teachers' control of pupils, into an impersonal problem: teachers needed no longer to impose their authority confrontationally, but could appeal to out-side forces, the examination board, the pupil's own interests, and the value of examinations in the job market, as an incentive to every pupil to behave well and work hard at the school syllabus. And it has worked extraordinarily well for many pupils.

Such motive-mongering is dangerous, of course; it may be more profitable to look at some of the *consequences* of this proliferation of examinations, among which I will discuss three. First, and perhaps most important, what can fairly be called the grammar-school curriculum continued to hold its central and dominant position in the secondary-school curriculum, despite comprehensive re-organization. In this it was helped by the fact that the heads of department in comprehensive schools were recruited almost exclusively from among the former grammar-school teachers. The comprehensive-school curriculum was to become monopolized and controlled by ex-grammar-school teachers whose previous experience had been with the 'top' quarter of the school population. There were, of course, some important curriculum changes during this period, and a flurry of curriculum development followed the raising of the school-leaving age, for no adequate curriculum was available for many of those who were compelled to stay at school for an extra year. The content was made more attractive and often adjusted to what teachers took to be adolescent interests; some subjects were integrated; and some new forms of examination, notably the CSE Mode 3, were developed. Despite all this the changes were relatively small, for at the 'top' end the 'O'-level courses were for the most part untouched and any radical experiments in curriculum construction were largely confined to 'early leavers' and 'ROSLA' pupils not entered for public examinations. Indeed, in some schools such classes were so unpopular with the teachers that any member of staff who was willing to teach them and had the enthusiasm to try something new would be encouraged to do so by a grateful headteacher. But for most pupils the grammar-school curriculum, albeit sometimes in a watered-down version, continued to hold sway in that – and this is what I mean by the grammar-school curriculum – the heavy emphasis on the cognitive-intellectual skills and abilities of the traditional school subjects was retained.

Other abilities and skills, apart from the intellectual-cognitive ones, were not, even in the most conventional of grammar schools, totally ignored. Schools have always recognized that at least four other types – the aesthetic-artistic, the affective-emotional, the physical-manual and the personal-social – have an important place in education. It is

51

by no means uncommon to hear teachers and headteachers extolling their importance, or to read books on the curriculum and its objectives making a very similar plea. *In practice*, however, they tend to be given a secondary importance. They can never be removed from the curriculum, for the distinction between these five types of ability and skill is only analytic, and it would be impossible to teach, say, English language and literature without paying attention to the aesthetic-artistic, the affective-emotional and the personal-social. Yet those school subjects in which these have a particularly strong if not primary significance, such as art, craft, music, woodwork, drama and physical education (to mention just traditional curriculum fare), tend to appear on the timetable in the lowly status of one-period-a-week subjects and, as pupils become older, to become *optional* subjects. They are not, in short, subjects which are seen as essential and thus compulsory to young people. The hidden-curriculum message is clear: the only knowledge and skills which *really* count in school, especially for the older adolescent, are primarily intellectual-cognitive in content. Teachers do not say this; nor, when the statement is so baldly expressed, would they all assent to it. But that, I believe, is the message many pupils receive, for the selective content and structure of the curriculum speaks much louder than the teachers' words. It is a greaty pity that teachers do not openly tell their pupils that they have other objectives than the cognitive-intellectual; but curriculum objectives are discussed with fellow teachers, not with the curriculum consumers. If teachers did tell their pupils, they might be in for a shock, for I suspect that many pupils would be amazed to hear that the school was deeply committed to other forms of knowledge and skill apart from the cognitive-intellectual; to them it would be news.

The hegemony of the grammar-school curriculum was sustained not merely by the fact that the heads of department in the comprehensive schools were drawn from grammar schools; that merely confirmed and supported a position with much deeper roots. One powerful outside pressure was that exerted by the examination boards (and behind them the universities), and a powerful internal pressure was that exerted by the headteacher. We shall shortly consider both more fully. At least as important was the general *political* pressure exercised from central and local government, especially from members of the Labour Party which had promoted comprehensive re-organization; and many of these men and women had representation among comprehensive-school governors.

Although comprehensive schools have a long history in British education – the earliest purpose-built comprehensive school was opened in 1954 – the heated public debate was sparked by Anthony Crosland's famous 10/65 circular which set in train compulsory re-organization along comprehensive lines. Within the Labour Party, however, discussions had been taking place for many years and only slowly did it adopt a commitment to the comprehensive school as the basic form for all state secondary schools. During the post-war Labour administration of 1945–51 the party had to come to terms with the then recent 1944 Education Act which was clearly committed to, but did not enforce, a system of secondary education along 'tripartite' lines of grammar, technical and modern schools. The minister, and the Ministry of Education itself, were quite open in showing a distinct preference for 'multilateral' rather than comprehensive schools. Many members of the party, including MPs, were strongly in favour of the retention of the grammar schools, for two main reasons. First, the absorption of the grammar schools into comprehensive schools could be seen as a handing over of the grammar-school tradition to the public and direct-grant schools, whose position might thereby be strengthened. If the grammar schools were retained, even in the form of a separate school on a multilateral base, and offered greater access to working-class pupils, then the recruitment of the elites from the public-school sector might be challenged. Second, many of the 'intellectual' elements of the Labour Party – and many teachers – had themselves moved into their social position on the basis of a grammar-school education and so were naturally cautious towards a policy which appeared to abolish them. Rodney Barker recounts the anxieties of the period:[4]

The demand for the common (i.e. comprehensive) school

arose primarily not from a rejection of the grammar-school tradition, but from a belief in its value and a desire for its wider dissemination. The multilateral system would make it, if not the experience of all, then at least the opportunity of all, whereas the tripartite system permanently denied such opportunity to the majority of children after the age of eleven. 'Why should we deny to our children the chance of having a grammar-school education?', [W.G.] Cove asked the 1946 party conference. Equality was not merely a matter of a single set of regulations or equal physical amenities – there should be access to a common curriculum and opportunity to take the same examinations. And that curriculum was to be the grammar-school curriculum. 'Are we going to deny the children in the modern schools the opportunity of taking the same examinations as the grammar schools?' Cove's reaction to the Ministry's decision to set sixteen as the minimum age for sitting the School Certificate was that this was a bad measure, in that it would prevent the pupils in the modern school from taking an examination open to the grammar-school pupils. His arguments in favour of multilateral schools made it quite clear that he saw them as, amongst other things, the solution to an unsatisfied demand for grammar-school education. The multilateral school was to provide for children of those parents of all classes who wanted an education for their children of a character and a duration which could not be provided in the modern school. Cove feared too that if the middle-class parent found that, owing to the inadequacy of the supply of grammar-school places, his child was unsuccessful in the competitive eleven-plus examination, then he would patronize the private, independent and fee-paying schools. Once again the solution was to be found in the multilateral school, where sufficient courses of the type and duration required could be provided. A similar attitude towards the grammar school and towards grammar-school education was revealed by other members of the Labour Teachers. Mrs Leah Manning, one of the earliest Labour advocates within the Commons of the common school, denied any suggestion that academic education was being attacked:'We are asking

that more and more children suitable for this type of
education should have it.'

It is not surprising then, that in 1949 the Ministry was
rejecting local authority schemes for comprehensive schools
or that in 1950 the Conservative Party approached the elec-
tion with a commitment to the preservation of the grammar
schools and with a determination to warn the electorate of
the 'impersonal' quality of large comprehensives. The public
proved to be very responsive. Whatever *organizational* form
secondary education might take, Labour politicians knew well
that the grammar-school *curriculum* could not be challenged.
The grammar schools might themselves be abolished in the
future, but the survival of the grammar-school curriculum
was ensured.

As a second consequence of the growth of public examinations, only those subjects, or more strictly those aspects of
subjects, which were readily and 'objectively' assessable
could be included in an examined curriculum. It was not so
much the grammar-school curriculum *per se* that mattered,
but the fact that it was the foundation of the School Certificate and later the General Certificate of Education. Yet it
was in the main only for these heavily intellectual-cognitive
subjects that generally accepted methods of examination had
over the years been developed. A grammar-school education
was desired because it led to a public examination; examinations were fully developed mainly in relation to intellectual-
cognitive subjects; so the intellectual-cognitive subjects
occupied the heart of the comprehensive-school curriculum
and the new examinations, such as the CSE which was
developed for those pupils for whom the GCE appeared to
be unsuitable. Lip-service continued to be paid to other
kinds of abilities and skills, such as the artistic-aesthetic,
affective-emotional, physical-manual and personal-social;
but it could be little more than lip-service because they had
a secondary position in the curriculum and (therefore?)
little effort was directed to generating adequate means of
assessing them, for public examinations relied heavily on
written examinations and of the five skills and abilities the
intellectual-cognitive is evidently most adequately assessed by

this form of testing. Again, the hidden-curriculum message
to pupils is clear: only knowledge, skills and abilities that
can be readily measured, especially in a written test, are to
be treated as *really* valuable.

In any examined course of study there is always a danger
that the final examination will come to dominate the processes
of the teaching and learning in ways which undermine the
original educational objectives. According to the 1979 survey
of secondary education by Her Majesty's Inspectors of
Schools – who are hardly the most radical of educational
critics – this point has already been reached in some comprehensive schools. They report that in a minority of schools
teachers attach little importance to anything but the public
examinations:[5]

> It was evident that in some schools pupils were being
> entered for examinations inappropriate to their particular
> abilities and some embarked on examination courses who
> would have been better suited by non-examination courses.
> Elsewhere, the range of programmes offered to some
> groups of pupils, usually the more able, was narrowed:
> these pupils were thought to have no time to spare for
> creative and aesthetic subjects and non-examination
> courses. Careers education, health education and religious
> education also tended to be excluded. The work attempted
> in the classroom was often constrained by exclusive
> emphasis placed on the examination syllabus, on topics
> thought to be favoured by the examiners and on the
> acquisition of examination techniques. In almost all the
> schools no time was made available in the fourth and
> fifth years for reflective work such as might be fostered
> by independent but carefully guided private study periods
> and the development of study skills which pupils might
> need later in school, or for future education and employ-
> ment. The pupils may be put at a disadvantage by this
> narrowing of their curricula and modes of work and the
> ensuing effects on the range of skills, values and attitudes
> which they have acquired. Certainly some pupils responded
> by showing little interest in anything which was not seen
> to be related to their examination work. Other pupils, for

example those leaving at Easter in the fifth year or not
intended to take examination courses, may also be at a
disadvantage in some schools where the examination objective has such primacy. . . . Many schools interpret, rightly
or wrongly, parental and employers' interest as a demand
solely for good grades in public examinations. . . . At
present too much reliance is placed on examination results.
Although these provide an important measure of pupils'
academic achievement they are inadequate yardsticks by
which to assess whether pupils are growing into responsible,
well adjusted and interested young adults, and can say
little about why a school is, or is not, succeeding in these
ways. [Italics added]

It is worth contrasting this contemporary inspectorial
criticism with the anxieties expressed in the Crowther Report
15 to 18 in 1959 – some years before comprehensive re-
organization – about a curriculum geared to an examined
minority becoming the diet of the majority:[6]

External examinations, then, tend to stabilize and make
uniform patterns of teaching and the content of a subject
syllabus. Once laid down, they tend to take a great deal of
altering. . . . External examinations not only tend to direct
attention, and attach value, to the subjects which are
examined at the expense of those which are not (and within the examined subjects only to their examinable aspects);
they also focus attention on pupils who are examined at
the expense of those who are not. . . . There is, finally, the
risk, well known if not always avoided in grammar schools,
that only the examined subjects and aspects of education
will be felt to have any real importance. These are risks
and it is essential that they should be observed. . . . Many,
probably more than half, of the pupils of the modern
schools would have their education deflected from its
proper lines by being prepared for an examination.

The Crowther Report did not contemplate that public
examinations would be taken by more than half of the
secondary-school population. One cannot but feel that they

would have protested more vigorously had they foreseen the place of public examinations in comprehensive schools. As it is, their observations are prescient; many teachers agreed with these views at the time. Nowadays the widespread teacher assumption about the importance of public examinations has provoked the HMIs' castigations reported above. For teachers, the consequences of the external examinations have tended to become part of the hidden curriculum of secondary schooling and so they often fail to perceive the message they are imparting to pupils.

A third effect of the spread of public examinations is that the everyday experience of young people has often been systematically excluded from the curriculum. At first sight this seems a strange claim, for in recent years there have been many attempts to make the curriculum, especially for the so-called 'less able', more relevant to their interests and experience. Too often, however, this took the form of adapting the core intellectual-cognitive elements into a more palatable form by linking them to what were taken to be pupils' interests, rather than by starting with pupils' interests and creating a curriculum from them. A telling illustration is provided in the work of Graham Vulliamy[7] of the University of York on school music. Here, surely, is a school subject that cannot sacrifice the aesthetic-artistic and the affective-emotional to the intellectual-cognitive. Vulliamy's work shows how that highly complex and varied form of music, which can be properly described as the Afro-American tradition, has been designated by music teachers and the leaders and experts in music education as 'pop' music. This label is overtly derogatory; it treats a highly diverse form of music as unitary; it suggests that this form of music is nothing more than a commercialized product, a claim that is only partly true. More important, so-called 'pop' music is taken by music teachers to be bereft of any artistic, creative talent and to be unworthy of serious attention. It is held in contrast with another musical form, the Western classical tradition, which is defined as 'real' or 'serious' music. It is this tradition which has a strong intellectual component because it is normally written down in the form of a score, whereas the Afro-American tradition is more oriented to improvisation – as is much modern 'classical' music, of which music teachers are so rarely admirers. 'Pop' music is not totally ignored by music teachers: pupils are allowed to play *their* records at the end of term, as a concession when 'serious' work is laid aside. So, for music teachers, musical ability is attributed to those pupils who can play an instrument in the school orchestra and can read the score of *Eine Kleine Nachtmusik* – or can pass the heavily intellectual-cognitive 'O'-level music examination. Not surprisingly, such pupils tend to come from middle-class homes where the parents send their children for private music lessons at an early age, sometimes in the hope of producing another Mozart, and more commonly with the sensible belief that an early musical education will provide an endless source of pleasure in later years. But other pupils, who cannot read music or play a conventional instrument and who know little about 'classical' music, are in real danger of being seen as musically 'thick' or stupid. And that judgment is made by many music teachers at a point in our history when we know that 99 per cent of young people spend an inordinately large part of their leisure time in listening to music and have highly selective tastes within that music. Again there is a clear hidden-curriculum message: only those aspects or forms of subjects which teachers regard as real and important are to be taken as real and important.

The proposition, then, is that the hidden curriculum *of* the formal curriculum transmits a message that schooling is principally ordered around a particular constellation of knowledge, skills and abilities, the intellectual-cognitive domain of propositional knowledge, which constitutes the central content of the main school subjects and which is assessed in public examinations. Other forms of knowledge, skill and ability are not by any means always ignored or excluded, but they are accorded a secondary position and are therefore less important. It is not always a message that is communicated intentionally by teachers, though they quite rightly hold the intellectual-cognitive in high esteem. Frequent attempts are made by most teachers to incorporate other kinds of skill and ability into their teaching and they avow a dedication to the education of the 'whole' child which necessitates a high valuation of the full range of human abilities and potentialities. Their sincerity is unquestioned and their aspirations are admirable. Yet in my view these are persistently contradicted by the very structure and content of the curriculum, by the nature and prominence of public examinations, all of which comprises an ineradicable, continuous and taken-for-granted reality which stamps itself on the minds of pupils and which belies the teachers' splendid ideals. Every day the pupils pursue a timetable in which the study of English, mathematics, science, history and geography occupy substantially more time than art, music, religious education and physical education. According to the 1980 DES survey 51.8 per cent of pupil time in the fifth year is devoted to the first group of subjects and 15.3 per cent of the time to the second group. Significantly the second group of subjects occupied 25.2 per cent of pupil time in the *first* year.[8] Is that balance, and change in distribution over time, the right one for comprehensive schools catering for all pupils? And when the second group of subjects is taken for public examinations, what is presumably the same standard of achievement as in the first group must be reached on the basis of far fewer lessons. It is these subjects which can be 'dropped' first, which tend to become optional or peripheral as pupils get older, which can be forgone when circumstances demand that a pupil miss a lesson.

The more profound and more disturbing message is that the very concept of ability becomes closely tied to the intellectual-cognitive domain. 'Intelligence' becomes defined as the ability to master the cognitive-intellectual aspects of school subjects. Pupils who experience difficulty in so doing are labelled with the euphemism of 'the less able' or even the overtly insulting epithet of 'the thickies'. And the pupils *know* they are so designated; they do not have to hear the labels applied to them by teachers, though most of them at some stage do so. 'Less able' becomes a diffuse and context-free description, not limited to the more accurate 'of below average attainment in mathematics', etc. or 'has difficulty with cognitive-intellectual elements', or the even more accurate 'of below average attainment in mathematics as taught by this teacher' and 'has difficulty with the cognitive-intellectual aspects in this subject taught by this teacher'. And we know that these labels are more likely to be assigned to working-class than to middle-class pupils, for there is massive evidence to show that the former are much more likely to be relegated to 'low' streams in all types of school.

It is an exceptionally narrow definition of ability and intelligence. In characterizing the values or 'focal concerns' of working-class life, W.B. Miller[9] drew attention to the high estimation of 'smartness' and the ability to outwit. He noted:

> Lower class culture can be characterized as 'non-intellectual' only if intellectualism is defined specifically in terms of control over a particular body of formally learned knowledge involving 'culture' (art, literature, 'good' music, etc.) . . . imparted by formal educational institutions.

Since the growth of the eleven-plus test intelligence has come, at least in educational circles, to be given a highly restrictive definition. Yet we must remember that intelligence tests were developed in the field of education in order to predict as accurately as possible the pupil's capacities to master the school's intellectual-cognitive curriculum of the grammar school. Given these aims, the directions taken by the intelligence testing movement were not entirely mistaken. The danger lay in the belief, common among teachers and by no means rare among psychologists, that the tests measured intelligence in a much more absolute way: on this view an IQ score gave an accurate index of most, and certainly the most important, aspects of one's general abilities. (We can leave aside the controversial issue of the extent to which intelligence is genetically inherited.) Since the IQ-test score is a moderately good predictor of pupils' abilities to master a cognitive-intellectual curriculum – and certainly a better predictor than teachers' own judgements – teachers were able to accept psychologists' notions about intelligence quite uncritically. Some writers perceived the limitations of this approach to intelligence. Herbert Blumer offered a much more balanced account:[10]

The concept or proposition that is being operationalized,

such as the concept of intelligence, refers to something that is regarded as present in the empirical world in diverse forms and diverse settings. Thus, as an example, intelligence is seen in empirical life as present in such varied things as the skillful military planning of an army general, the ingenious exploitation of a market situation to a business entrepreneur, effective methods of survival by a disadvantaged slum dweller, the clever meeting of the problem of his world by a peasant or a primitive tribesman, the cunning of a low-grade delinquent girl moron in a detention home, and the construction of telling verse by a poet. It should be immediately clear how ridiculous and unwarranted it is to believe that the operationalizing of intelligence through a given intelligence test yields a satisfactory picture of intelligence. To form an empirically satisfactory picture of intelligence, a picture that may be taken as having empirical validation, it is necessary to catch and study intelligence as it is in play in actual empirical life instead of relying on a specialized and usually arbitrary selection of one area of its presumed manifestation.

Teachers are often aware of this; they employ a fairly sophisticated concept of intelligence when they make sense of pupil achievements in terms of concepts such as 'imagination', 'insight', 'sensitivity', 'maturity', 'incisiveness', and so on. But teachers can at the same time adopt the much blunter working vocabulary which speaks of the 'less able' in a blanket way.

This very narrow definition of ability, grounded in the curricular elevation of the cognitive-intellectual, has its effects on pupils. Ability labels are not seen by pupils as mere *descriptions* of part of their total set of attributes as human beings; they are seen rather as generalized *judgments* upon them. Because the mastery of the cognitive-intellectual domain is so essential to success in school, ability labels carry rich connotations of pupils' moral worth. Those who are designated as 'bright' know that by that very fact they are being complimented and credited with a valuable attribute. The 'less able' understand that they lack the very quality on which the school sets most store; a sense of failure tends to permeate the whole personality leaving a residue of powerlessness and hopelessness. It is here that dignity, as I have defined it, is most severely damaged. Many teachers work hard to counteract such tendencies, especially where the pupil concerned has a likeable personality. They look for opportunities to praise and to encourage. Teachers who teach those subjects with a weaker cognitive-intellectual bias and those who, despite teaching 'main' subjects, are sensitive to the importance of other skills and abilities can do much to sustain what is often a failing self-confidence in the pupil, but they are rarely entirely successful. And they know it.

Most teachers have little personal experience of systematic failure; as pupils they were almost always relatively successful – though they are anxious to tell us that they too were rebels in their own way. Some, like me, have a skeleton or two in their academic cupboard. I was not successful, during my schooldays, at woodwork. Slowly I grew to dislike and then to hate the subject at which I was failing; and so, not surprisingly, what few skills I had deteriorated rapidly. Soon I was a target of teacher criticism. 'Everyone stop work', the teacher would announce, 'and look at Hargreaves.' I knew I was to be the exemplar of what not to be doing. Naturally I gave up woodwork at the earliest opportunity and forgot about it. When I grew up and bought a home, I found I needed to re-hang a door; suddenly long-forgotten phantoms from my woodwork lessons besieged my mind. My hands trembled as I bought my Black and Decker tools in the shop. Not until I had successfully completed the work did I dispel my fears and sense of incapacity. But with my renewed feelings of competence came another realization, that I had been able to consign my experiences in woodwork to distant corners of my subconscious only because in most of my other school subjects I had been relatively successful. My conspicuous failure had been drowned in a sea of moderate success. Suppose, however, my failure had not been confined to woodwork lessons; suppose that experience had been replicated in art and music, in French and physics, in English and mathematics: what then? For the first time in my life I realized how little I understood what a persistent experience of failure in school could mean to a pupil. Even now I am not sure that I can perform that feat of imagination required to put myself in the shoes of such a pupil.

The nearest I can come is to imagine a school in which the aspects in which I was least successful (the physical-manual) replace those aspects in which I was most successful (the cognitive-intellectual). In this nightmare my secondary school's timetable is dominated by periods of compulsory woodwork and metalwork, gymnastics, football and cricket, drawing and painting, technical drawing, swimming and cross-country running. Sandwiched between these lessons, but only in thin slices, appear welcome lessons in arithmetic and English, in French and history. Some of these, however, cease to be available to me after the third year; they clash with the more important subjects of technical drawing and gymnastics which I need for higher education and a good job. I enjoy most lessons very little; I am bored and make little effort in areas where I seem destined to fail. The temptation to 'muck about' in lessons, and even to truant, is almost irresistible. My friends soon matter to me much more than anything else in school and our greatest pleasure is in trying to subvert and mock the institution which we are forced to attend for five long years. I don't think my teachers, who seem so strong and so clever with their hands and feet, really understand me at all. Quite often they are kind, but I know they look down on me and think it's all rather hopeless in my case. I'll be glad to leave school.

Is this too fanciful? Or do we all have within us the making of our own nightmare through which we might catch a glimpse of how easily, had the education system been built on alternative narrow premises, we might be such very different people? The construction of alternative worlds in imagination may help us to see why many 'less able' pupils cease even to try at school, despite teachers' exhortations. It may be not so much that they lack the ability to succeed, but that they are deeply afraid that they will not. In such circumstances it is rational not to try, since if one tries and fails it merely confirms one's lack of ability and sense of worthlessness. If one does not even try, then poor attainment can be easily explained by the refusal to try. It is a masterly sense of retaining the last vestiges of a crumbling dignity. Teachers' constant complaints about laziness are a small price to pay for a pupil in such desperation.

Some teachers, especially in secondary-modern schools, understood these matters. They had come to recognize both the absurdity of making the modern school a miniature grammar school and the urgent need to provide a different curriculum content and new teaching methods if they were to provide their pupils with an adequate education. But their voices have been strangely muted in comprehensive re-organization. In part this is because, with some important exceptions, they have not held positions of power in re-organized schools; and in part it is because comprehensive schools have intentionally obliterated the concept of the modern school and many of the experiments that prospered there. The very term 'secondary-modern' has in many quarters become a term of opprobrium, associated with failure and the second-rate. It is a gross injustice. The best secondary-modern schools avoided two extremes: that of seeing their clients as the unteachable 'rejects' who had to be kept off the streets until they were fifteen, and that of trying to ape the grammar school, creating within the school an educational race, premised on the graduate, in which a sequence of hurdles progressively eliminated all but the chosen few who were then deemed fit for higher and further education. (Most comprehensive schools have successfully avoided the first extreme, but often because they have opted for a modified version of the second.) In the best secondary schools con-siderable effort was expended to create vocationally oriented courses. Indeed many of the examinations specially designed for such children were tests of occupational skills. It is un-fortunate that in some comprehensive schools the very concept of 'vocational education' has become a dirty word and has sometimes been displaced by impoverished courses in 'vocational guidance' and 'careers education'. A few comprehensive schools have built upon the vocational orien-tation of good secondary schools, but even they tend to be constrained by the non-vocational bias of most of the GCE and CSE public examinations. When these two public exami-nations are combined into a single public examination, the anti-vocational bias is likely to get stronger since in the amalgamation the more powerful 'O'-level academic orientation will be the dominant partner in this marriage.

This drift away from the best secondary-modern school practice and from vocational education in many of our comprehensive schools was not a carefully planned or intentional change. Indeed, surprisingly little of the detailed operation of comprehensive schools was ever laid down in the form of a blueprint or a model that comprehensive schools should enact or follow. This accounts for the remarkable diversity among comprehensive schools, whose style and character is much less monolithic and predictable than that of the old grammar schools. One of the relatively few things that comprehensive schools have in common is the importance assigned to the sixteen-plus public examinations. Much recent educational change is best seen as a process of drift: the current of educational practice flows in a rather tortuous stream between the constraining banks of political rhetoric and criticism and perceived parental demands.

Leading members of the Labour Party, from Hugh Gaitskell to Harold Wilson, proclaimed to the public that the comprehensive schools would be 'grammar schools for all'; this not merely silenced the critical voices we have noted in the party itself, but it also appealed to growing demands for a more meritocratic system of secondary education and at the same time allayed the fears of parents who greatly resented the abolition of the grammar schools. The slogan was a sophisticated one for it capitalized on the contradictions in the public's mind: parents were in favour of the retention of the grammar schools and their public examinations but opposed to the eleven-plus selective test as the basis of a 'once-for-all' allocation.[11] If the comprehensive schools could be seen by the public as 'grammar schools for all' then the contradictions could be solved. Many people seem to have accepted this argument, at least for a short period, and at least in principle. But public opinion is notoriously fickle and when comprehensive re-organization began many grammar schools had to be closed, as part of their amalgamation into the new comprehensives; immediately a strenuous defence of the grammar schools was activated. Many parents with children at these schools, as well as former pupils, believed the schools to be good ones and so not surprisingly fought against the closures. Harold Wilson's claim that the grammar schools would be closed over his dead body now seemed to be a thin and superficial assertion. Most people were delighted to see the demise of the eleven-plus; but many remained sceptical that the amalgamation of grammar schools and (usually several) secondary moderns actually constituted the provision of 'grammar schools for all'. Since the public had been persuaded into comprehensive re-organization more on the basis of the unpopularity of the eleven-plus rather than the positive virtues of the comprehensives, the stage was now set for two further developments. The first was for the upper sections of the middle class to increase or transfer their loyalties to the independent sector, the direct-grant schools and the public schools, especially those which accepted day boys. The second was a determination that the promises made for the comprehensive schools should be kept: 'standards' would have to be maintained and this, it was said, would require constant public scrutiny, especially of the examination results.

Yet in one sense the comprehensive schools did indeed become the grammar schools, for the comprehensive schools were to become dominated by the grammar-school curriculum, which was now available to all. The comprehensive-school system no longer required the eleven-plus selective test, but the problem of selection was not thereby dissolved away. Selection would inevitably continue in some form; the difference was that now it would take place *within* the single comprehensive school. In practice selection is now operated in a new 'thirteen-plus', when pupils are segregated into 'O'-level, CSE and non-examination groups.[12] Parents are aware of this and it is by no means uncommon for parents to demand that the teachers enter their child for 'O'-level courses, whatever the teachers believe to be in the best interests of the child, because the parents know that the 'O' levels are the first academic grammar-school step on the rungs of the educational ladder that leads to social and occupational success. So for the grammar-school curriculum to be available to all it had to be *imposed* on all for as long as possible. All pupils were to be compelled to have the chances that the grammar schools had denied to some. The meritocratic demand for greater equality of opportunity resulted in a convergence on the academic curriculum.

Most teachers and parents cling tenaciously to the rhetoric of meritocracy. The comprehensive school allegedly avoids the sharp differentiation of pupils at eleven and (if one cannot afford private education) offers greater chances to all pupils, through education, to get on in life. This meritocratic conception rests on its appeal to middle-class parents to obtain for their children at least as good an occupation as their own, and to working-class parents it offers an opportunity for their offspring to rise in the world, to 'get a better job than his dad's' – as the grammar schools had done for so many of their working-class pupils. In theory the comprehensive schools had other objectives – creating a social mix of children from different backgrounds and with different abilities, an opportunity to create a social sympathy and harmony that might help to eradicate old social divisions between 'them' and 'us'.[13] To many teachers these social aims were a primary justification for comprehensive schools. Parents, I suspect, saw these as no more than peripheral aims: their real commitments were to meritocratic principles.

Popular adherence to meritocratic ideas is grounded in experience. Middle-class parents naturally want to keep their children at their own social level at least, and many working-class parents understandably seek to realize through their children ambitions which had to be forsaken in their own lives. We have to remember that in the post-war period between one-half and two-thirds of the places in grammar schools were taken by pupils who were working-class in origin.[14] It was thus a very common experience for working-class families, especially where the father was in a skilled or semi-skilled occupation, to have one child in a grammar school. We know, of course, that some of these children were neither happy nor successful in the grammar school, for a complex variety of reasons. But many of them were successful, achieved distinguished performances in public examinations, and so moved directly into 'white-collar' occupations or proceeded to higher education. Almost every working-class family had some relative who had been to the grammar school and who had thereby risen to a higher occupational level. This appeared to be convincing evidence that, relative to the first quarter of this century, the education system was helping society to become more just and meritocratic than it had been. On this view the comprehensive school was but the latest in a series of reforms and one which would widen opportunities still further: it would be a natural next step in our slow progress towards a more open society.

Recent work, however, suggests that this general conviction of our slow movement towards greater meritocracy may be illusory.[15] At the period when our secondary schools were, by a long sequence of reforms, beginning to offer greater opportunities to working-class pupils – and the Open University was doing so for adults who were too old to make use of the improved provision in schools – the structure of the labour force in Britain was undergoing some marked and very important changes. There was to be a sharp contraction of low-level manual jobs, indeed of almost all kinds of manual jobs. At the same time middle-level white-collar jobs, especially in administration, public service, and some technical jobs, were expanding. It is because of this expansion that so many working-class pupils became socially mobile. It was not a change created by working-class boys with talent and a grammar-school education actually *displacing* middle-class pupils with less talent – as the meritocratic principle would require; rather, the occupational structure created a kind of vacuum in its middle into which many working-class grammar-school pupils were sucked, along with their middle-class peers who were, of course, merely arriving at their traditional occupational destinations.

But the signs are that the occupational structure is now moving towards relative stability. The period of boom and expansion is, at least for the immediate future, over. The problem will not be a vacuum to be filled: it will be the surplus of the unemployed. There will be some dramatic consequences. Almost certainly the rate of social mobility for working-class pupils will decline: the opportunities for a working-class pupil to 'get a better job than dad's' will deteriorate. Objective chances of mobility become worse precisely at the period when the comprehensive system is ostensibly providing greater opportunities for working-class pupils. Hopes and aspirations are likely to outrun available opportunities.

In the past the coincidental changes in the occupational structure created the illusion that substantially greater opportunities were being provided for the working classes through education. It was wrongly assumed, we now know, that reform in educational provision *caused* our society to become substantially more meritocratic. If, as seems likely, the creation of comprehensive schools coincides with a reduction in opportunities for working-class pupils to be socially mobile, then many people are likely, once again, to make an unwarranted causal link. It is easy to see now the judgment that some observers will be making in ten years' time: the creation of the comprehensive schools has caused a reduction in the provision of equality of opportunity for working-class pupils.

Even in the shorter term there will be problems. That there was considerable social mobility for working-class pupils in the recent past is certainly true: but it is also true (though less often mentioned) that the *majority* of working-class pupils are destined to remain working-class. It has been true in the past and will be true in the future. But pupils may be seen to end up as working-class, not as could be argued in the past because they were denied a fair and equal opportunity by the structure of secondary education, but only because in contemporary comprehensive schools they did not make use of the opportunity. To leave school with very few 'qualifications' and so enter the ranks of the semi-skilled or unskilled or unemployed is, some will argue, a consequence of personal choice or wasted opportunities. Such people, it will be said, have only themselves to blame. Indeed I have heard too many teachers offering this cautionary tale to their present pupils as an incentive to work hard at school. A school with a strong meritocratic ideology is inevitably implying that there is something *wrong* with being working-class, for this is a state that any sensible pupil will work hard to escape from. But of course many working-class pupils will not be able to escape; they will continue to be, and have little choice but to be, working-class. The stronger the meritocratic ideology of the comprehensive school, I suggest, the greater the threat to the dignity of those pupils who do not succeed in the school's terms and who move into the less skilled working-class job or into the ranks of the unemployed. In consequence the greater the meritocratic ideology of the school, the greater will be the tendency for an alternative, compensatory counter-culture to emerge amongst the 'failures'. It is one of the saddest ironies of our age that the comprehensive school should become so dominated by the academic, grammar-school curriculum, when (as I shall argue) it is least suited to the needs of our time and least likely to pay occupational dividends to that section of working-class pupils who have the capacity to master it.

Teachers, much more than parents, are beginning to see through the political rhetoric of the school as a meritocratic agency, and indeed the creation of the comprehensive school may have helped them to this insight. Teachers' beliefs in the genetical basis of intelligence are less firm than they used to be, not least because of the work of sociologists of education in uncovering the importance of home background in its influence on educational attainment. Teachers do not differentiate pupils' home background in sociologists' social-class terms but rather in terms of the home being 'good' or 'bad'. This is not a reference to the family's social or economic standing, but the parents' interest in their children and their education and the relevant supportive attitudes. Teachers know that pupils are greatly privileged or handicapped in their school progress by parental attitudes. It is not that the capacity to profit from school is transmitted from one generation to another exclusively by the genetical inheritance of intelligence; nor is it simply transmitted by the inheritance of money which gives access to the best educational institutions (as was true through the nineteenth century and the first half of the twentieth, though it must be recognized that a powerful rump survives in the form of the public schools). Rather, it is transmitted, to use Pierre Bourdieu's[16] felicitous term, in the form of *cultural capital*. On this view, which goes beyond most teachers' current conceptions, the capacity to succeed in school is transmitted by parents, mainly from

71

the upper and middle classes, as a particular style and manner of thinking and speaking which is consonant with the culture of the school. In terms used in this book, middle-class parents are themselves highly skilled in the cognitive-intellectual mode, partly because they are themselves products of such an educational system.[17] It is transmitted before the child ever reaches school and continues to be transmitted throughout the child's educational career. Indeed, it can be argued that this 'cultural capital' of the cognitive-intellectual mode of the parents increases during secondary education since the school curriculum begins to converge on these skills and abilities in a way in which primary schools do not. The pupil who cannot obtain such cultural capital from home, or cannot absorb it directly from the school, will become progressively disadvantaged as he gets older – which is perhaps why 'compensatory education' schemes addressed to the pre-school child can have very limited effects. The claim that the comprehensive school is an instrument of greater meritocracy becomes, for many children, a myth which convinces the public that 'equality of opportunity' is being provided when, in fact, the school serves to preserve, stabilize and legitimate the social structure as it now exists. With the French educational system in mind, Bourdieu writes:[18]

> The culture of the elite is so near to that of the school
> that children from the lower middle class (and *a fortiori*
> from the agricultural and industrial working class) can
> acquire only with great effort something which is *given*
> to the children of the cultivated classes – style, taste,
> wit – in short, those attitudes and aptitudes which seem
> natural in members of the cultivated classes and naturally
> expected of them precisely because (in the ethnological
> sense) they are the *culture* of that class. Children from the
> lower middle classes, as they receive nothing from their
> family of any use to them in their academic activities
> except a sort of undefined enthusiasm to acquire culture,
> are obliged to expect and receive everything from school,
> even if it means accepting the school's criticism of them as
> 'plodders'. . . . By awarding allegedly impartial qualifica-
> tions (which are largely accepted as such) for socially
> conditioned aptitudes which it treats as unequal 'gifts', it

transforms *de facto* inequalities into *de jure* ones, and *economic and social* differences into *distinctions of quality*, and legitimates the transmission of the cultural heritage. In so doing, it is performing a confidence trick. Apart from enabling the elite to justify what it is, the *ideology of giftedness*, the cornerstone of the whole educational and social system, helps to enclose the underprivileged classes in the roles which society has given them by making them see as natural inability things which are only a result of an inferior social status, and by persuading them that they owe their social fate (which is increasingly tied to their educational fate as society becomes more rationalized) to their individual nature and their lack of gifts. The exceptional success of those few individuals who escape the collective fate of their class apparently justifies educational selection and gives credence to the myth of the school as a liberating force among those who have been eliminated, by giving the impression that success is exclusively a matter of gifts and work. . . . The school . . . is in truth a conservative force which owes part of its power of conservation to that myth. . . . By giving cultural inequalities an endorsement which formally at least is in keeping with democratic ideals, it provides the best justification for these inequalities.

Bourdieu's thesis is, at least as far as Britain is concerned, an overstatement. The fact that so many working-class pupils successfully completed their grammar-school education demonstrates that being working-class is far from constituting an absolute bar to social mobility. In his concession of 'the exceptional success of those few individuals who escape the collective fate of their class' Bourdieu certainly underestimates the sheer number of working-class 'exceptions' in Britain. It can be argued[19] that the grammar schools have been an important force in the active dissemination of 'cultural capital'; indeed, this research finding is in line with the arguments of those working-class ex-grammar-school contributors to the *Black Paper* defence of the grammar schools. It remains an undisputed fact, however, that these 'exceptions', numerous as they may have been, are a minority of working-class pupils. The comprehensive school by definition must give a major part of its attention to the majority; it cannot obtain its justification for what it achieves for a minority. The grammar school could do so with greater justice, but since most of the pupils in comprehensive schools would in former days have gone to secondary moderns, the comprehensive school has a moral duty to consider that majority and to do so it must go beyond meritocracy. No one has ever been very clear about the purposes of the secondary-modern schools. Today we know what the comprehensive schools were designed to be *against.* Until we ask ourselves what comprehensive schools are *for*, they cannot go beyond the meritocratic principles on which at present they somewhat uneasily rest.

For the school to continue to act as a conservative force which legitimates inequalities it is essential that teachers maintain a belief in the myth of meritocracy *and* preserve the cognitive-intellectual domain at the heart of the curriculum. Comprehensive re-organization, which is supposed to lead to a more just society, has ironically *increased* the very forces which it is supposed to weaken. Headteachers are under pressure to demonstrate to a sceptical public, which is kept on the alert by the *Black Papers* and the barrage of polemic from Dr Rhodes Boyson, that the comprehensive schools can do at least as well as the former grammar schools, and preferably better. The key index of this is held to be success in public examinations. The major immediate task of the comprehensive school is getting as many pupils as possible through CSE, 'O' level and 'A' level. Until success has been established by these criteria, it is felt by head-teachers, the comprehensive school will not be accepted by the public. In consequence the myth of the meritocracy and the pre-eminence of the cognitive-intellectual curriculum must be maintained at all costs – on the clear direction from the headteacher. The triumphant announcement on 'Open Day' of a 5 per cent increase in examination passes will be to declare the comprehensive school a successful innovation. The upheaval of re-organization is finally justified and the faith of the public in state secondary education restored.

Some pupils know better. The members of the counter-culture penetrate the mists of this grand rhetoric, as the work of Paul Willis has indicated. And in some schools pupils are beginning to realize, because of the huge increase in unemployment among the young school-leavers, that a few CSE passes are not a passport to a job any longer – so what is the point of working for them? The school has its own powerful critics from within, but not many teachers listen to the unfavourable notices proffered by their clients.

Peter Wilby, the education correspondent of *The Sunday Times*, is, I believe, a more accurate observer of our comprehensive schools when he suggests that:[20]

> The trouble with our comprehensives is not that their academic standards are too low but that they are too high. Academic standards still have a virtual stranglehold on English education – and they are the enemy of genuine educational standards. Our secondary education is organized to select those few who will go to university and, ultimately, the even tinier minority who will approach the frontiers of theoretical knowledge. For their sake, all our children are being put through an over-blown, over-academic syllabus, in which the dominant experience, for the majority, is one of failure, not of achievement.

But the English educational system has a very long history of organizing itself around the needs of the minority. It is not surprising that the innovation of the comprehensive school failed to exorcize this obsession overnight. Many years ago Jack Common understood perfectly well where he, as a working-class boy, stood in the educational system.[21]

> The week's curriculum, I fancy, must have been a bit of a conundrum to all concerned. Why were we learning or not learning these things? Of course, reading, writing, arithmetic have their own sense to them . . . but drawing, but history, but grammar, botany, singing, geography, geometry, recitation – what mortal use could they be to the likes of us? Our parents said, to help us get better jobs. . . . Our teacher said it was a fine thing to be educated. . . . The fact is, not they nor anybody could say plainly what we

75

were being educated for. In a few schools up and down the country, teaching is a simple matter because the pupils have a reasonably foreseeable future which can be contemplated cheerfully. They have waiting for them the same assured position in adult society that their parents had. The teacher must prepare them for that position by the appropriate character-conditioning, initiation into the peculiar code of behaviour which is the mark of their kind, and a laying-on of the gold leaf of culture to make them look worthy of the job already picked for them. But our lot of kids were just going to be ordinary workers. . . . Now what character, what code of behaviour, what culture is appropriate to the worker?

They hold revolutions about that in some places. You couldn't expect our teachers to have the answer. Of course they hadn't, so in practice the school unconsciously orientated its teaching to the exceptions among us . . . who were going to be lifted up into a higher social class. How many of these? That was the point. Our school was doing well it considered, by the only practical test that existed, if it managed to raise the proportion of pupils capable of winning scholarships and getting thereby possible passports to Better Things. . . . Always the pride that prevailed in this working-class school was that it succeeded in turning out less recruits for the working-class than any other of its kind in the district. That less was still the majority, mind you. . . . But the school's official boast was not of them.

The commentary refers to an education in the early part of the twentieth century. Since those days we have had over fifty years of educational reforms. Yet do not Jack Common's words apply with a devastating fit to the condition of many working-class pupils in a contemporary comprehensive school?

4

The culture of individualism

The re-organization of secondary education into comprehensive schools has been accompanied by a startling dissensus on educational matters. Primary schools have, for the most part, been left to get on with their work in relative peace, but almost every aspect of secondary education has been the subject of dispute, bitter fighting and (too often) uninformed debate. In the early days there was considerable enmity between the Labour Party and the Conservative Party about re-organization itself; but today it is generally accepted that the comprehensive schools are here to stay. Whilst the broad principles of comprehensive education are now in most circles *hors de combat*, the particular pattern of its implementation which was left to the discretion of local authorities – 'all-through' 11–18 schools, 11–16 schools feeding a sixth-form college, a tiered system with middle schools, neighbourhood community schools, etc. – remains a controversial issue. Moreover at the very point of comprehensive re-organization, or immediately afterwards, a number of important social changes and developments have affected secondary education. Some of these have been direct educational decisions, such as the raising of the school-leaving age; some have been social changes with a profound effect on schools, such as changes in the birth rate, which had dramatic consequences for schools affected by falling rolls; others have been less direct, but no less consequential, such as declining resources for schools; the demand for better links with, and a more responsive attitude to, industry; public criticisms about a decline in academic and behavioural standards in schools. All this occurred at the very moment when schools were facing what for many teachers was the traumatic upheaval of re-organization.

When the secondary schools are under such stress and in the midst of change, challenge and criticism, it is particularly difficult to keep one's eye on the total picture. Most teachers and educationists have inclined to take highly defensive postures against external criticism or to fight bravely on for yet further changes. All of us become enmeshed in minor struggles over this or that detail. These worthy causes are real enough; they are not trivial, but nevertheless they are often details on the wider canvas of secondary education. Our loss of focus on the whole picture was not entirely caused by the many social changes to which I have referred; a principal cause was the lack of any generally agreed set of aims or purposes for the new comprehensive schools. For many teachers and most parents there has simply been no explicit and clear rationale for the comprehensive school. And when aims and purposes are clouded, we lose our way, and there are no clear directions either for the resolution of disputes or for the many positive innovations which (perhaps surprisingly) have been generated by re-organization and its concomitant stresses.

Several guidelines may be suggested for helping us to keep some sense of direction in such foggy educational weather. First, we must strive very hard to keep the total picture in mind and take care not to get lost in what are relative details. Second, we must as far as we can retain the best of present practice in secondary education. Further reform may eliminate a present evil but, if the cost of so doing is the elimination of a present good of equal or greater magnitude, then the value of the reform is doubtful. We must not, as did Ivan Illich with his notions of 'de-schooling', throw out the baby with the bath-water. In terms of my own argument so far, we must not damage the cognitive-intellectual aspects of education irreparably in searching for a more balanced curriculum. Third, we must be willing to apply the above argument retrospectively. It may well be that some of our past reforms had undesirable consequences or side-effects. We may have to recover from the past those desirable features which have been discarded or destroyed by earlier reforms. The 'old' is not always 'bad'; to look backwards for inspiration is not always to be naively reactionary. Fourth, we have to consider the feasibility of reform; we cannot, like Illich once again, afford to be too utopian and propose changes that are so politically naive that they have not the slightest hope of implementation. Educational dreamers are not to be despised, but too many of them will only create a nightmare.

Comprehensive re-organization has not been easy for most teachers and it has coincided with what I believe is a more important problem for them, namely all the changes to which I referred above. On my visits to schools I am often tempted to think that the dominant concern of teachers over the last fifteen or twenty years has been their relationships with their pupils. This is hardly remarkable, for teaching is a pre-eminently social activity requiring extensive social skills, sensitivity and resourcefulness. The great changes in authority relations, the so-called decline in deference, that have affected our society in the post-war period have been nowhere more forcefully felt than in our secondary schools. Despite some early ups and downs, and with a few exceptions still here and there, our teachers have responded to this change quite magnificently and often at considerable personal cost. They have not, it must be said, received the applause from parents and politicians that they merit. It is, I suspect, this challenge at the interpersonal level, combined with the difficulties of re-organization, which has distracted teachers from other major changes (such as the increased dominance of public examinations) and from the fragmentation of educational development and change in recent years. And who can, in all fairness, blame them?

The implication of the last chapter is that the examined curriculum is in need of some reform. Most of the teachers I know take a similar view; they feel a deep unease both about the academic curriculum and about the constraining power of the public examinations. At the same time they feel entirely powerless to make any significant changes – and so inevitably allow the issue to slide to the back of their minds – and in any event feel very unsure about the directions in which we might go. Perhaps, then, there might be a more positive lead from Her Majesty's Inspectors. After all, they are distanced from the immediate, day-to-day constraints of the practising teacher, and they are a small body with a potentially powerful voice at the Department of Education and Science. In the summer of 1978 the HMIs produced a document entitled *Curriculum 11–16*, which, as one of the products of the Great Education Debate stimulated by Prime Minister Callaghan in 1976, was to discuss the case for, and content of, a 'core curriculum' for the secondary school.[1] It was a damp squib. Perhaps it was too much to expect the HMIs to take a fresh, vigorous and comprehensive view of the curriculum for what after all are new comprehensive schools. Perhaps they, like teachers, felt under too much pressure to produce the 'right' answers for their political masters – for it is very unlikely that the agenda for the Great Debate has been constructed with no probable answers already in view. Five of the six secondary-school headteachers invited by *The Times Educational Supplement* to comment on the report found it distinctly unhelpful. Mr Patrick Eavis, the head of a school in Newcastle upon Tyne, pointed out with evident disappointment that the report seemed merely to justify, yet again, the traditional academic curriculum:[2]

> These people have obviously read Hirst and Peters and all that. I was brought up on it myself, but all it does is look at what is in the curriculum and find good reasons for it being there. They wrap it all up in words like objectives and skills but it tells you nothing about what precisely we should be doing, or how. It is just a nice safe traditional view of what is taught. The truth is that most kids are bored out of their mind with this stuff. It's OK for those who know they only have to put up with it for a few years to get a nice job like mine, but what are the other eighty per cent here for? Nothing in this report is going to cause a revolution in terms of motivation; getting kids interested in what they are doing and actually wanting to do it. What I am concerned about is just what sort of science should we do and how can we make it relevant to the twentieth century, let alone the twenty-first. Teaching them about pop groups and football is no answer either. Of course we have got to expand their horizons and offer them genuine choices in life, but how do you do it? This report is no help in this respect at all.

It is, I suspect, a view with which many teachers agree. Mr Eavis shows the limitations of attempting to reform the curriculum by refusing to question the contents of the conventional academic curriculum. Despite the improvements in teacher–pupil relationships, the needs of 80 per cent of pupils cannot be met simply by changes on that front. It is probably a counsel of perfection to ask for more inspiring teachers and more resources. The curriculum itself must be revised, but it is not clear how it might be.

Many new curricula have been developed in recent years and some of them are very impressive. It has, however, proved much more difficult to disseminate these innovations widely. Teachers who were personally involved in curriculum development, whether at the Schools' Council or in regional curriculum-development centres, have found the experience as exhilarating as it was demanding; but it has been difficult to persuade other schools, not associated with the development work, to adopt the finished product. I believe, though curriculum theorists may find the judgment harsh, that too much of this development work, like the report of the Inspectorate, took too much of the present selected content and structure of the present curriculum as unquestioned and unquestionable. In too many cases, even though it was recast in new, more interesting and more attractive forms, it was still the same old familiar curriculum which was taken for granted. Sugared as it is, the pill remains bitter for many pupils; they cannot be bribed by superficial novelty. A new curriculum format is often attractive to teachers; it may produce more exciting lessons than any of us can remember from our own schooldays; the 'trial' runs may be especially successful when administered by enthusiastic teachers committed to the experiment's success. But none of this ensures a more general success for the curriculum scheme when taught by more cautious and sceptical teachers who are distanced from the original innovation and played no part in its construction. And teachers' attitudes to a new curriculum are soon transmitted to pupils.

The cardinal error, I submit, was to see most curriculum reform in terms of *subjects* and to organize curriculum development among teachers committed to the same subject.

81

To do so kept the assumption, that these are the right subjects which must continue to be taught as distinct subjects, completely unchallenged. Even where two traditionally distinct subjects were 'integrated', there was a constant danger that the integration existed on paper only, the 'geography' and 'history' components (to take one example) being clearly visible beneath the new surface of 'social studies' and in practice being taught by teachers whom the pupils knew to be 'really' a geography and a history teacher. The integration of several different subjects was attempted occasionally, but this could not be very attractive to the many teachers who think of themselves as subject specialists and who are aware that most public examinations are still in the format of single subjects. The inevitable consequence is that the major achievements of curriculum reform and development have been too often to put old wine into new bottles.

We must conclude that any adequate curriculum reform must be prepared to challenge the traditional subjects of the academic curriculum, the core of which we have inherited from the last century and from the early part of this. But what is the alternative? As Mr Eavis pointed out, we cannot construct this around the obsessions of young people, such as pop music and football. That might (though I doubt it) be seen by the young as a relevant and interesting curriculum, but it does not constitute a justifiable formal education. There is, I shall argue, a way out of this artificial choice. But before describing it, I must attend to some preliminary considerations, of which the most important is to ask what we are educating young people *for*. Whilst one would hope that relevance and interest would be characteristic of any new curriculum, they cannot be the criteria with which we begin. To establish a curriculum on what happens to interest young people is to risk trivializing the curriculum into a content (such as popular music and football) for which they require hardly any formal education at all.

It seems sensible to start with the *aims* of secondary education and then seek a curriculum content which will realize those aims. This is, of course, the path advocated in much curriculum development. The initial step is to formulate such admirable abstract aims as 'the realization of pupils' aptitudes and abilities' or 'the preparation of the young for active participation in a democratic society', then to operationalize these into more specific objectives from which the precise lesson content can be derived. This curriculum content can then be evaluated to test how far the objectives are being achieved in practice. This is one theory of how one should proceed. The practice is not, as so often in education, in accord with the theory. The trick is to *reverse* the steps proposed in theory. A teacher is trained to teach a subject; that subject will continue to be taught in the new curriculum. This sets a severe limitation on *what* can legitimately be taught as that subject, though the form in which it is taught, the order in which it is taught and the methods by which it is taught are all open to revision. With such a limitation one is forced to work backwards in curriculum development so that often the abstract aims appear as mere rhetoric which justifies the unquestionable content of the syllabus that is to be taught. If one genuinely began with the aims, and sought to work out logically and with an open mind what content might most adequately realize those aims, there is a real risk that the eventual syllabus would not correspond to the content that the teacher is trained, qualified and used to teach; the 'subject' might disappear. It is a risk that most teachers, for understandable reasons, cannot afford to take.

This unkind (and partly unfair) caricature of curriculum development does not mean that we must not have, or even begin with, abstract aims. The moral, rather, is that we must not prejudice the conclusions, that is the syllabus or curriculum content, which may be entailed. If we set ourselves certain aims and then find ourselves forced to a curriculum content which is beyond teachers' powers to teach, then at least we can be honest that those aims cannot be realized through secondary education. At least we avoid the hypocrisy of pretending to have aims that we know are not being, and cannot be, achieved.

If the earlier argument that schooling tends to damage dignity is sound, then we might take as our principal aim for secondary education the promotion of dignity. This was defined earlier as 'a sense of being worthy, of possessing creative, inventive and critical capacities, of having the power to achieve personal and social change'. It seems admirable, but it is very woolly. That it emphasizes a personal state in the pupil and the possession of skills rather than knowledge makes it remarkably vague as a definition. We can make it a little more concrete if the conditions under which dignity is likely to be achieved are specified. I suggest two such conditions. First, the person must acquire competencies and a sense of making a valid and valuable contribution to the life of the groups and institutions of which he or she is a member. Second, the person must have a sense of being valued by others in the groups or institutions of which he or she is a part. When these conditions do not obtain, a person will experience great difficulty in maintaining dignity as it has been defined. There seems to be nothing startling here; these are aims which are probably acceptable to most teachers. One feature stands out, however; both conditions have a strong *social* or corporate element; the individual person is carefully tied to social groups and institutions. The aims are not directed, as is usually the case in lists of aims, to the development of the *individual*. Instead, the individual and his development are seen to be contingent on the location of the individual in a social context. At first sight, the change is but a slight one, no more than a difference in emphasis. I want to argue that it is very much more.

Mass schooling was introduced in the nineteenth century after a long, tortuous and heated debate. Simplifying the complexities of history we can say that it was a struggle between two deeply opposed views. On the one hand, it was held that the introduction of compulsory mass education for the labouring classes would destroy the social fabric and threaten the interests and power of the middle and upper classes. Social disorder, anarchy or revolution would ensue. On the other hand, it was held that without mass education of the poor, Britain would be unable to compete as a modern industrial society; we could survive only with a better educated work-force. It was a profound dilemma for nineteenth-century capitalism. The second view prevailed, as we know, and perhaps only because elementary education was to be accompanied by a religious education which would teach the labouring classes the providential basis of their lowly social status. In the early teacher-training colleges student teachers were subjected to a similar religious regime; they too must not aspire beyond their station.

I refer to this debate in the last century not to make the now fashionable point that from its very beginnings mass education was conceived in terms of social control of the upper classes over the lower classes. That is self-evident, though it ignores the genuinely humanitarian and philanthropic motives which also helped to generate reforms. My point is to stress that the debate was about the *social* functions and consequences of mass education. Both sides showed broad agreement on these terms of the debate, which focused on two general questions. First, what sort of society do we want to create or maintain? Second, what is the role of education in creating or maintaining such a society? Once the social objectives of the kind of society to which we were aspiring had been determined, then as a second step the aims of education to realize such a society could be clarified. It was an overt attempt, on both sides, at social engineering. We hear relatively little about what mass education will do for *individuals*; the development of individual talents and the liberation of individual minds is a minor consideration.

In the following hundred years the balance between individual and social ends for education was to change dramatically. The shift towards a concern for the individual pupil has been of inestimable benefit. The movement towards individualism in education was impelled by many influences, such as Rousseau's romantic stress on self-development and growth, on which many leading educationists and innovators relied in various ways. It became allied to the so-called Protestant ethic, which celebrated hard work and self-reliance; in the United States in particular social barriers could be broken by those with talent and industry. New democratic ideals spawned a new child-centredness in education and the 'progressive' educational ideals of John Dewey. In more recent times the child-centred movement in education found new support in the developmental psychology of Jean Piaget. The paths of these various forces cannot be traced in detail here. My object is to show a clear link between a progressive child-centred educational philosophy and a meritocratic conception of the relation between education and society; that link is not accidental. It has left us with a particular understanding of education's contribution to society. In crude terms it is this. We make society more 'open' by limiting the power and the privileges associated with birth, mainly the social position of the parents and wealth. All positions and occupations must be open to those with the appropriate abilities and qualifications. We can achieve this negatively, as in the abolition of fee-paying grammar schools, or positively, as in the provision of additional resources to the underprivileged in the form of grants, social-priority schools and compensatory education. The comprehensive school is merely one change in a long line of reforms directed to the same end. These reforms are, we should note, almost exclusively structural, administrative and financial. The teacher in the classroom, it seems, is now free to get on with what he regards as his real work: the cultivation of the individual child and his various abilities and aptitudes. If that task is accomplished, then the 'system' can do the rest: every teacher must do his very best to tap the potential of every individual pupil and when that is achieved the pupils will slot 'naturally' into the right channel of the education system and thus into his rightful (that is just and merited) position in society.

Some teachers, not least those in urban secondary schools, know this ideal has not been reached, for they experience daily the lack of equality of opportunity and the existence of barriers which keep many of the doors in the 'open' society firmly closed. Yet they are aware, on good grounds, that progress has been made. We may not have reached our goal of a true meritocracy, they concede with some sadness (or even anger), but things have improved more than the Marxist critics seem to allow. In any case, the necessary structural, administrative and financial changes still needed cannot be initiated by the practising classroom teacher. At this level, the work of the teacher remains unchanged: it consists in the cultivation of the individual. As we have noted, in recent years schools have taken on many additional duties in relation to 'pastoral care'; the individual can be cultivated adequately only if teachers are prepared to act, with remarkable generosity, as welfare workers and parent-substitutes as well as academic instructors. The individual pupil must be cared for in all aspects of his life, not just the academic and intellectual ones.

Secondary schools and their teachers are, I propose, deeply imbued with a *culture of individualism*. The origins stretch back, as I suggested earlier, at least to Rousseau; the growth of the culture of individualism has been very slow and tortuous and in our secondary schools the most rapid phase of its development followed the Second World War. It was no sudden change, no sudden acceptance of a new educational philosophy: there is no equivalent in the secondary-school sector to the enormous influence exerted by the Plowden Report on primary schools.[3] The change evolved so slowly and so unevenly, yet most teachers have been deeply influenced by it, especially younger teachers. One index of the change is the shifting working vocabulary of teachers. In schools today one hears much less of the once-common corporate vocabulary: 'the honour of the school', 'loyalty to the school', 'team spirit' and *'esprit de corps'*. These terms tend today to have a rather old-fashioned ring to them. Loyalty and honour have been satirized away. (Even when they do survive they are often debased, as when a teacher appeals for loyalty when he is demanding nothing more than mindless conformity – and the pupils can, in private, translate the lofty concept to the more crude demand that it is. For there is, of course, a substantial difference between the subjugation of personal interests and preferences to collective and institutional pride and the blind acceptance of teachers' unreasoned demands.) As these corporate concepts vanish, so too do the collective rituals with which they have traditionally been associated: the daily school assembly of all pupils and staff, Speech Day, the school song, school uniform. It is indeed the battles between teachers and pupils over school uniform which has led to the debasement of the concept of loyalty, for headteachers autocratically *ordered* the wearing of school uniform as a symbol of institutional pride, ignoring the fact that real loyalties spring from allegiances which are naturally called forth. Too often our headteachers saw the pupil resistance to school uniform as a symptom of incipient rebellion rather than as a symptom that the school was failing to excite pride in the pupils. They forgot that the notion of a uniform is not in itself alien to the young: they ignored the ubiquitous wearing of blue jeans.

There are other indices of the growth of individualism in comprehensive schools. The development of 'pastoral-care' systems at first sight appears to be a strongly corporate innovation. In practice they are not always so.[4] The division of pupils into 'tutor groups' or 'house groups' or 'year groups' has often meant little more than the allocation of pupils to particular groups which meet just once a day for registration and other administrative functions, groups which have little significance for pupils and little impact on their school lives. The pastoral-care staff have also often found themselves assigned 'disciplinary' as well as 'caring' functions, a hazardous combination for a year tutor. It is not difficult for 'pastoral care' to comprise little more than allocation to a tutor group and some provision of 'personal counselling' for those with problems. Ironically pastoral-care systems are often referred to as 'house systems', based of course on the houses in the public schools. But in most comprehensive schools the 'houses' are relatively inconsequential: they are not the distinctive, physical houses where the pupils actually live and to which they give their loyalties. The comprehensive school's imitation of this feature of the public schools is often little more than titular.

Perhaps the most startling change is the disappearance in many schools of the form, or the class unit. Most adults remember their schooldays in terms of the class of which they were members for many years; they passed through the school in general with the same group of boys or girls. I can still remember the roll-call of my class-mates: Aitken, Billington, Biltcliffe, Blackburn, Bonsor . . . and so on through the list: I can even remember the desks in which they sat. These fixed classes or streams in the small grammar and secondary-modern schools are fast disappearing in our larger modern comprehensives, which are much more likely to have staggeringly complex combinations of bands and sets and mixed-ability groups and options, with the poor old tutor group as the one isolated experience of continuity. In its more extreme version we speak of the 'individualized curriculum', a unique programme for every child. In schools of the past each class had its own classroom where most of the lessons, with a few specialist exceptions such as science, would be conducted by the teachers who moved round from room to room. In many schools today it is the teachers who 'own' the class-rooms and the pupils who move round the school. This is not merely an important loss of corporate territory for each class, but it guarantees the Paddington Station effect every forty minutes: the bell rings and hordes of pupils pack into the narrow corridors as they search for their next teachers. If pupils do not have their own classrooms, they do not have their own desks. So the desks are replaced by tables (which are cheaper anyway), and the pupils keep their belongings in the impersonal space of locker-rooms. But the lockers are a target for thieves and become vandalized, and so cannot be used. As a result in some comprehensive schools at the end of every lesson the Paddington Station effect is transformed into the Luton Airport effect – the children stream round the building, but are now armed with huge cases, bags, carriers, hold-alls in which all their belongings are kept. There is no corporate home, no collective responsibility and yet teachers are puzzled that there is low institutional pride.[5]

This comparison between our own experience of school with that of many of today's children sounds nostalgic; but it is the loss of the corporate elements in the wake of the culture of individualism that I want to evoke, not nostalgia.[6] Nor do I want to argue that the culture of individualism has been a grievous error *in toto*, for in many respects it has brought untold benefits, just as the more corporate schools of yester-day could be and sometimes were oppressive in their imper-sonality and their conformity. My contention, rather, is that we have gone to the opposite extreme of the nineteenth-century debate and that any educational system which is premised on either extreme position alone is defective. An educational system which is entirely determined by its social functions in society will become merely an instrument which furthers the interests of those who determine the content of those prescribed social functions, and the education of the individual will be sacrificed to these social ends. Equally, an

89

educational system based on the cultivation of individual pupils will forget that the system will inevitably have social functions and consequences and these cannot be ignored or handed over to others. This is the most important insight of the Marxist critique discussed earlier: teachers become blind to the social functions of education because it is not part of their conscious intentions any longer. Being lost in the culture of individualism, teachers in effect consign the social functions to the hidden curriculum of schooling. We have reached the position today where most secondary-school teachers treat the concept of 'social engineering' with considerable distaste; that, they assert, is not what education is about. Retreating into the culture of individualism, they can wash their hands of such horrid 'manipulative' ideas. They are, of course, in serious error. Under pressure teachers will admit that the educational system involves a degree of social engineering, but they see this as apparently restricted to the slow improvement of the system in accord with meritocratic principles and believe that this is effected at the structural and administrative levels; it is not something that affects the classroom work of the ordinary practising teacher. This ignores the mounting evidence that our progress towards meritocracy is to date very limited, illusory or even misguided. And it ignores that there are many other elements to social engineering through education. In a modern industrial society the education system is, and cannot be other than, a form of social engineering, for whatever teachers think and feel and prefer, the educational system will have social functions and consequences. The question is not whether school is a form of social engineering or not, but whether or not teachers are going to be aware of, and take part in shaping, those features of schooling which represent social engineering.

Teachers can effectively shield themselves from the notion of social engineering by the style in which and the rhetoric with which reforms are introduced. The establishment of the comprehensive school, such a major instrument of social engineering, can be accomplished, even against considerable opposition, because it is accompanied by a rhetoric of expanding opportunities for *individuals*, an idea which is highly consonant with the culture of individualism. In a similar way, when there is an urgent need in society for more highly qualified personnel, as was true in the late 1950s and early 1960s, this is easily achieved by encouraging teachers to develop individual talent the more vigorously and by providing more resources to that end. Again, the culture of individualism is not in any way challenged. Social engineering takes place without in any way threatening the autonomy of the school (or university) which is so jealously guarded; this freedom buttresses the culture of individualism and leaves the teacher with the sense that he is promoting the development of individual pupils to make their own choices rather than playing a key role in shaping society.

The extent to which the culture of individualism has permeated the thinking of teachers is illustrated in the *Schools Council Enquiry 1* by Morton-Williams and Finch, in which pupils, parents, teachers and headteachers were asked to rate in importance various school objectives.[7] On a number of these there were marked disparities between teachers and their clients. Pupils and their parents show an instrumental attitude to school – education, in their view, provides a pupil with something that can be of direct use in the labour market. Two-thirds of the pupils (and even more parents) saw helping a pupil to do very well in examinations such as the GCE or CSE as a very important educational objective; but less than 20 per cent of teachers and headteachers believed this to be very important. (It is almost certainly true that the percentage of teachers who rate examinations as an important objective would today be substantially greater than in 1968.)[8] Over 80 per cent of pupils wanted school to teach them things which will be of direct use in a job; but less than half of teachers and just over a third of headteachers perceived this as a very important objective. On the other hand, 92 per cent of teachers (and almost all headteachers) believed the development of the pupil's personality and character to be a very important objective, whereas less than half the pupils subscribed to this view. It is clear that the culture of individualism, in the form of a liberal, humanitarian and child-centred philosophy, holds teachers firmly in its grip. Teachers know that for many pupils and their parents public examinations constitute the primary purpose of secondary

91

education; but they know, too, that some pupils will not succeed in these examinations and that an education which is reduced to the passing of these examinations is not an education worthy of the name. They fear narrow vocational training and resist the thesis that a function of schooling is to fit pupils into particular positions in the occupational (and therefore also the social) structure. The world beyond the school is seen as threatening and hostile: the best that teachers can do is to provide pupils with a self-confidence and maturity (that is, a development of personality and character) which will allow them to survive in that world and, with luck, reach some kind of happiness and self-fulfilment. This pedagogical philosophy appears in its strongest form among those teachers who work with pupils who are not entered for, or who will achieve little of value in, public examinations. Since the dice are loaded heavily against such children, it is they more than others who are in urgent need of the survival kit of a well-developed character. For many such teachers, the formal curriculum assumes peripheral importance; their real task is educating their charges in personal development.

Seen in this light, the consequences of the culture of individualism are profound. It leaves the teachers with the false impression that they do not need to ask the two key questions – what kind of society do we want, and how is education to help us to realize that society – and can instead ask only – what kind of individuals do we want and how can education help to create such individuals? Once the social questions are put aside, teachers can ignore the *political* functions of education.[9] Today teachers are impatient with the 'politics' of education, because they use the term political to refer only to *party* political matters. Understandably they resent many educational issues being dominated by the vagaries of party political antagonism. Yet this very common tendency among teachers to contrast *educational* with *political* issues is to indulge in a naive and false antithesis. On the definition of political as concerning how a society is structured, maintained and governed, educational issues will in many cases become entangled with political issues. Politics cannot be kept out of education, and those who argue that it should are

merely defending an educational debate in which the underlying political assumptions are not exposed as part of that
debate. This panders to and trades upon a depoliticized
teaching profession which is addicted to the culture of individualism, and which in consequence sees the educational
system as self-contained, the leaven in the lump of an un-
healthy society that constantly threatens to engulf defence-
less individuals.

The fault with the culture of individualism, let me repeat,
does not lie with the humanistic sentiments and ideals which
it enshrines; in themselves they are far from being reprehensible. The error lies in the repudiation of the nineteenth-
century concerns with the social functions of education and
the attempt to substitute individual functions in their place.
In somewhat simplistic terms, if an excessive and exclusive
attention to social and societal needs jeopardizes the education
of the individual, then an excessive and exclusive attention
to individual needs jeopardizes those of society. There is an
unremitting tension between society and the individual which
cannot be solved by ignoring one of these two elements. The
nineteenth-century obsession with social functions was, to
our advantage, corroded by the increased attention of educationists to individuals. Our present obsession with individuals
has led teachers to deny and fear the social functions of
education, and sociological critics to point out that some of
those nineteenth-century functions are still operative within
our society and must be rooted out.

The consequence is that we fall into what I shall call
the *fallacy of individualism*. This is the belief that if only
schools can successfully educate every individual pupil in
self-confidence, independence and autonomy, then society
can with confidence be left to take care of itself. The good
society will be automatically produced by the creation
through education of good individuals. Education, it is held,
cannot directly change society; it must do so *indirectly* by
creating the kinds of individual who will then possess those
qualities which are a prerequisite for the realization of the
good society. This belief can then be used to justify a range
of divergent teacher perspectives. The 'liberal' teacher interprets his task as the preparation of self-confident autonomous

adults; the 'radical' teacher interprets his task as, in addition, the provision of the pupil with an insight into inequalities and injustices which prevail in contemporary British society.

This is shown in two accounts of the aims of education of two distinguished headmasters which, significantly appeared in a book entitled *Education for Democracy*.[10] John Mitchell, the primary-school headteacher claimed:

> The modern primary school aims to awaken the child's interest in learning, to view each child as an individual and cater for him accordingly, to give each child the opportunity to produce creative work and to experience the satisfaction which accompanies the achievement of original and valuable work. The school in no way aims to compare one child with another, but only to compare what each child is now producing with what he has previously produced. As well as producing children who are capable of working on their own intellectual level, the school must give emphasis to the development of the child in other fields – self-confidence, initiative, responsibility, respect and understanding for others are amongst the things we hope to foster.

The aims suggested by Albert Rowe, the highly influential former secondary-school headmaster, seem consonant with these:

> Our society needs intelligence and expertise, *but allied to a new democratic concern for others.* Not trained intellects alone, but *feeling intellects*, able in empathy to put ourselves in other people's shoes and act in the light of the knowledge that we are members of one another, and so treat others as they'd like to be treated. Of course we depend on the intellectuals, but equally we depend on 'the others', upon their skills and qualities as human beings also. . . . This is a multi-directional multi-dimensional view of human nature, flexible enough to embrace life in all its infinite variety and richness. The price of education is life itself. So the purpose of education is life itself. So the purpose of education must be to help each pupil to develop to maximum length as many strands of excellence

as possible. Schools which adopt an ethic of co-operation and community can create a milieu which is quickly accepted as natural and which will in time change class-biased assumptions into humane and democratic ones, accepted implicitly and unconsciously. A milieu in which all their pupils will grow, not only in brotherly awareness of one another as of equal ultimate worth, but also in generous and sensitive recognition of each other's valuable and infinitely varied qualities and gifts. [Italics in the original]

The first view outlines a primary-school progressivism which draws on Piaget's developmental psychology. In the second quotation, we see the same breadth of vision in relation to the diversity of pupil talents, but with a stress on tolerant and empathetic social relations based in a spirit of co-operation. Once this ethos is established in the school it will inevitably 'in time change class-biased assumptions into humane and democratic ones'. The good society is just round the corner, if only we can transform the milieu of school. Educated in such a climate, the child will become the father of democratic man.

As is usually the case in essentially individualistic, child-centred accounts, society and social relationships are not ignored. Reared in the right educational climate, the individual pupil will naturally develop his talents and live in a spirit of harmonious co-operation with his fellow men in a society grounded in the ethic of the Sermon on the Mount. This model of society is naive. We hear little about inequalities and injustices, or of the deep conflicts between those who govern and those who are governed, between employers and employees, between different interest groups competing for incompatible ends, between officials and clients, between rich and poor. All this, it seems, will wither away when individuals become autonomous and treat others with humanity. The thesis is vague and almost certainly fallacious.

We cannot slough off the past so readily, not merely because the hand of history lies so heavily upon us (true though that be), but because the vocabulary of the progressive teachers discards, or treats as peripheral, a set of concepts and ideas with which we must come to terms – power

95

and authority, privilege and disadvantage, order and control. These concepts are more easily found in the vocabulary of more traditional and conservative teachers. Whereas the progressives celebrate freedom, autonomy and individual development as the prerequisites of an unfolding future utopia, the conservatives celebrate control by those whose duty it is to exercise power, and obedience from those whose duty it is to submit, so that on this basis we can escape our present 'anarchy' and recover a past utopia which will save us from our steady decline into chaos. These two polarized positions (which in practice rarely appear in so blunt a form) are presented to us by teachers as incompatible alternatives from which we must choose one as a direction both for education and for society.

For a small, but growing, section of teachers there is a third possibility, that of the 'radical' teacher.[11] In its Marxist form, it simply dismisses the traditional position for obvious reasons, and accuses the progressive of naivety. Like the progressive, the Marxist radical places his utopia in the future but, unlike the progressive, does not believe that it is in the near future or that it can be realized through educational reform. By asserting that the necessary social change can come only from fundamental changes in our economic and political life, the Marxist radical is left in an awkward predicament, namely what can such a teacher actually do in schools? If the school merely reflects capitalist society, must not his work as a teacher merely serve to perpetuate the very system which he wants to see destroyed? There is an easy escape route in defining the radical teacher's task as the explicit demystification of capitalism in his classroom teaching. Pupils are to be prepared not with the qualities of utopia, to ensure its emergence, as in the case of the progressive, but with the knowledge and skills to fight capitalism, to ensure its defeat, for that is the first and primary step in the creation of the utopia. The personal qualities needed for that utopia can be decided later when the possibility of its existence comes into sight. Like the traditional teacher, the radical Marxist is happy to use the obsolescent vocabulary of power, authority, discipline and control, but as a means of displaying and analysing the exploitation to which people are subjected in the present social system. Nevertheless, the radical Marxist, like the progressive, falls neatly into the culture of individualism, though it takes a different form, and they are uneasily united in a common espousal of the fallacy of individualism.

It is clear that we must transcend these different ideological positions by wresting from each the important truths which they possessively appropriate to themselves. From the progressive movement I take the emphasis on caring for the individual pupil and the cultivation of his rich and varied talents, not just cognitive-intellectual ones. I take also the progressive's belief that education can help to change society other than by assisting a Marxist revolution. Later I shall take from the Marxist the need to demystify for pupils the world in which we live. In the rest of this chapter I want to explore the more traditionalist position to see what we can learn from the concern with the social objectives of education.

We can begin with three contemporary sociologists who have sought to chart the impact of a technological society upon the modern consciousness; society has changed and it has changed our experience. In *The Homeless Mind*, Peter and Brigitte Berger and Hansfried Kellner[12] try to account for the feelings of helplessness, frustration and alienation experienced by many in our society. They suggest that modern man's identity, or the way in which an individual defines himself, is *peculiarly open*. We are no longer born into a clear social position in which we will live and die. Today we are born into possibilities and our biography can become a migration through several successive social worlds in which we take on different identities. At the same time man's identity is *peculiarly differentiated*. Because we can live in several social worlds, sometimes within a single day, we lack the experience of a coherent and stable world. It is never clear where our 'real' identity is located. This makes the modern identity *peculiarly reflective*. Because our world is not neatly integrated, it presents us with a constant need to make choices and decisions. Finally, modern identity is *peculiarly individuated*. The importance of individual freedom, autonomy and rights have come to be taken for granted.

All these changes reflect the weakened power of institutions to allocate man to clear and fixed roles. Berger, Berger

97

and Kellner trace these changes through the demise of the concept of *honour* and its replacement by the concept of *dignity*. Honour is often associated with a hierarchical society, as in medieval codes of chivalry. It is something that is possessed not merely by an individual but by an individual who occupies a particular status or standing in society and who shares the honour with others of the same status. Honour is something that a man can bring not just to himself, but to the group of which he is a member – the family, the group, the school, the occupation, the nation. When honour is defended, it is defended on behalf of the group. When honour is lost, others in the group share in the shame.

Even those at the lowest levels of a social hierarchy have held strong conceptions of honour. For example, in Robert Roberts's *The Classic Slum*[13] the working-class poor would protect honour fiercely. The book is replete with examples:

> Over our community the matriarchs stood guardians, but not the creators, of the group conscience and as such possessed a sense of social propriety as developed and un-erring as any clique of Edwardian dowagers. Behind the counters of a corner shop one learned to realise their power. In and out they trailed from early morning to an hour before midnight, little groups that formed and faded, trading with goodwill, candour or cattishness the detailed gossip of a closed society. . . . Each would be criticised, praised, censured openly or by hint and finally allotted by tacit consent a position on the social scale. Misdeeds . . . were mulled over and penalties unconsciously fixed. . . . Parents of the most respectable and conformist families were the staunchest upholders of 'discipline', though adults whose social standing was suspect or who had in any way transgressed against the accepted conduct would often brag about the severity of the chastisement meted out to their erring young, in an effort to restore tarnished prestige. . . . If a single girl had a baby she lowered of course not only the social standing of her family but, in some degree, that of all her relations, in a chain reaction of shame.

As Berger, Berger and Kellner note, honour occupies about

the same place in current usage as chastity: it is hardly something one boasts about.

As our strong attachment to institutions declined, our concepts of honour became obsolescent. (How many nowadays speak of the 'honour of the school' except in a satirical tone?) It was replaced by the discovery of dignity which took place amid the wreckage of our debunked conceptions of honour, because, unlike honour, dignity is tied to individuals rather than social positions and institutions. Dignity is associated with individual rights, with individual self-realization against the pressures of institutions requiring conformity. It is the free man who achieves dignity; it is this word which becomes the shibboleth of individualism.

Our authors understand very well that the modern spirit yearns for a safe home, and that the natural temptation is to dream nostalgically of the securities and certainties of the past or to turn to socialism with its promise of a new home in the future. Neither will do:[14]

It seems clear to us that the unrestrained enthusiasm for total liberation of the self from the 'repression' of institutons fails to take account of certain fundamental requirements of man, notably those of *order* – that institutional order of society without which both collectivities and individuals must descend into dehumanizing chaos. In other words, the demise of honour has been a very costly price to pay for whatever liberations modern man may have achieved. . . . [The] rediscovery of honour in the future development of modern society is both empirically plausible and morally desirable. Needless to say, this will hardly take the form of a regressive restoration of traditional codes. . . . Man's fundamental constitution is such that, just about inevitably, he will once more construct institutions to provide an ordered reality for himself. A return to institutions will *ipso facto* be a return to honour. It will then be possible again for individuals to identify themselves with the escutcheons of their institutional roles, experienced now not as self-estranging tyrannies but as freely chosen vehicles of self-realization. The ethical question, of course, is what these institutions will be like. Specifically the ethical test

99

of any future institutions, and of the codes of honour they entail, will be whether they succeed in embodying and in stabilizing the discoveries of human dignity that are the principal achievements of modern man.

That is our task, perfectly articulated, to see how the school might be just such an institution. There will be no attempt to put the concept of honour into circulation among teachers, however. Rather, we must rescue the concept of dignity from its individualistic connotations. The conditions of dignity, specified in earlier pages, can now be more fully justified. They were that to acquire dignity a person must achieve a sense of competence, of making a contribution to, and of being valued by, the groups to which he or she belongs. On such a definition dignity is a property of the experience of an individual pupil; but it can be acquired and maintained only in the context of collective life in a group.

It is not a contemporary insight; it belongs, more properly, to the founding father of the sociology of education, Emile Durkheim (1858-1917). Marx, Weber and Durkheim are the hallowed trinity of the founding fathers of sociological thought; but of the three only Durkheim was a former teacher and a professor of education as well as sociology. From his earliest studies Durkheim was concerned with the nature of social solidarity in modern society. Like his predecessors, he sought an explanation of how a complex industrial society, with its specialization of functions and elaborate division of labour, could be an integrated society. The apparently simpler, smaller, pre-industrial societies could be held together by common ideas and sentiments shared by everyone; how does rapid urbanization and industrialization affect social cohesion? Durkheim did not believe that, in principle, the division of labour in advanced industrial societies necessarily involved a breakdown in social integration and solidarity, but it was clear to him that in his own society there were indications of a serious threat of social disorganization. An index of this was the growing crime rate, and Durkheim devoted a whole book to a sociological analysis of suicide, in which he explained the origins and social distribution of suicide in terms of the pathological state of modern society and used *egoism* and *anomie* as his principal explanatory concepts. We must note that Durkheim was not interested in what he called egoism and anomie merely because they provided an explanation of suicide; he was interested in suicide because the suicide was (for various reasons) a convenient phenomenon through which he could document the power of egoism and anomie. For these two concepts are fundamental to his much more general diagnosis of the ills of his society and his fear of social disintegration.

According to Durkheim egoism and anomie are merely different aspects of the same social state. Egoism is a form of excessive individualism. It arises when the individual becomes detached from social life and his private goals become preponderant over those of the community:[15]

> The more weakened the groups to which he belongs, the less he depends on them, the more he consequently depends only on himself and recognizes no other rules than what are founded on his private interests.

Anomie refers to a lack of social regulation, through which:

> greed is aroused without knowing where to find its ultimate foothold. Nothing can claim it, since its goal is far beyond all it can attain. Reality seems valueless by comparison; reality is therefore abandoned, but so too is possibility abandoned when it in turn becomes reality.

To what extent might such egoism and anomie be said to characterize the conduct and attitudes of pupils in contemporary British secondary schools? To answer this, we must consider more carefully than we have done so far, the different kinds of pupils in school. I shall suggest that there are four types of pupil. These are, of course, merely analytical types; pupils cannot all be easily assigned to one type and the distribution of such types varies from school to school. The types are merely a convenient way of examining the range of pupil orientations to school.

The first type I shall call 'the committed'. In school they are generally conformist, though I dislike that term which often has unfortunate pejorative connotations. They share the values and ideals of the school and the teachers; they enjoy school in all its aspects. Little needs to be said about this type, for such pupils are readily recognized by teachers, since they are but miniature versions of themselves.

The second type can be called 'the instrumentalists'. These pupils lack any profound commitment to school or its ideals and staff; but they know that school potentially offers them much, particularly the qualifications of examination results and teacher references that give access to higher education or desired and desirable occupations. They are not much excited by school, but neither do they offer much resistance. They are content to play the game of school by the teachers' rules.

The third type I shall call 'the indifferent'. Their most striking characteristic is that they are bored by school. 'It's boring, sir' is their most common complaint. They display a persistent lack of enthusiasm to most of what school offers, though a skilful teacher or carefully planned lesson may capture their imagination and attention, for a moment. Whilst examinations and other incentives tend to be ineffective with them, they show little active resentment or opposition. They seem to be overwhelmed by lethargy, lacking the energy to praise or condemn. They drift through their schooldays. In consequence, whilst they avoid anything more serious than a half-hearted, game-like resistance to teachers, they are nevertheless not easy to teach. Quite often they come from relatively affluent working-class homes, and they worry their parents as much as their teachers for their lifelessness and lack of initiative. It is my impression that this type has grown in numbers during recent years.

The fourth group contains 'the oppositionals' about whom much has already been said. They turn in overt and sometimes powerful resistance to the school and to teachers. Their antagonism is overt, pronounced and prolonged. They become defined, individually and collectively, as a 'discipline problem' for teachers – and sometimes for their parents.

Which type or types most closely correspond to Durkheim's description of egoism and anomie? Although to some degree they characterize the oppositionals, the fit seems rather weak. Whilst such pupils display a very low commitment to school, we know that they maintain a very profound allegiance to their peer group and its counter-culture to which they become highly conformist. Their resistance to social regulation by adults is high, but it is replaced by strong social controls exercised by friends. Since they are so closely bound into their group life, they do not show untempered greed or the pursuit of private individual interests, since the group's needs must constantly be taken into account. And if it is sound to suggest that their counter-culture is an attempt to restore, in some primitive and 'magical' manner, working-class community, then we can interpret the counter-culture as a creative, if somewhat limited and misdirected, search for some kind of social solidarity. The concepts of loyalty and honour may be dying in many of our schools and elsewhere, but they are not dead: they are alive and well in the counter-cultures of young people. Once they were more vital, as they were in schools, in those adult-controlled youth organizations such as the Scouts and Guides and the cadet forces of the Armed Services, whose mass appeal has now begun to fade. But young people are not so easily deprived of their group loyalties; they have not disappeared, but have merely been displaced into various relatively unorganized (at least by adults) associations of young people on football terraces each Saturday afternoon and into the disco world of popular music. Much of what we see as 'football hooliganism' can be interpreted as a spilling over of excessive team loyalties.[16] The violence must be deplored, but it must not blind us to the ritual aggression by which a youth defends the honour of his group or his team. The tragedy is adults have failed to find the new forms which will command the loyalties and sense of honour of the young. There is a distinct pathos to the fact that many an adolescent male will, if his professional football team loses its match on a Saturday afternoon, be dismayed and downcast until the following Saturday.

In June 1980 an adolescent boy was gaoled for three years after admitting throwing a petrol bomb into a group of West Ham supporters. It was an appalling act.[17] His defending counsel offered the usual mitigation of home circumstances and personal disadvantages, but added:

> He appreciates he could have caused harm and knows he
> has done wrong. This young man is devoted to his team.
> He knows more about this team and has more love for it
> than anything in his life. He has an idea in his mind about
> eleven heroes and as a consequence he has allowed himself
> to get carried away.

Even the *prosecuting* counsel seemed to understand this.
He said:

> He decided that he was, to use his own words, 'going to
> put Newcastle on the map' and was sick of them being in
> the Second Division. To put them on the map he was going
> to throw a petrol bomb in the crowd – something which he
> had never done before.

Without in any way condoning this act, one can legitimately
wonder how our society has deprived this young man by failing to offer him some institution or social purpose which
could command his sense of loyalty and honour and direct it
in more positive and constructive channels. And our schools
contain many more counter-cultural, oppositional pupils
who, I fear, are similarly 'at risk'.

There is, however, a much better match between egoism
and anomie and the indifferent and instrumental pupil
types, who in most schools appear in far larger numbers than
oppositionals. In some schools it is they who are the 'normal'
or typical pupils, with the committed and oppositionals as
much smaller extreme groups. The indifferent is much more
likely than the oppositional to be a 'loner' with weak ties to
family and friends; it is he who is more likely to indulge in
fantasies of wealth and fame, and who is likely to find the
work, as he finds school, just plain boring. At home he will
become absorbed in the fantasy world of American television programmes rather than being out on the streets with
the 'gang', and at school he is in trouble for his inattention
and passivity. The instrumental pupil is much more likely
than the oppositional, who understands his future with a

stark realism, to indulge in unrealistic academic occupational aspirations and is quite ready to sacrifice group affiliations for his 'private interests' of getting on in the world. The instrumental wants personal success and intends to get it. Egoism, Durkheim noted, is strongly associated with the Protestant ethic, with its high valuation of knowledge and education and with the readiness to be dislocated from family of origin. Such values, it can be argued, are more strongly entrenched in society and in meritocratic comprehensive schools than was true in Durkheim's day. The school has become increasingly individualistic and the instrumental pupil is one of most typical, though not most preferred, children. The instrumentalists identify with the school's meritocratic ideals; it is the oppositionals who deny and resist them.

If this is a legitimate interpretation, then it seems that the 'normal' and 'typical' pupils in our schools with their high levels of egoism and anomie should in many respects be of much greater concern to us than the oppositionals who are usually designated as the 'social problem' in spite of their lower levels of egoism and anomie. Perhaps schools are failing *most* pupils, not just the working-class counter-culture members to which so much attention has been given. Seen in this light the culture of individualism has damaged the very heart of our educational system; for Durkheim, I suspect, contemporary schools would provide one index of the slow but unbridled growth of egoism and anomie which he detected as the major threat to social solidarity in advanced industrial society.

In much of his work Durkheim appears to be pessimistic concerning the fate of modern society. Durkheim considers, and then rejects, the state, the family, and religion as potential inhibitory agents. Nor has he much faith in attempts to restore local communities. Yet he is equally sceptical about education; to put faith in education to undertake the task of preventing the slide into increased egoism and anomie is to ascribe to schools a power that they lack, for education:[18]

is only the image and reflection of society. It imitates and reproduces the latter in abbreviated form; it does not create

105

it. Education is healthy when peoples themselves are in a
healthy state; but it becomes corrupt with them, being
unable to modify itself. If the moral environment is
affected, since the teachers dwell in it they cannot avoid
being influenced; how then should they impress on their
pupils a different orientation from what they have
received?. . . Education, therefore, can be reformed only
if society itself is reformed.

The culture of individualism may strengthen egoism and
anomie in school, but school is merely a reinforcing, not the
main causal, agent. We cannot, it appears, change society by
changing schools; if we wish to change schools, we must
change society first.

Durkheim searched for an answer to social change which
would arrest these destructive forces and found it, though
without much conviction, in the development and growth of
occupational groups and associations. Only they, he argued,
could effectively resist the forces towards centralization,
bureaucratization and the breakdown of social solidarity;
only they could create the plurality of local and voluntary
associations that would command allegiance and loyalty and
thus provide the necessary social regulation; only they could
act as the essential buffers between the individual and the
state that was too remote to exercise these basic social functions.

Yet Durkheim had more to say on the relations between
education and society and we must look closely at this, for
it is clear that his own preferred answer for social solidarity
has failed. Trade unions and professional associations can
indeed create a degree of solidarity, as we saw earlier and as
we shall see again later, but they have not stemmed the tide
of egoism and anomie. Indeed, today many such associations could with justice be indicted as centres of a new
corporate egoism and anomie. In his book on moral education, however, which is a collection of lectures to teachers,
Durkheim suddenly adopts a much more positive approach to
the role of education in shaping society. We can understand
this only if we first accept Durkheim's unusual and very
sociological conception of morality.[19]

Everything which is a source of solidarity is moral, everything which forces man to take account of other men is
moral, everything which forces him to regulate his conduct
through something other than the striving of his ego is
moral, and morality is as solid as these ties are numerous
and strong. . . . Society is not, then, as has often been
thought, a stranger to the moral world, or something
which has only secondary repercussions on it. It is, on the
contrary, the necessary condition of its existence. It is not
a simple juxtaposition of individuals who bring an intrinsic
morality with them, but rather man is a moral being only
because he lives in society, since morality consists in being
solidary with a group and varying with this solidarity. Let
all social life disappear, and moral life will disappear with
it. . . . As for what is called individual morality . . . that is
an abstract conception which has no relation to reality.

This conception of morality may seem foreign to many
teachers who have become attuned to a more psychological
individual-ethical orientation that dominates much of the
moral education now given in schools. The task for Durkheim
is to translate his notions of morality and solidarity into
educational practice, for he believed that in the modern
world morality can be based not simply on religion, to which
many no longer assent, but on a secular and rational morality.

The first element, in Durkheim's view, is the spirit of
discipline; moral conduct consists in following a system of
rules which carry the compelling influence of authority. At
the very start, here is a vocabulary – discipline, authority,
duty and will – quite alien to many progressive teachers. It
is a vocabulary which is even more distasteful to contemporary sociologists; these are words no self-respecting
sociologist of education would dare breathe, unless it be in
denunciation of our 'authoritarian' schools and teachers. It
is no doubt for this reason that this aspect of Durkheim's
work is now almost completely ignored by contemporary
sociologists; it is written off as 'conservative', as an unfortunate aberration which shows how even one of the greatest
sociological minds can be limited by the presuppositions of
his age. But such an interpretation can be warranted only by

the most superficial reading of Durkheim. It soon becomes apparent that discipline is to be understood as a condition of, not a barrier to, freedom; it is unrestrained egoism which is the true tyranny and which robs us of true freedom. Nor does discipline involve blind and slavish submission to immutable rules; when a society freezes its morality into fixed rules a Christ or a Socrates is needed to restore morality to its proper course.

The second element of morality is the attachment to social groups. Moral ends are to be seen as collective not individual ends:[20]

> Morality begins, accordingly, only insofar as we belong to a human group, *whatever it may be*. Since, in fact, man is complete only as he belongs to *several* societies, morality is complete only to the extent that we feel identified with those different groups in which we are involved – family, union, business, club, political party, country, humanity. [Italics added]

It is thus from the social, from society, that authority emanates, from collective ends rather than those persons who happen to be in power at a particular time or place.

The third element of morality is autonomy. In Durkheim's scheme authority must be obeyed not in a spirit of passive resignation but out of enlightened allegiance: rationality must play a central role in moral conduct. The teaching of morality should be neither preaching nor indoctrination; it is a rational activity of explaining and helping the learner to understand moral demands. Children at school will not become moral through the exercise of coercive control of the confrontational imposition of teacher power. If Willard Waller's 'conflict model' of the school and his description of the school as 'a despotism in a state of perilous equilibrium' are accurate accounts of secondary schools today, then for Durkheim this would be an index of how far schools have strayed from their true purpose. Rather the teacher must present the rules and moral obligations as binding on all, including the teacher, who is merely their instrument, not their author. The function of punishment is thus not to intimidate (or deter) or to retaliate; that might induce conformity and obedience, but not morality. The whole purpose of punishment is merely to affirm the importance and sacredness of the rule that the offence denies:[21]

> Severe treatment is not an end in itself; it is only a means;
> consequently it is justified only to the extent that it is
> necessary to attain the end which is its raison d'être – the
> end of giving the child the most vivid impression possible
> of the feelings evoked by his behaviour. It is not a matter
> of making him suffer, as if suffering involved some sort of
> mystical virtue. . . . Rather, it is a matter of reaffirming
> the obligation at the moment when it is violated, in
> order to strengthen the sense of duty, both for the guilty
> party and for those witnessing the offence. . . . Every
> element of the penalty that does not promote this end is
> bad and should be prohibited.

For this reason Durkheim was deeply opposed to the use of corporal punishment in school.

From this very brief outline of Durkheim's views it is evident that he is no crude, nineteenth-century authoritarian. Our contemporary young sociologists of education see the words 'discipline', 'authority' and 'duty' and are instantly inflamed by them. They simply assume that this is a defence of authoritarianism, whereas in fact the authoritarian teacher will find no comfort or support whatever from Durkheim's book. It is no exaggeration to say that Durkheim was making a most powerful indictment of authoritarianism in education, thus transcending the popular educational assumptions of his times. But more than this, Durkheim was offering a carefully argued and constructive alternative to the 'progressive individualism' which was later to prove so enormously influential. He was not opposed to the individual pupil: autonomy, rationality and dignity are central in his thinking. Morality and solidarity can be achieved only through enhancing the dignity of man; and dignity can be provided for individuals only through their association with moral and solidary groups.

Part of the difficulty in understanding the thrust of Durkheim's originality of educational thought is that he uses the term 'individualism' in a pejorative sense, to embrace

egoism and anomie. In modern educational thought the concept of the individual is essentially and thoroughly positive,
not least because in recent times we have become sensitive to
the negative effects of group life and the constraining weight
of pressures to conformity. To modern man the concepts of
individual and group (or society) are sometimes seen as
contradictory and are associated in the mind with other antitheses, such as self versus system, man versus machine,
creativity versus conformity, freedom versus tyranny, autonomy versus control, independence versus incorporation. For
Durkheim such antitheses can be dangerously superficial and
even false. Such contrastive opposition of the individual with
the social can mask an important truth: that our individual
identities are profoundly social in their origin and their
maintenance. The social institution we call marriage can be
highly destructive to the individuality of the partners; but
marriage is so very popular precisely because it is a social
arrangement in which both individual identities can flourish
and find a unique expression. Marriage is, as Durkheim knew,
a powerful protection against egoism and anomie. To appreci-
ate Durkheim's position we must compare the antitheses
offered above with another, less commonly cited set –
isolation versus integration, insularity versus community,
self-centredness versus altruism, alienation versus commitment, competition versus collaboration. Excessive individualism and excessive corporatism can both be stifling and
oppressive: the problem is not to choose between the two,
but to discover the conditions under which individual and
group life can be mutually beneficial.

That Durkheim is no crude collectivist became clear during
the Dreyfus affair. The anti-Dreyfus argument was simple:
in times of national crisis it is legitimate and right that one
individual can be sacrificed to the needs of the nation.
For Durkheim this stance was not merely morally repugnant,
but also deeply erroneous in its understanding of how true
national solidarity is to be achieved. In his defence of Dreyfus,
Durkheim argued that there is another or second individualism,
which is radically different from egoistic individualism.
Whereas in the latter everything is subordinated to the
private *interests* of the individual, this second individualism

is concerned with the fundamental *rights* which are basic to the dignity of all men.[22] This individualism is concerned 'with the glorification not of the self, but of the individual in general'. In other words, true community and true social solidarity are achieved only when they are founded upon the respect for individual rights, for only then is society moral and just. If such basic rights are violated, as in the Dreyfus affairs, then solidarity and morality are perverted into injustice and so become malformed. Liberty, individual freedom and the rights of man are not just ends in themselves, but the proper foundation, and the means of promoting and maintaining, society's solidary character.

Durkheim did not fully resolve the tensions between the two kinds of individualism, between the individual and the group, between independence and obligation, between basic rights and superficial interests. But he did understand that true dignity and morality have a social and corporate aspect. Genuine individuality must be rooted in group life. Moral education, in the Durkheimian sense not the ethical individualism of today, thus becomes one of the central objectives of schooling. But it cannot be achieved by conventional, direct teaching: it cannot be inculcated by exhortation or even by cognitive-intellectual efforts alone. It must come through the direct experience of group life. And group life was not merely a means of giving people the social skills of co-operation and empathy, but of generating solidarity. For Durkheim, then, schools must give pupils the clearest possible idea and experience of the groups to which they belong, and to which they will belong when they have left school. For he realized that his hopes that occupational associations would provide the solidary base of modern man could not be realized unless the spirit of association is already aroused, but it would have to be aroused in children and within the context of experience provided by the living groups of which children were members. It was a vicious circle: groups rest upon the spirit of association, but the spirit of association can be aroused only in groups. It was thus that Durkheim revised his earlier pessimistic conclusion that education could not contribute to social change. Now the school's key function would be to 'breathe life into the spirit of association':[23]

It is precisely at this point that the role of the school can be considerable. It is the means, *perhaps the only one*, by which we can leave the vicious circle. [Italics added]

It is an unexpected, challenging and optimistic conclusion. But it is a challenge, not a blueprint. Durkheim was a great thinker and explicitly stated that his own detailed ideas for moral education were limited to his own time and place. This concession to the future shows foresight as well as humility, for the central element in Durkheim's scheme was none other than the class unit. It is for us, in spite of the growth of individualism and the decline of community both in school and society since Durkheim's day, to find the means whereby that challenge can be met in the new comprehensive schools of our own age.

5　The curriculum and the community

If we are to provide a rationale and set of purposes for comprehensive schools, we cannot be content with the limited justification that the comprehensive system permits us to abolish selection at eleven-plus, that it furthers meritocratic ends, and that it is somehow a good thing that all secondary-school pupils should be educated in a common school. At this point in our history we must enter once again into the debate that preceded mass schooling over a century ago, namely: what kind of society do we want to create and how can the education system help us to realize such a society? The answers we reach will determine the relation between education and society into the twenty-first century.

So far we have considered a number of themes of significance to contemporary society and education: the persisting damage that school does to the dignity of many school pupils, especially those from working-class homes; the erosion of working-class culture and community; the preservation of and dominant emphasis given to the cognitive-intellectual domain in the school curriculum; the growth of the cult of individualism and the failure of the school to make its proper contribution to social solidarity in society. In all these matters comprehensive re-organization has promoted little change for the better or has even made matters worse.

Some educationists take the view – and it is one which I share – that comprehensive re-organization has distracted public attention in most areas of the country from what may in the longer term, prove to be one of the most important innovations of the time: the emergence of the community school.[1] The very title of the community school suggests that in this reform may lie some of the solutions to the problems we have already discussed at length. Are community schools the answer? Do they provide, within the broad comprehensive framework, the pattern of future reform and development which we must now follow?

The concept of the community school, like the concept of community itself, is a flabby and sometimes vacuous one. This history of the community school is long and goes back at least to the pioneering establishment of the famous village colleges in Cambridgeshire by the great Henry Morris in the 1920s.[2] In more recent times we have become familiar with the names of Countesthorpe College in Leicestershire, Sidney Stringer School in Coventry and the Abraham Moss Centre in Manchester. The community school, like the comprehensice school, is a loose term which covers a wide variety of changes and developments. We may, for analytical purposes, divide these into four groups.

The first change is concerned with the promotion of a community *within* the school, and on the whole this has taken the form of increased democratization within the school, especially between teachers and pupils. Most commonly a school council has been created, often consisting of elected pupils and staff. In this forum problems and complaints can be aired and resolved. In most cases, the council has few executive powers; its major duty is to advise the headteacher in whom, as the person accountable for the school to the governors and local authority, all major powers reside. The number of schools with a vigorous school council is probably still small; in some instances it was introduced by an enthusiastic headteacher, but in others it was conceded by a reluctant headteacher as a skilled move to take the sting out of the activities of the National Union of School Students.

In a few community schools this trend to democratization has been pushed much further. In Countesthorpe College, for example, the principal, whilst technically holding all the powers of a headteacher, in practice passes many of these powers to the staff as a whole in their 'moot'. In effect, the principal acts as a kind of chief executive of a staff body which must take an active share in all major decision-making, especially in matters of general policy.

In themselves, these reforms are insufficient to meet the problems and tasks I have outlined, though I shall have more to say about the role of the headteacher later. Within twenty years, I suspect, all secondary schools will have a school council and pupil governors, but that change could occur with no more than a few minor repercussions.

A second development involves greater participation in the school by the outside community, especially where the comprehensive school is a neighbourhood school. The Taylor Report of 1977[3] has undoubtedly encouraged the importation of parents and other community representatives onto governing bodies. This reform takes a weak (or 'liberal') and a strong (or 'radical') form. In the weak version, community participation is orientated to greater parental involvement, sometimes in the traditional structures of parent-teacher associations and occasionally in the active involvement of parents in classroom activities. Here parent-governors are a natural next step. In the strong version of this reform, parent-governors are but the first step in a process of *community control* of the secondary school. To understand this we must examine the third type of reform.

This is concerned with the school as a community centre. On this view the school premises do not belong to the teachers and pupils. Rather, the school premises are located in and shared with many other community services in one set of buildings. Libraries and swimming baths and various leisure facilities, such as sport and drama, belong both to the relevant community groups and the schools, who jointly share and control what is seen as common property. The major justification is that this makes economic sense, encourages greater use of the facilities, and breaks down the barriers between the school and its host community. In some versions of this reform the artificial boundaries which separate secondary schools, further education and adult classes are destroyed. A single class of students may contain a wide range of adults, full-time or part-time further-education students, and conventional secondary-school pupils. Again it is said that this yields important economic advantages and integrates different age

115

and status groups in a common learning enterprise. This aspect of the reform I believe to be of far more importance than the use of shared facilities, for it can reintegrate sections of the community which are at present carefully segregated. After the age of sixteen many people pursue educational courses in colleges of further education, technical colleges, colleges of technology, and polytechnics; their links with school pupils are thereby severed. Even within secondary school the careful age-grading of year-groups ensures that most young people spend most of their time with, and find their friends among, others of the same age. We have witnessed the decline of institutions, such as churches, which cut across these age-groupings, and even in that most popular of community institutions, the pub, nowadays young people are to be found at separate tables or even in separate rooms. The community-school classroom which contains people of different ages and interests potentially challenges these artificial divisions and offers its own contribution to community solidarity. Moreover, the presence of committed adults in classrooms might greatly reduce the problems of indiscipline and lack of motivation with which teachers have to contend; the most salutary lesson for apathetic adolescents might be working alongside those who have left school but who now recognize a need for and have developed an interest in education. The wonder is that teachers have shown such little interest in this innovation; their indifference and even resistance to the idea requires explanation, which we must reserve for a later section.

In such a community school, with shared facilities and 'mixed' classes, the most distinctive feature of the present secondary school – an isolated building shielded from the world by its protective playground and playing-fields and containing a small number of teacher-adults supervising a large number of adolescent-learners – would fade rapidly. Instead of the school cultivating greater community participation within itself, as in the second kind of reform discussed above, the school would be dissolving itself within other community institutions. It is at this point that demands for community control of the school are likely to be most insistent – and most threatening to teachers. A sophisticated plan for such a community school controlled by its own community was sketched by Eric Midwinter in 1975.[4] The school in this scheme is linked to a much wider decentralization of other services, such as health, to a local community with new financial and administrative powers. The plan has many attractive features and it is surprising that it has not stimulated much more discussion in educational circles. Perhaps it challenges too many vested interests and was proposed at an inauspicious moment when, in fact, powers were being moved away from local authorities to metropolitan and regional centres.

The fourth development is that of the community-centred curriculum. The reform is focused on the content of the curriculum itself rather than on the structure of the school as an institution and its relation to the community. In the weak (or 'liberal') version of this reform, pupils may be required to follow, or are given an option in, a new school subject called 'community studies', which may be examined. Alongside this there may be voluntary schemes for community service, directed especially at the old and the very young. Community service and community studies seem eminently sensible. The danger is that these become options open to, or even compulsory for, the 'less able' or 'non-academic' pupils who are not working on courses leading to public examinations. Pupils quickly learn the meaning of this. A group of pupils on examination courses are talking about those who are not:[5]

> *Pupil*: I think they do more social work – learning about the community more than actual education, Maths and English and that.
> *Pupil*: They've been going out a lot, and been doing work around the school, going out for community service.
> *Interviewer*: Is it as worthwhile as the programme you've been on?
> *Pupil*: I think it's worthwhile in their own way, because a lot of them aren't intelligent enough to take exams, some of them are, but not all of them . . . and they spend their time doing a worthwhile programme really. They can't learn in Maths and English, that sort of thing, but they learn about the community.

117

And a member of the course comments:

> I think the community service was just to get us out of
> school so that other kids could have a lesson, just to let
> other people look after us for a bit so other children could
> have the teachers.

The moral is clear: academic education is to be contrasted
with 'learning about the community' which is for pupils
who are 'thick' and who waste teachers' time and efforts.
The hidden-curriculum message being transmitted to *both*
groups of pupils is a disastrous one.

In the stronger version of this reform 'community studies'
or community service is rejected as an appendage to the
traditional curriculum; instead, a major part of the curriculum is organized around community themes and interests and
needs. This has been proposed, from a relatively conservative
position, by Geoffrey Bantock.[6] His analysis is founded on a
blunt recognition that for many pupils 'the watered down
academic education we still provide as the core of the curriculum would seem to have failed'. The failing pupils are the
'bottom 50 per cent of pupils', those who come from 'culturally deprived' homes, and those who wish to leave school
as soon as possible, and will enter unskilled or semi-skilled
jobs – in short, mainly working-class pupils. A grammar-school
academic and cognitive-intellectual curriculum, which is
partly defined as 'high culture', is not, according to Bantock,
at all suitable for these pupils. Instead, they must be provided
with a 'popular education' which is closer to their own culture,
life styles and capacities; it will be a curriculum which is
oral rather than literary, concrete and practical rather than
theoretical and abstract. Various sociological and psychological theories, of Bernstein, Eysenck and Jensen, are drawn
upon to justify this position. The content of the curriculum
for those pupils assigned to 'popular education' will be concerned with the development of critical attitudes towards
the mass media, especially television, films and the popular
press; the education of the emotions; crafts, drama and movement studies; domestic studies (for girls) and technical studies
(for boys). In effect, most working-class pupils would follow

a separate and distinctive curriculum based in affective-artistic and physical-manual knowledge and skills, whereas a small minority of 'bright' working-class pupils and most middle-class pupils would pursue a different curriculum grounded in cognitive-intellectual knowledge and skills and in 'high culture'. Bantock is, rightly, impatient with the view that the education of the working classes can be transformed by getting rid of the 'middle-class culture of the school' (about which a good deal of nonsense has been written) and educating working-class children in their own working-class culture. The working classes have a culture, in the anthropological sense that I described earlier. Most children learn their class culture in this sense without any help from the school and there is certainly not enough working-class culture that is worth turning into a formal school curriculum. Brass bands are a notable working-class musical form which schools could use more fully, but bingo and greyhound-racing or pigeon-fancying have little to offer to a formal, institutional education which lasts for over a decade. Bantock's alternative curriculum is not, strictly speaking, a programme of community studies; rather it is an education in the expressive arts, related directly to the lives pupils will lead as adults in the community and to the finer elements and traditions of working-class culture. As an educationist must, but a sociologist need not, Bantock has to make value-judgments about the worth of the different elements of what we loosely call working-class culture, and some of these have to be rejected as irrelevant to schooling. The emphasis Bantock assigns to the expressive arts is both important and unusual, and I shall later adopt a similar emphasis for the comprehensive-school curriculum.

A more 'radical' interpretation of the strong version of a community-centred curriculum is provided in the work on Educational Priority Areas, led by A.H. Halsey, who has been extremely influential in educational reform during the last twenty years. The EPA project was an offspring of the Plowden Report on primary schools and marks a shift away from simpler notions of equality of opportunity towards a policy of positive discrimination. Working in 'socially deprived' areas, the EPA teams vigorously fought to improve education.

119

Very quickly they recognized the need to revise educational objectives if any of the enormous obstacles they faced were to be overcome. The school curriculum must be based on the community and its objective must be the development in children of a critical and constructive understanding of the environment in which they live. A change of emphasis was essential, from academic to social subjects, and from the learning of information to the acquisition of skills. In the words of a justly famous passage of the report:[7]

> If we are concerned with the majority of children who will spend their lives in EPAs, rather than only with the minority who will leave them for universities and colleges and middle-class occupations elsewhere, then the school must set out to equip their children to meet the grim reality of the social environment in which they live and reform it in all its aspects, physical, organic, technical, cultural and moral. Only if they are armed with intimate familiarity with their immediate problems may they be expected to articulate the needs they feel and create the means for satisfying them. The obvious danger here is that of creating a second-class education for second-class citizens through curricula restricted to local horizons. But what we intend is the opposite of a soporific: it is not to fit children for their station in life in an ascriptive sense. It is to accept that many children must live out their lives in deprived areas and to inspire them to think boldly about it rather than lapse into resigned apathy.

Pupils are, in stirring words unusual in an education report, to be 'forewarned and forearmed for the struggle'.

Members of the EPA project recognized that the schools in most urgent need of help served communities where the sense of community and community resources were most depleted. It is natural, therefore, that they should assign to the school an important task in the regeneration of those communities. Against the general tide in comprehensive schools the EPA projects urged an explicitly political and collective function for schools in deprived areas.

It is too early to give a balanced assessment of the effect

of the EPA projects and the reports. But few would deny that the effects on secondary comprehensive schools have been disappointing so far. The scheme was limited by its terms of reference, which included raising the educational performance of pupils and the morale of teachers. Further, the scheme was under-financed from its inception. But much more important is that the project was concerned with primary not secondary schools and was linked in the public mind with 'deprived areas' and 'compensatory education' not with the educational system as a whole.

There is much of merit in the arguments which favour a less academic and more community-centred curriculum. The proponents cannot be accused of any foolish romanticism that all children are really the same. Over the years Bantock has acknowledged the stark fact, well known to teachers, that for some pupils, who are in disproportionate numbers working-class in origin, the bookish, academic curriculum – 'primarily cognitive in orientation' – is simply inadequate. Many of these pupils remain uninitiated into the intellectual worlds which schools represent to them; and teachers know that the attempts at inculcation of such a curriculum are doomed to failure since the ensuing achievements will be so low. Bantock stoutly refuses to turn the known fact that some working-class children possess capacities which are underestimated by teachers and which could, with more concerted teaching effort, be fostered to much higher levels of achievement, into a more general and foolish proposition that the known differences in pupil achievement and motivation are merely a result of a class-biased system of schooling which is open to remedy. Like many others, Bantock knows that it is both pointless and unnecessary to make all children jump through a long sequence of academic hoops in order to get a relatively small number of university entrants. Yet the various proposals, whether in a 'strong' or 'weak' form, whether 'conservative' or 'radical' have a common fault: they tend to prescribe what amounts to a special curriculum for most working-class pupils.

Such an educational apartheid – the term is surely not too strong – is unacceptable. If we are to offer a community-centred curriculum to those schools in deprived, urban

121

working-class schools, how then do we decide what constitutes the clear definition of such a school? Where do we draw the line between such a school and an 'ordinary' school? The practical problems are immense. And what would happen to academically oriented pupils in such schools? For they do exist, though their number may be small. Are they to be denied an access to an academic curriculum because they live in a district where the school does not provide such a curriculum? Bantock's alternative curriculum for the 'less able' has similar problems. His target seems sometimes to be the 'low achiever' and sometimes the lower working-class pupil and sometimes those pupils who do not like their schooling: he has in mind 'the bottom 50 per cent'. How do we decide to withdraw a pupil from the academic curriculum to allocate him to the alternative curriculum? Bantock seems happy to leave this to the teachers and suggests they could use reports from primary schools, the results of intelligence and achievement tests, knowledge of home background and parental support, all of which could be available to the teachers of our eleven-year-olds. It is quite evidently a new eleven-plus selection test, with the difference that this one will be used to allocate half the pupil population to the academic curriculum, whereas the old eleven-plus selected about a quarter for the grammar school. Any attempt to introduce this new eleven-plus would almost certainly be strongly resisted by most parents, and I think rightly so. It would once again be an almost irreversible decision made when children are eleven years old; even worse, it would be left to the subjective judgment of teachers, which would undoubtedly be much less trustworthy than the use of the standardized tests of the old eleven-plus. The number of 'errors' of selection – and of parental objection – would be enormous.

There is, I believe, no future at all in the suggestions of a community-centred curriculum or an alternative curriculum for the less able and for most working-class pupils, and I am glad of it. The principle of *early* selection has, one hopes, been destroyed for all time. There are other objections to Bantock's scheme, ones of a more logical kind, but we may leave these until later. For the moment we must not lose sight of an important advance made by all these suggestions. We may reject the idea of these alternative curricula for the 'less able' and for working-class pupils on the grounds that the problems of selection and allocation would introduce an evil which would be greater than the good of such a curriculum, but that does not in any way undermine the idea of community-centred and alternative curricula and show them to be inherently unsound. We are perfectly at liberty to retain the ideas whilst simply refusing to allocate children to such curricula on the basis of a new eleven-plus or the district where these pupils happen to live. The very fact that these ideas of a less academic, alternative curriculum have been proposed by esteemed educationists of very different persuasions indicates that an important direction for secondary education is being explored, and we would be very foolish to ignore it.

There are, then, four analytical dimensions to the concept of the community school. Any school may adopt one or two of these dimensions and ignore the others; and it may adopt a particular dimension in a 'strong' or 'weak' version. In certain aspects community schools appear to provide solutions to some of the problems exposed in our earlier analysis of secondary schools, but they certainly do not provide the whole answer. In fact as yet we have no clear image of what a community school is; there are in existence a small number of schools who give themselves that title, but in detail they often differ quite markedly from one another, which is perfectly appropriate during an experimental and pioneering stage of their development. When we consider the movement as a whole, as in the four analytical dimensions suggested here, a number of basic contradictions become exposed; for the community school is not a single and coherent reform but a constellation of reforms, some of which are in tension with one another.

A good example of such a contradiction is the tension between participation and the community-centred curriculum. A school may begin with a 'weak' version of *participation*, which is defined as greater parental involvement. It is, however, easy to pass from this phase into one of greater *accountability* to parents and community representatives.

123

From here it is but a short distance to *community control* of the school. It is clear that at this point, assuming for the moment that it is a desirable change, there will be a considerable shift in power from the headteacher and his staff to parents and other community representatives. Yet at the present time it is very unlikely that parents would be strongly in favour of a community-centred curriculum in a comprehensive school; it is much more likely that they would show a strong preference for the traditional curriculum, high academic standards, and an emphasis on results in public examinations. A community-centred curriculum is much more likely to be developed in a school where the headteachers and staff are committed to the notion but are highly insulated from relatively powerless and non-participating parents.

In part this was the problem faced by Countesthorpe College, which is probably the best-known community school. Their high degree of internal democratization was inevitably very controversial and it was fully understood by all the staff that unless the school could produce acceptable public-examination results, the axe would be brought down mercilessly upon their heads. The book, *The Countesthorpe Experience,* is at pains to protest that none of the school's many innovations was ever introduced at the cost of academic standards as measured by examination results:[8]

> It is not surprising that innovations of this character
> should give rise to conflicts. . . . When appointed as the
> second principal, John Watts had a different row to hoe.
> However, this he has done triumphantly, so that today one
> can say without doubt that the College has won the massive support of parents – an outcome partly due to the
> nature of student-teacher relations, and more recently to
> overcoming the natural anxieties of parents concerning
> examinations and their children's future careers. Examination results in the last two years, covering O level GCE and
> CSE Grade 1 passes per head, are now clearly above
> the national average. (Professor Brian Simon)
>
> Two years of results at GCE O level and in CSE, respectable if not generally spectacular, have given confidence

to students and their parents where any of them had
suspected that the more tangible dividends might not be
forthcoming. (If not *generally* spectacular, it might none-
theless be worth noting two points. One fifthformer
found it possible to pass eight subjects at O level at Grade
1. And . . . about half of the total comprehensive intake in
both years passed GCE O level in English.) (Staff Report)

Without sacrifice of examination results, university and
college entries or employment prospects, relationships
of unusual trust have been established between teachers
and students. (Staff–student statement to the Education
Committee)

The pressure on comprehensive schools to 'prove' themselves
by examination results is exerted *a fortiori* on a community
school. As long as this continues there can be no full development of a community-centred curriculum in the *secondary*
school; it can achieve no more than a minor or peripheral
position in relation to the grammar-school curriculum. Had
Halsey and his EPA project teams made their plea for a
community-centred curriculum in secondary rather than
primary schools, their efforts would probably have been
predestined to failure.

We thus reach an impasse. It is the community school and
a community-centred curriculum which seem to be one of
the most promising ways in which to reform secondary
schools in order to mitigate the negative effects of schooling
and to promote the objectives outlined earlier: yet the growth
of the community school and the community-centred curriculum are stunted by the dominance of the national examinations, especially GCE 'O' level and CSE for the nation's
sixteen-year-olds.

In his book *School is not yet Dead* Harry Judge, a former
comprehensive-school headmaster, does precisely that. As its
title suggests, the book is a riposte to the 'de-schooling'
thesis of Illich and Reimer; it is a staunch, balanced and
sober defence of secondary schools and their teachers. It is in
no way a defence of community schools and a community-
centred curriculum; indeed, much of the book is highly

acceptable to those who are suspicious of these reforms. After a careful review of the history, purposes and functions of these examinations, Judge concludes that we would on the whole gain from their abolition:[9]

> Benign results would flow from a simple decision to put the machinery into reverse, and allow the sixteen-plus national examination, having outlived its usefulness, to wither away. What would these results be? First and foremost . . . examinations would cease for pupils and teachers alike to be an illusory goal for five years of secondary schooling. At present, they operate both as a restraint on freedom and a convenient excuse for avoiding radical and constructive thought about the content of the curriculum. Their disappearance would remove an unhelpful myth from secondary education, and free teachers and pupils to think more carefully about what they are in fact doing, and why. A teacher would no longer be able to insist, to himself and his pupils, upon the value of any piece of work simply because 'It is part of the syllabus'. Nor would he be ale to yield to the temptation, as we all gracefully do, of using the examination as a piece of blackmail to squeeze work from the unwilling. . . . A pupil conversely would not be falsely encouraged to remain in full-time schooling simply to improve his certificated performance, without any genuine interest or belief in what he might be doing, or in order to demand some further certification for extra time he spent in school. . . . If the sixteen-plus examination system were to be dismantled, it would simultaneously become easier for teachers to understand in themselves what they were trying to do for all the pupils in the comprehensive school, and less tempting for them to develop half-unwittingly a system that might have been purpose-built to produce rejection and failure.

For many teachers and parents the idea of abolishing the national sixteen-plus examinations is startling, and much more radical than comprehensive re-organization or the community school. To those who bitterly opposed re-organization, the call for the abolition of 'O'-level examinations is just one more threat to national academic standards. We forget, however, for how brief a time these examinations have been with us and have been so readily accepted by the teaching profession. The National Union of Teachers has a long history of opposition to the extension of public examinations and took the view that if they were to be adopted by the secondary-modern schools they would narrow the curriculum and inhibit experimentation. And as we saw earlier, the Crowther Report of 1959 endorsed these fears. But both the educational establishment and the teachers underestimated the demand for public examinations, which in our booming economy were becoming the new selective device for employers. The teachers' determination to retain a broad curriculum for most adolescents inevitably collapsed in this pincer movement of parents and employers. Access to good jobs mattered to pupils and their parents, and the sixteen-plus examinations became the new occupational qualifications. For a period pupils could be prepared for work at sixteen *and* for 'A' level and higher education by the common route of the public examinations. The influence of teachers was restricted to some small reforms within these public examinations. In the CSE some new and imaginative curricula were developed and the Mode 3 style of assessment was introduced: but it was the GCE 'O' level which remained at the apex of the system.

The sixteen-plus examinations are not necessarily here to stay as the immovable foundation of secondary education. Many now believe they exert too strong an influence, or even constitute a new tyranny. They no longer, in a period of mass youth unemployment, provide automatic passports to good jobs for those who leave school at sixteen. The growing doubts of teachers combine with external changes and lead to a questioning about the purpose and functions of these examinations. It may be the first step towards their abolition. As Judge reminds us, an economist who had questioned the future of the canal system in 1790, or a journalist who in 1920 had doubted the future of the British Empire, or an educationist who in 1950 had prophesied the demise of the eleven-plus, would all have been greeted with dismay and disbelief.

127

The abolition of the sixteen-plus examinations would provoke fear and excitement, rejoicing and opposition among teachers. A consideration of the important objections that can and would be brought against such a reform must be postponed for a little while; instead we must concentrate on the more immediate task of considering how the freedom from external examinations at sixteen-plus could be used to advance some important educational purposes. We must, on the one hand, explore how this reform might help to eliminate some of the undesirable features to which I have drawn attention, and, on the other hand, ascertain the extent to which it would allow us to incorporate into secondary education those objectives and functions which are neglected in the present secondary school. The not uncommon 'progressive' view that *all* examinations are in principle educationally unsound and their abolition would automatically permit a 'true' education to flourish is naive and must be rejected as an unreasoned slogan.

It seems proper at this stage to make an open declaration of the general direction of the argument. I am not advocating examination-free community schools. As I have shown, the concept of the community school is vague; whilst I favour many of the innovations associated with community schools and believe that they entail much more significant reforms and developments than comprehensive re-organization, any attempt to transform all our secondary schools into community schools would be a slow and difficult change, which would not solve some of our problems and would generate many new ones. My main proposal is that all secondary schools should have a central, core curriculum, for pupils between the ages of eleven and fourteen or fifteen, which should be organized around community studies and the expressive arts. These would be part of the curriculum, not the whole of it, but there should be no public examination at sixteen-plus. The exact proportion of school time devoted to this might vary from school to school, in accordance with the needs and interests of the staff and the pupils, but I envisage that up to one-half of the first three or four years would be devoted to this work. However it should be a *compulsory* curriculum for *all* pupils of whatever abilities and social back-

128

ground. The notion of a compulsory element in the total curriculum is not new; the 1944 Act made religious education such a subject. (In practice, of course, English and mathematics tend to be compulsory subjects, though they are not legally required.) Parliament made religious education a compulsory subject because, for a variety of reasons, it was held that some religious education was an essential prerequisite of an educated person. It is my view that community studies and the expressive arts, and the knowledge and skills which they would teach, are now the *sine qua non* of an educated person in the last part of the twentieth century.

The assumption (or taken by many to be an implicit assumption) in the EPA work is that working-class pupils in 'deprived' areas have a need for a more community-centred curriculum because the communities in which they live are in urgent need of regeneration, but that this need is not shared by those who do not live in 'deprived' areas. It is this assumption that must be questioned. There is little doubt that erosion of community has been most severe in inner-city areas; and it is this sector which has, of course, been most extensively studied by sociologists. But the middle classes have not remained entirely unaffected by many of the same social forces and changes that have transformed working-class life. We cannot assume that all is well with the middle classes and their communities. Indeed, a neglected part of the sociological argument is that, in their traditional cultures, the working classes had a more highly developed sense of the local community than the middle classes. If it is true that the middle classes have not been insulated from social change and often display a singular lack of community spirit, then *all* children, including middle-class pupils, require community-related knowledge and skills. This may involve the careful investigation of middle-class communities where there can be found isolated old and retired people; business men under severe stress; frustrated, well-educated housewives tied to the house by young children; and latch-key children with both parents out at work. Behind the oak doors of detached houses on fashionable housing estates are hidden many personal and social problems which require solution: loneliness and distress and neglect do not belong uniquely to

129

the working-class 'deprived'; it is simply that the middle classes are more skilled at hiding their problems. It is true, of course, that in general the middle classes have many more privileges and opportunities than the working classes; but it is sheer perversity to imagine that there are no problems among the middle classes. Some of their problems are ones which they share with all sections of society.

Further, as part of community studies – not least because many communities are a mixture of middle-class and working-class groups – middle-class children would need to explore their own privileges and advantages. Middle-class pupils need a curriculum which will help them to uncover and demystify *their own* powers and privileges, and to face the problem of justifying them. There is a special kind of deprivation in being middle-class, one in which prejudices harden into certainties and privileges into rights. We can move towards being a better society only when there are changes in all sectors of it; an exclusive focus on community regeneration in deprived areas distracts attention away from national regeneration. A community education which loses sight of the nation as a whole as a community is not worthy of its name and can justifiably be condemned as parochial.

A compulsory community studies must be free from public examinations at sixteen-plus. If it is made a compulsory yet non-examined course whilst all the traditional subjects continue to be examined, then it will soon cease to be seen to have any importance. It will, as religious education has tended to do, soon fall into decay and neglect. But we cannot simply add it to the examined subjects. Any such course needs to be rather diverse in content, varying markedly with the skills and interests of the teachers, and the needs of the pupils and the communities in which they live. There might well be some common guidelines, but the exact content and the way in which it was sequenced and taught needs to be adapted to each individual school. A public examination soon acts as a constraint towards a common content; but community studies can never be as sharply defined as, say, a study of the history of the Tudors and Stuarts. Further, much of the knowledge and skills with which this topic must be concerned are not readily testable by written examinations. And most of all, this is not a subject in which some children could be destined to 'fail'. It would be unwise to label pupils as social and community failures by mid-adolescence.

Much of the content of a course in community studies will almost certainly have to be team-taught by a group of teachers with expertise in different subjects. We do not have teachers who are already experts qualified in community studies. There needs to be much joint learning, both between teachers, and between teachers and pupils. The pattern should be that which has already been established by 'integrated studies', in which we have in recent years been acquiring considerable experience. The innovation of 'integrated studies' has not been without its critics, especially in the field of 'social studies' (usually history and geography, but often including several other subjects). Bantock has offered a sustained critique of some current fashions in contemporary education, with its obsession with the temporary interest and immediate needs of pupils: he is impatient with what he calls the 'fragmentation and trivialization' of the curriculum, which then becomes 'a magpie curriculum of bits and pieces, unrelated and ephemeral':[10]

> Let us, with this indictment in mind, consider the current
> fashion for the interdisciplinary. Subject divisions are
> often dismissed as 'artificial' largely on the grounds that
> everyday living constantly involves the crossing and
> recrossing of subject boundaries and 'life as real as the
> home or the playground' is the object of our endeavour.
> But, of course, our 'living' is only interdisciplinary, as it
> were, in our moments of inattention and of imperfect
> consciousness. As soon as we focus our attention, seek to
> transcend the often mindless play of our daily existence,
> we enter an essentially specialised world. . . . A study of
> 'Our Town' (a popular subject) involves historical, econo-
> mic, geographical features (among others) that, to take
> on significance beyond the superficial, imply some degree
> of inwardness with the concepts and developments of the
> various subject fields involved; otherwise all that occurs is
> a meaningless copying from books and authorities (a not

131

infrequent manifestation, it can be said), in undifferentiated enthusiasm. The error implicit in an exclusive diet of this sort of thing lies in its haphazardness – and its subjectivity.

This paragraph raises a number of problems. First, it displays one of Bantock's most skilful, rhetorical tricks. To argue against something he dislikes he carefully selects the least successful example of it, implies it is typical, and then uses such bad practice to demolish the original justification for it. The form of the argument is: X is held to be a curricular good; here is a typical bad example of X; therefore X deserves no further consideration. This argument will not do at all. Mathematics is held to be a curricular good by all; it is very easy for me (or for you or for Bantock) to find an example of very bad teaching of mathematics; but none of us would be justified on this basis for changing our belief that mathematics is a curricular good. All we would have shown is that mathematics can be, and sometimes is, badly taught. Bantock brings no evidence at all that in general 'integrated studies' takes such an impoverished or trivial form, and I challenge him to do so. There are, needless to say, some available examples of bad practice in 'integrated studies', as in every subject known to me. But there is some extremely good practice too; and it is naturally the good practice which one will choose as the pattern for a new course in community studies.

Second, advocates of integrated studies do not reject the barriers between subjects on the vague grounds that they are 'artificial', though they sometimes can be so. It is rather that no single discipline has an obvious pre-eminence in the study of the community. If the course is taught with a sharp separation between each discipline, then it is left to the pupils to face the major task of *integrating* the different disciplinary perspectives into a coherent whole. In practice this is far too difficult for most pupils, with the result that the integration does not take place at all. It is only when teachers with different subject backgrounds work closely together on the problems of integration that the problems of creating coherence become visible and can be dealt with.

Moreover this integration does not, as Bantock implies, necessarily involve the abandonment of the *disciplined* basis of study. An adequate understanding of one's own community and social condition does indeed require the most careful study of how the community came to be as it is. History is needed for that task, but it does not have to be any less disciplined just because its point of departure is an understanding of the present or because it is being undertaken in concert with (say) geographical and economic perspectives. Indeed it may well be that integrated studies will stimulate in pupils a recognition of the need for, and the point of, the disciplined study of the single-subject specialization. At their best integrated studies and community studies will also introduce into the curriculum some elements of disciplined fields of study which take their full place in the university curriculum - archaeology, the history of science and technology, philosophy, politics, anthropology, sociology, psychology, government, international relations - but which sometimes do not appear in the school curriculum at all. As for Bantock's objection to such a course being the 'exclusive diet', I know of nobody who would devote the whole of secondary education to integrated studies or community studies; it is certainly not being suggested here.

Integrated studies - and community studies - thus require considerable expertise and a flexible openness if the course is to succeed. It should lead not only to relevance, but to depth and integration; whenever it can be shown to lead to trivialization and fragmentation, we must happily condemn it with Bantock. But to decide, on the basis of a little bad practice, that the enterprise is inherently flawed in principle, is to display a reprehensible prejudice against attempted innovation in our present limited curriculum.

We can now see why, in the case of community studies, there can be no detailed answer to the question posed by a teacher, 'But what would you have me teaching next Monday morning?' Only general objectives can be established, not a blueprint. The problem, in practice, is not the determination of the detailed content of the course, but rather coping with the problems of 'integrated studies' and team-teaching. Almost certainly we shall have to revise our notion of the timetable of forty-minute periods. Community studies (and the expressive arts as we shall see later) cannot be fitted neatly into the odd forty-minute period here and there. It often requires much longer stretches of time, probably whole days, not least because sometimes the pupils need to be taken out into the community and sometimes the community needs to be brought into the school. I am often tempted to think that the most conservative force in British secondary education is the constraint of the timetable of forty-minute lessons: one can, as a teacher, make almost any change or innovation one wishes, but only so long as one does not have to ask the deputy head to alter or amend the timetable. Officially it is said that the forty-minute period is there because pupils cannot concentrate on one topic for longer than this. I doubt it. It seems much nearer the truth to suggest that it is teachers who need the break every forty minutes, they who need the rest and the change. Those teachers who have experimented with teaching in day or half-day blocks know very well that the most important change demanded is one in teaching methods. It has to be admitted that a reform which increased the time devoted to community studies and the expressive arts as part of a compulsory core curriculum would entail some major changes also in pedagogy and school organization.

If a community-centred curriculum aims to endow children with the knowledge and skills to be active and useful members of their communities, the fundamental questions are: of which communities are the pupils now members and which communities are they likely to join when they leave school? Until these questions are answered in some detail, we cannot be in a position to specify the knowledge and skills that are needed. Yet curiously in some of the community-studies courses known to me these questions are not asked. Rather, two answers are presupposed – the pupil will be a member of his local community or will become a 'citizen'. The first answer is parochial and begs the question of whether there is a clear, local, residential community; the second answer is trivial in its vagueness. Both can easily lead to courses in 'civics' in which knowledge, such as the workings of Parliament or the local sewage system, is given pride of place. We cannot so easily dodge the difficult question of how community is to be defined.

For many the instant connotation of community is a local residential community, that is, a small and bounded territory. This can be reduced in size to a district, an electoral ward, a neighbourhood or a street. It can be expanded to a village, town or city, a county, a region, a nation, a continent, a world. This spatial conception of community is of self-evident significance, but it far from exhausts the conception of community. It ignores the small communities which we most value – family, kinship networks, friendship groups. We are also members of institutional communities – classes, year-groups, houses, teams, and so on in schools; the typing pool, the shop floor, the work group and the trade union at our place of work. For many people institutional forms such as churches, clubs, parties are expressions in community of their religious, leisure and political interests. Any adequate conception of community must include all of these, and more, if it is to be the foundation of a compulsory curriculum. Three things are at once apparent: we all belong to multiple communities; our community membership often changes; the communities of which we are members may be in conflict with one another.

The knowledge and skills required to participate successfully in such a variety of communities are extremely diverse; it would be difficult to find a 'common core' of knowledge and skills. 'High culture' and a knowledge of conventional subjects are prerequisites for membership in some but by no means all of these communities; even literacy and numeracy are not the most important requirement in many of them. It is precisely the task of a community-centred curriculum to expand its conception of community and to unravel the skills and knowledge that are required for participation. In so doing, we shall probably transform our conceptions of knowledge and skills, of 'intelligence' and 'success'.

It is through this enterprise that we can come to reformulate the position of the cognitive-intellectual domain in the secondary-school curriculum. Such knowledge and skills cannot be discarded, since they play an important part in so many communities. But it is not always *the* most important knowledge and skill. The community-centred curriculum will set the cognitive-intellectual into a new balance with the other forms of knowledge and skill. As part of this the conventional 'subjects' of the curriculum are likely to be re-shaped; much of what they contain will in fact be retained, but will arise in different contexts and in new forms. This has often been the experience of those teachers who have taught 'integrated studies', though these are usually limited to the first two years of secondary school or to the non-examinees, since the sixteen-plus examination constrains the re-emergence of the traditional subject labels in whose terms most examinations are organized. For me one of the most depressing features of contemporary secondary schools is the very large number of pupils who by the age of twelve have developed a marked dislike of a 'subject'. 'I hate it' is a common reaction to many subjects, when frequently what the pupil really means is that he or she dislikes the teacher and/or the way it is taught. Once the pupil develops this distance, interest and performance decline, which exacerbates the dislike. A few recover when they meet a different teacher, but for too many the aversion becomes permanent. One of the major benefits of dispersing subjects into a topic-based and more community-centred curriculum is that pupils can grow to dislike topics or teachers without discarding huge fields of knowledge and skill at the same time.

The father of community schooling, Henry Morris, understood the danger of the cognitive-intellectual diet of the conventional curriculum, leading to a force-feeding of the young on material for which they were intellectually and emotionally too immature:[11]

> For twenty years I have been fired by the belief that the school in England, and indeed in every country of the world, has to be re-made. The school has been dominated by the needs of the 'brainy' boy or girl, who is good at books and comes out well in examinations, and who wins prizes at the university. For millions of boys and girls who learn by practice and action this is a gigantic error. . . . Our State educational institutions and particularly our schools are classroom ridden, lesson ridden, textbook

ridden, information ridden, and given over to incessant
didactic discourse and discursiveness. Even in the best
schools . . . the element of discourse is overwhelming.

Once take away the neat 'subjects' and textbooks from the
teachers, and they are free to end this obsession. Almost
every teacher has that disconcerting experience of finding
himself in an exciting discussion with pupils only to have to
curtail it because it is not strictly relevant to the examination
syllabus. Almost every teacher discovers remarkable knowledge, talents and skills in pupils – and sometimes they are
well hidden – and yet knows that those cannot be accorded
any formal recognition. It is not much of a consolation to a
pupil who is failing at a narrow cognitive-intellectual curriculum to which he has taken a strong dislike to be told by his
teachers that he has 'a lovely personality' or 'some unusual
talents'. But in a community-centred curriculum there is a
real possibility that a much wider range of human talent can
come to be recognized, and thus prestige and praise can be
distributed more widely to more children. Children are quick
to spot differences among one another in knowledge and
skill – I suspect they do it more quickly than teachers in
many cases. Differences in cognitive-intellectual differences
cannot be masked from them by disguised names for streams
and ability groupings; it may make the teachers feel better
about it, but the pupils are totally undeceived. Only if we
diversify the knowledge and skills that we value can we hope
to make most children in school develop a sense of worth
whilst at the same time understanding that in some fields
their knowledge and skills are more limited. The only way in
which we can prevent so many pupils leaving school with a
sense of failure and inferiority is to make sure that there are
many more opportunities in school for pupils to experience
success, and it is wrong-headed to believe that more success
can be offered without broadening the curriculum to cover
skills and qualities which are peripheral or irrelevant to the
dominant cognitive-intellectual mode. And if some of the
pupils who are now defined as 'brainy' and steal all the
prestige accorded to cognitive-intellectual achievements have
their sense of superiority tempered by learning that other

pupils have remarkable skills which they themselves lack, so much the better.

The sense of failure and worthlessness which many pupils now derive from their educational experiences can be reduced by a diversification of the knowledge and skills cultivated in school. But will this help pupils to become the kind of adults who would be able to regenerate community life? As we have seen, the work of Halsey and Midwinter has emphasized the importance of this objective for working-class pupils in deprived areas. If the school really can play a role in helping to break the 'cycle of deprivation', in association with other (especially economic) reforms, then any curriculum programme which will help to achieve this objective will surely command our wholehearted assent. It is becoming clear to all that as these inner-city communities deteriorate it is costing enormous sums of money and human energy (in the form of social and community workers) merely to slow down the speed of deterioration.

Such an objective cannot be achieved by a relatively tame programme of small doses of 'civics' plus some community service. A programme of community studies with the slightest chance of achieving this objective will inevitably have a radical thrust. Children need, both for their immediate work and for use in their lives after school, the motivation and skills to build up appropriate community groups and the capacities to identify and influence the real power sources in the community. Very often these are elected representatives and officials in local government. The political dimensions of community studies immediately become apparent. But many politicians are nervous about political education, for they fear that this will become 'party political' and open the door to the political indoctrination of the young. Moreover most politicians prefer to be influenced and pressured through normal party political channels, that is, their own rank and file members. They do not like direct confrontation and negotiation with other kinds of community pressure group. In this they show their narrowness of conception of political life and their ambivalence towards full community participation. Politicians tend to be suspicious of party politics in schools and yet they also expect the schools to educate young people to take a genuine interest in politics, at national and local levels, and to play active roles as participants in democratic society. They bewail the widespread ignorance and apathy concerning political life and yet refuse to let the schools do the work that is essential to making improvements in the commitments of the young in the political arena. I fear that many politicians are open to accusations of bad faith. They do want more political commitment and participation, but they do not want to lay themselves open to criticism, challenge and change. The truth is that political cynicism among people will persist until we give political education more attention and until politicians themselves show more willingness to be accountable.

The vast majority of teachers, whatever their own political beliefs, seem to have little interest in political indoctrination. For them political *education* means leaving the choice of party political commitments entirely open to the pupil. One of the tasks of a political education is an understanding of, and even a demystification of, *all* power bases in society, only some of which are strictly speaking party political. Most of us have in recent years become more sceptical of and less deferential towards those in positions of power and authority. The Watergate scandal in the United States came as the ultimate confirmation of a mistrust of those in power which had become widespread throughout Western democracies in the previous decade. The task of political education within community studies would be to prevent this mistrust from lapsing into cynicism and instead use it as the foundation of healthy, critical yet positive commitments. In every school the pupils are encouraged to formulate reasoned criticisms of novels and plays, of scientific experiments and theories, and (as in Bantock's proposals) of radio, television and newspapers. This is surely a good thing, and to exclude political and economic life from reasoned criticism would be to draw an arbitrary boundary and to teach pupils that school is unconnected with social, political and economic realities. The problem is how we teach 'reasoned criticism' *and* the positive commitments to social solidarity which I have emphasized so strongly.

It is here that Durkheim's plans for the school as a source

139

of solidarity are open to the charge of naivety. He wanted education to inculcate national solidarity ('the political society as a whole') and also the more localized solidarities ('the special milieu for which one is specifically destined'). But there is inevitably a tension between these which Durkheim failed to explore in depth. Society is not so monolithic as Durkheim suggests; it is in many respects deeply riven by conflicts. Some groups are much more powerful and privileged than others and these groups will fight to maintain their advantage and to deny the exploitation and neglect of which we are aware. It is thus that the concept of the 'national interest' becomes a tired and irrelevant slogan, an appeal which becomes debased when it is used to preserve an unjust status quo. The phrase 'society as a whole' can become the means by which the powerful legitimate their position: consensual national solidarity becomes a conservative defence against the changes needed for greater social justice. Durkheim would probably have approved of Edmund Burke's claim that:[12]

> To be attached to the subdivision, to love the little platoon
> we belong to in society, is the first principle (the germ as
> it were) of public affections. It is the first link in the
> series by which we proceed towards a love of our country
> and to mankind.

In our terms, the assumption is that solidarity in school can be extended to community solidarity and that *automatically* leads to national and international solidarity.

This assumption is not warranted. Let us suppose that a small residential community, aided by a school system that helps to promote solidarity and offers a course in community studies, achieves solidarity and an understanding of its problems, what is needed to solve them, and the skill and confidence to seek out that solution. There is a good chance that this residential community will quickly come into conflict with the wider community (say at the level of the town) and those who exercise power there, local officials and councillors. There is no automatic transfer of solidarity at the level of the local residential community to solidarity at the level of the town. Suppose, further, that local officials argue that the solution does not lie within their powers, but at the level of central government. Town solidarity might be achieved, but only in conflict with the national level. The growth of solidarity at any level may well increase the conflict at the next level.

It is the recognition of this that leads powerful groups to fear the solidarity of the less powerful; and classroom teachers have a daily reminder of this elementary principle, for they know that if pupils really made use of their own collective power then the teacher's power, much of which rests on assertion and bluff, would soon leak away. So Durkheim was wrong to imply that a growth in solidarity would necessarily lead to a reduction in social conflict, and Marx was more realistic in seeing solidarity of the working classes as a necessary precondition of the revolution by which they would improve their condition. Yet I cannot help feeling that Durkheim was right in seeing national solidarity as an object for our strivings; the Marxist view that an idyllic state of solidarity free from conflict would naturally arise after the revolution seems naive. Durkheim underestimated the existence and inescapability of social conflict; Marx reduced social conflict ultimately to *class* conflict, which is an important but not the only form of conflict – or of solidarity. In our own time the popular conceptions of both conflict and solidarity are, with the help of the mass media, heavily concentrated on industrial relations, the battles between the 'bosses' and the 'workers' – two solidary opponents in conflict. It distracts our attention from the many other conflicts and solidarities that do exist, and should exist, in a healthy democratic society.

There are, then, many difficulties with a programme of community studies which seeks to take its political aspects seriously. It is dangerous simply to encourage pupils to develop sceptical and critical attitudes to those in power, for this soon slides into a generalized debunking of all forms of power and authority, which feeds the cynicism and sense of powerlessness that create egoism and anomie. It is futile to debunk those in power unless it is accompanied by a conviction that change can be made and by a knowledge of how to set about making that change. On the other hand, a community-studies programme which actively seeks to build up the solidary relations by which such change might be achieved runs the risk either of restricting its target to the immediate local context in defiance of the fact that many local problems occur as a product of larger, structural forces, or of creating wider conflicts in which each solidary community tries to further its own interests in blatant disregard for the rights and interests of other communities.

Durkheim emphasized that we all belong to multiple communities, and it is here that the seeds of the solution are to be found. Significantly this was also understood by John Dewey, the father of the progressive movement in modern education:[13]

It is the office of the school environment to balance the various elements in the social environment, and to see to it that each individual gets an opportunity to escape from the limitations of the social group in which he was born, and to come into living contact with a broader environment. Such words as 'society' and 'community' are likely to be misleading, for they have a tendency to make us think there is a single thing corresponding to the single word. As a matter of fact, a modern society is many societies more or less loosely connected. Each household with its immediate extension of friends makes a society; the village or street group of playmates is a community; each business group, each club, is another. Passing beyond these more intimate groups, there is in a country like our own a variety of races, religious affiliations, economic divisions. Inside the city, in spite of its nominal political unity, there are probably more communities, more differing customs, traditions, aspirations, and forms of government and control, than existed in an entire continent at an earlier epoch. . . . The school has the function also of co-ordinating within the disposition of each individual the diverse influences of the various social environments into which he enters. One code prevails in the family; another, on the street; a third, in the workshop or store; a fourth, in the religious association. As a person passes from one of the environments to another, he is subjected to antagonistic pulls, and is in danger of being split into a being having different standards of judgment and emotion for different occasions. This danger imposes on the school a steadying and integrating office.

Dewey specifically notes the solidary character of a delinquent gang or deviant group; but this praiseworthy character is marred by the negative ends to which these energies are directed and by the isolation of such a group from other groups in society. Both Dewey and Durkheim are concerned to harness and direct solidariness to higher social and individual purposes, and both assign to the school a major role in this social reconstruction. The contemporary culture of individualism in education is unfaithful to Dewey's vision of progressivism; it has stripped away the social and political character of education in which Dewey and Durkheim - whom we so readily place in opposite positions - both profoundly believed. Durkheim would surely have subscribed to Dewey's image of a modern, complex and democratic society, which:[14]

> makes provision for participation in its good of all its
> members on equal terms and which secures flexible
> readjustment of its institutions through interaction
> of the different forms of associated life.

Here, then, is a programme of tasks for secondary education as we move to the twenty-first century. First, in all groups each person must learn to subordinate his private interests to the needs of the whole group in order to achieve solidarity; and different groups will involve the subordination of different private interests and wishes. Second, the person must learn that different groups are sometimes in competition with one another. He has to learn to acknowledge that equivalent groups have equal rights and to avoid the rationalization that one's own solidary group can exercize its rights or further its interests without regard to equivalent groups. We see such rationalizations frequently in the form 'My pay rise has been fully earned and is justified; yours is a selfish demand against the national interest.' Third, each person must learn that different groups collide in attempts to further their interests. Thus a man belongs to a ratepayers' association which aims

143

to avoid increases in the rates, but other communities to which he belongs and which require financial help from local government suffer because the financial support is reduced or withdrawn. It is only when all are active members of several groups that the experience of collision between groups and their mutually contradictory objectives can be fully appreciated. Fourth, each person can learn that sometimes groups must combine forces and dissolve their boundaries if either group is to have any chance of realizing its interests. Greater industrial participation and the blurring of the sharp boundaries between 'workers' and 'management' might well yield common benefits to both these traditional opposing parties. In short, it is when we belong to many groups and communities, and play an active role within them, that we are most likely to learn about, and resolve, the tension between solidarity and conflict.

Durkheim offers a further insight in his conception of 'the other individualism'. We discussed earlier the notion of egoistic individualism which arises when the individual is divorced from group life and seeks to further his private interests free from social regulation. The second individualism rests upon a distinction between rights and interests. Rights are basic and inalienable; every individual and group has human rights which must be respected by other groups. Interests lack the fundamental character of rights. Interests can be legitimately furthered and negotiated, but only if they do not involve the infringement of the basic rights of others. Yet we are aware that in our society some groups and communities, especially those that are small and lacking in power, have their rights infringed by larger or more powerful groups which ruthlessly further their own interests. It is this which most damages national solidarity. For people to be truly responsible, they must learn that sometimes interests have to be abandoned because they encroach upon or negate the rights of others.

All this alerts us to the dangers of a programme of community studies which could become naively radical. It would not be enough for the school to be concerned with itself as a solidary community, nor to direct its forces towards trying to create a solidary local residential community. It must prepare pupils for membership of several communities and, in anticipation of this, must offer pupils meaningful membership in multiple groups and communities within the school. Each pupil must be provided with the vital experience of learning about the tensions which arise between solidary sub-communities within the school and how those conflicts must be resolved in a way that respects the rights of individuals and groups. It is of such stuff that the school as a solidary community will be made.

It is a bold vision and a daunting challenge for education. But if I am right in believing that one of the most central problems of our society is increasing active community participation from its members and securing the means and skills by which the inevitable conflicts can be resolved whilst respecting basic human rights, then what other major agency apart from the school has any hope of success? Sometimes external forces can induce similar changes. It is interesting that in time of war there can be a considerable increase in social solidarity and a degree of liberation for oppressed groups. Those who experienced the Second World War know that in many respects social solidarity was enhanced as we united and co-operated against the enemy. But it is also true that the liberation of women in our century owes much to the two world wars, which demanded that women enter what was traditionally 'men's work'. Women began to realize their own talents and skills and could be freed from their standard and restricted domestic roles. And men, with some reluctance, had to acknowledge some of their prejudice and self-interest. The wars did affect the class structure and gender divisions. Can the schools now undertake that same great work of improving solidarity *and* helping groups to enjoy their rights?

One of the most consequential by-products of a more community-centred curriculum, I hope, will be a considerable diversification of occupations and social positions to which teachers expect their pupils to aspire. In the conventional cognitive-intellectual curriculum, the implicit 'role models' tend to be those of the established professions – doctors, lawyers, dentists, architects, teachers, scientists, and so on. This is a reflection of nineteenth-century secondary schools,

145

which prepared their pupils for such positions, which were indeed the most powerful and prestigious positions. Since then there have been some shifts in power, in particular to national and local politicians and to trade union leaders. Most teachers known to me show little enthusiasm for trade union officials and often show a distinct (and sometimes quite justified) contempt for local councillors, whom they meet as school governors. I have never come across a single lesson in which a trade union official or a local councillor was held out to a pupil as a position to be sought. Yet it is surely in these positions that we need able and imaginative people with a finely educated capacity to understand and work for community needs and interests. And are not these people who must be most deeply committed to the exercise of participatory democracy, who must be open in their decision-making, and who must be willing to face the rigours of being more accountable to their electors? How much are they served by their present educational experiences? A trade union education officer points out that:[15]

> the TUC estimated that while some basic education was needed for 80,000 people a year – some training, that is, for one in five of all the country's stewards, officials and lay branch officers each year – in 1973–4 provision was made only for 30,000. In 1975 there were only facilities for less than half a day for every union office-holder in the year, or two and a half days for every hundred trades unionists. This compares pretty dismally with the provision made by the unions in every other West European country. . . . The glaring need is without doubt for the present meagre provision to be expanded. At the moment it's an uphill task to meet the immediate needs of only a small proportion of shop stewards – thousands of whom will have left school as soon as they could, and for whom a union education course is the first formal study they have done since.

Is there not an urgent need for the school to prepare the very best of its pupils for such roles, and might not a more community-centred education be an ideal preparation? It was believed by influential thinkers of the last century, such as Mill and Arnold, that power would inevitably pass from a small elite to the mass of the people. Revolution and social disharmony could be averted if the masses were given a suitable education. They may still be right, but an education based on the cognitive-intellectual grammar-school curriculum has been found wanting as the most appropriate education.

The number of working-class pupils who today leave school bored and alienated by their education experience may not be significantly greater than it was in the past. But the attractions which the school lacked could once be found elsewhere; there were alternative causes which inspired service and commitment. The churches and the unions (sometimes in combination) acted in this way, and many found a sense of mission in the promise of socialism, as Jeremy Seabrook has recently recaptured for us. Here is an extract from one of his informants, now aged eighty-four:[16]

I went to my first socialist meeting when I was five years old: I went to hear Ramsay MacDonald. He should have been a poet rather than a politician. I heard Jimmy Maxton, oh he was full of passion. So many of them were. People made such sacrifices for what they believed in. I've been speaking myself when the snow was coming down on the street corners and you've longed for the crowd to go away, but they wouldn't. We had something to say and I loved it. I spent my holidays working for the ILP. I could raise money from a crowd just by talking. In fact, a Salvation Army captain once said he wished I'd joined them – I was known as the champion beggar.

I joined the ILP at sixteen. At the same time they had formed a branch of the Women's Social and Political Union, the suffrage movement, in Glasgow, and of course I joined with great enthusiasm. They asked me if I was interested in the more militant side. I didn't think I could, being in service. They said, 'Well, you can drop these things in pillar boxes' [bottles of acid]. And so it was that I used to walk down the street in my servant's uniform at the appointed time, I'd take the cork from the bottle and put it in the pillar box, and then after a time it would begin to smoulder and burn. I'd walk demurely back to my place of employment and take a peep out of the basement window to see what was happening. They'd never suspect a domestic servant of doing anything so outrageous. Then of course they smashed windows – I never did that. They always went for property though, never never to hurt people. . . .

When I was a girl of twelve I remember one night I was selling the *Labour Woman* outside St Andrew's Hall, and Kier Hardie was speaking. When he came out, he saw me selling the paper and he said, 'That's right, my lassie, you'll be a credit to the movement yet.' I was so proud; I could hardly wait to get home to tell my dad that he'd actually spoken to me. Eventually I worked for the ILP. We went on different missions each week round the country. Every meeting would be crowded, and when we spoke, we spoke to make converts. The speakers were dedicated. . . .

The old ILP finally ceased to exist only about three years ago. That was a sad day. It gave us substance and background in our fight. I think a lot of people now prefer slogans to doing hard work. We worked, we went on marches, we knocked on doors, we spoke on street corners. We'd get a hundred thousand people marching on May Day in Glasgow.

The political parties nowadays attract very few young people; like many other institutions, they lack the means to draw out of the young any conviction, passion, dedication and sheer hard work. Those qualities are still needed. A community-centred curriculum might just provide the young with the challenges they are denied elsewhere. It might even help to restore to the trade union movement those wider social and community aspirations and ideals of which it was once proud. It is difficult to deny that some of those humanistic dreams have faded among some trade unionists who have more and more concentrated their energies on the immediate interests of their members. It is right that unions should exercise this function for, if they did not do so, the exploitation of ordinary workers would increase unchecked. It is the lack of the broader vision that I deplore. Unquestionably the middle classes hypocritically invoke the concept of 'the national interest' when they want to defend their own interests and position against the legitimate demands of poorer and less privileged sections of the community; but such attitudes are mirrored by trade unionists.[17] How often today we hear a union official, when asked to justify the union's demands in relation to the needs of the whole community, neatly avoiding the issue by a blunt assertion that his job is to improve the pay and conditions of his members and it is someone else's job 'to run the country'. A genuine commitment to the needs and rights of the whole community is not, in our society, an exclusive property of any one section of the community. The trade unions are now powerful and influential and they need such a commitment.

Community schools and community education are in their infancy; courses in community studies are still few and somewhat experimental. There is an emerging literature on community education which is rich in ideas, cautious in its pretensions and critical of the achievements so far; and that literature treats in depth many of the issues and arguments that have to be neglected here. Changes in curriculum and pedagogy are substantially slower than changes in structure and organization, as we learned in the case of comprehensive re-organization. Change in the content and method of teaching has to be grafted onto existing practice. Or, to put the matter another way, existing practice can show a remarkable resistance to apparent change. Teachers, like everybody else, do not much care for having their deep assumptions questioned and changed. The culture of individualism is as deeply ingrained into the fabric of schools as the cognitive-intellectual tradition and can easily survive what appear to be radical changes. We would perhaps expect to see little of this culture in the famous community school, Countesthorpe College; but a careful reading of *The Countesthorpe Experience* betrays its continued salience in the life of the school. The accent in teacher–pupil relationships was on trust, co-operation and democratic, joint decision-making. This, we are told, would maximize pupil autonomy; every pupil would be encouraged to take personal responsibility for the choice and direction of his work, though naturally with the supportive advice and help of the teachers. But this is just another version of the fallacy of individualism. It is good that pupils should not be too dependent upon their teachers, but a collection of autonomous and self-reliant individuals does not and cannot produce a community. Countesthorpe College sensed some of the dangers, it seems, for it created 'teams' of staff and students, little schools within the one big school, and I admire the way in which the teachers shunned any sharp separation of academic roles from pastoral ones. But it is simply not enough merely to provide 'a smaller unit within the school as a whole to which both staff and students can feel a sense of belonging'. The removal of a sense of loneliness and isolation does not create a community. 'A sense of belonging' is a *passive* concept, something which is provided by the school against excessive individualism. Communities command loyalties, and loyalty is an *active* concept, something which the school inspires and commands. A pupil *receives* a sense of belonging, but loyalty is something he must *give* by intent. It is clear from the accounts of the college that the staff have not as yet succeeded in finding the new equivalents to 'loyalty to the school' and 'corporate pride' which characterized the best schools in former times. Such equivalents must be found if the school is to provide pupils with a rich and direct experience of the solidary community.

Because, as we have seen earlier, comprehensive schools have tended to discard some of the most promising bases for corporate experiences such as the class unit and collective rituals, we shall have to find new and imaginative ways in which the corporate spirit can be revived. There can be no simple turning back of the clock. In our former schools the corporate elements often took a structural or organizational form, such as an assembly or the class unit; they were essentially external to the content of the formal curriculum. In our age, I suspect, the corporate elements must penetrate into the curriculum, both in its contents (as in community studies) and into the ways in which lessons are managed and taught. This is why co-operative project work is potentially so important. Here work is interdependent, the success of the whole resting on the success of the individual contributions. We know too little about how effective such projects might be in the promotion of group solidarity. We know that in some cases projects might have the opposite effect, as in project work I have witnessed where a few able members do all the work and the rest sit back and do little. Research has uncovered some of the conditions under which project work can promote group solidarity, but it has not fully been applied to project work in schools.

Solidary experiences can, however, be found in some unlikely places. Let us take the case of the expressive arts to which I want to give a central place in the core curriculum. They are often seen as being profoundly concerned with individual development, fostering emotional development, self-confidence and aesthetic sensitivity. Now I do not wish in any way to decry these aims in the teaching of drama; I merely want to note how the primary aims are focused on the individual pupil and the social element is reduced to the acquisition of certain interpersonal skills. Thus we are told that the main purpose of drama is:[18]

> developing and bringing out the child's personality and qualities of character. All the creative arts should be approached in schools with this attitude of mind; but drama is closest of all to this development.

One authority cites nearly thirty aims for the teaching of drama, but only one – to help pupils to 'come to terms with groups and society, to accept discipline' – comes close to solidary functions.[19] Much more typical is the argument that drama confers:[20]

> direct experience, transcending mere knowledge, enriching the imagination, possibly touching the heart and soul as well as the mind. . . . Education is concerned with individuals; drama is concerned with the individuality of individuals, with the uniqueness of each human essence.

Drama teachers, like their colleagues, have unwittingly become victims of the cult of individualism, and in so doing they are in real danger of ignoring the powerful corporate potentials in drama. Let us consider the performance of a play, which we can use as a paradigm for other aspects

151

of the creative arts, such as operas, choral music, orchestras and bands. In the performance of a play there is a highly elaborate distribution and specialization of labour: there are actors, with large and small parts; a stage staff of those who build and paint scenery, lighting technicians, dress designers, and so on; a 'house staff' who deal with programmes, tickets and refreshments. It is like society in miniature, with its differentiation of function, and some participants having more central roles than others. But for a play to be a success each contributor must give of his best and be correctly integrated with all the other elements. If the person with the smallest contribution to make 'fluffs' his lines or is neglectful of his contribution, the enterprise as a whole is in danger of being ruined. Anyone who has been involved with a school play production knows what a tremendous and exciting corporate spirit is generated, particularly just before and during the public performance. It is an exemplar of differentiated team-work.

Individual performers may be outstanding and get credit for it. But the success of a few does not, as happens in class-rooms, automatically generate a sense of failure in the rest. Those with more lowly contributions know perfectly well that they could not be the 'star' of the show, but they know that they have been making a contribution which is essential to the whole enterprise and which is thus known to be valued. A play thus gives the participants dignity in the sense in which I defined it earlier. Each makes a contribution, the competent execution of which brings a sense of being valued. Solidarity and dignity are conferred simultaneously.

Pupils and their parents know the deep impact of public performances of the arts. Pupils see the last night of the play as a time for regret and sorrow; it will be plain old school again tomorrow, back into classroom lessons. It is not at all uncommon for parents to report to staff how the play has engendered a new pleasure, interest and commitment – and sometimes a new willingness to come to school. Pupils tend to remember these events longer than almost anything else about school: photographs of them are treasured. Yet in most schools the play is part of the *extra-curriculum* – an optional and occasional (perhaps annual) activity involving a minority of the pupils in their spare time. A unique contribution to dignity and community solidarity is made simply an 'extra'.

The number of drama teachers in schools has grown rapidly for many years. But they are severely constrained by the timetable of forty-minute periods. School plays cannot be produced within such a framework. It is not surprising then that school plays ('theatre') must in practice be given a low priority. Most pupils' experience of drama must be confined to 'drama lessons' and the easiest way to conduct such a short lesson is to devote it to *improvised* drama and movement, with its focus on individual objectives. One of the central functions of drama is thereby distorted.

Play-reading in the classroom is no substitute for drama or for the performance of plays. Pupils often find such play-reading rather dull, especially when the teacher takes the main part. Yet the public performance of a play can make an inestimable contribution to a pupil's literary and cognitive-intellectual education. My own fascination with Shakespeare began not in the classroom or at Stratford-upon-Avon, but on the stage as a non-speaking member of the Roman mob in *Julius Caesar*. I came to love (and incidentally to learn by heart) the great 'Friends, Romans, countrymen' speech. Yet every year we still send away from school thousands of children with a strong dislike of Shakespeare instilled through the classroom reading of dead texts examined in the sixteen-plus examinations.

Bantock rightly wants to give drama and movement a central place in his alternative curriculum. But that is for the 'bottom 50 per cent', not for all. He cites evidence that it can be extremely beneficial for those who find the more academic curriculum difficult and dull. No doubt he is right and would approve of the Department of Education and Science's survey of school drama which reported that:[21]

When young people are working together in unstreamed groups of all but the lowest ability it is often found that the boy or girl most ready to give a lead in a dramatic situation is from the less able group. Such leadership needs a marked combination of qualities. The boy or girl must

153

have grasped the whole situation imaginatively. He must then have the penetration – for it is more than just the imagination – to realise in a moment how that situation can be developed – simply to be able to imagine what happened next. An intelligent child can usually be counted on to have a bright idea. But we are speaking of more than this: the ability to have the idea and to be able to give expression to it in 'acting', that is, physically and vocally. This ability depends not only on a full grasp of the situation but on a kind of intuitive awareness of what will be acceptable to the rest of the group. There are children who produce ideas that the rest of the class are unable to accept. Among a class of so-called less able children in a [secondary] school in the north-east one little boy stood out from the class for the intense vitality of his movements, his deep involvement in everything that he did, and the vigour of his speech. In all these respects he was far ahead of anyone else in the class. On being asked about him his teacher replied that he was 'best at drama' (best of all the children and best in all his work). But his headmaster said that he was 'a boy of little ability, a nuisance, a show-off'.

This is not uncommon and it neatly displays how head-teachers and others persist in their narrow definitions of intelligence and how drama is assigned peripheral importance in making our educational assessments of children.

This quotation seems to support Bantock's thesis; but if the 'top 50 per cent' of pupils are to be given a more academic curriculum, there is a danger that they will be deprived of drama which they will learn to see as unimportant for bright and brainy pupils. The DES report continues:

In many streamed secondary schools, the A stream pupils, whose seven years at school are milestoned with examinations, often have fewer opportunities to take drama than their less able comrades. In some schools the amount of timetabled drama increases as the ability of the pupils decreases. This is accounted for partially by the enormous pressure on the time of the able children . . . and partially by the assumption that drama is a kindly way of keeping the backward pupils out of trouble. But in a growing number of schools the remedial values of drama are becoming recognized, and while it is encouraging to note that it can make a substantial contribution to the education of the less able, it is becoming increasingly apparent that drama can contribute to the education of the most gifted. Unfortunately much of the drama that was seen in grammar schools and the top streams of the bigger schools was disappointing.

Evidence and good sense undermines Bantock's argument. His scheme rightly broadens the curriculum of the 'bottom 50 per cent', but it threatens to deprive the 'top 50 per cent' of a most important educational experience after the age of eleven. Why should intellectually gifted children suddenly, at this age, lose their needs for, and rights to, drama? Bantock correctly claims that the academic curriculum is an unsuitable exclusive diet for many pupils and so suggests an alternative curriculum grounded in the expressive arts. But it does not follow from this that all is well with the academic curriculum for half of our young adolescent population. My argument is that all children need more community studies and more expressive arts in the core curriculum that is followed by all. Bantock does not question the old grammar-school curriculum. Raymond Williams does:[22]

> The fact about our present curriculum is that it was essentially created by the nineteenth century, following some eighteenth-century models, and retaining elements of the medieval curriculum near its centre. A case can be made for every item in it, yet its omissions are startling. The social studies, even of an elementary kind, are virtually omitted at the level which every child can be certain of reaching, yet it would be difficult to argue that a detailed description of the workings of parliamentary and local government, of the law and public administration, of the organization of industry, of the evolution and character of modern social groups, of the techniques

155

by which a modern society is studied and influenced, is less relevant than, say, the detailed descriptions of the geography of South America which now have traditional sanction. Where education in the social studies is given at all, except in exceptional schools, it is outside 'business', as modern languages and science were outside 'business' in the nineteenth century, and its teaching varies in quality from simple description to the casual and hortatory process – a true descendant of 'moral rescue' – known as 'civics'. In the arts, similarly, it is a meagre response to our cultural tradition and problems to teach, outside literature, little more than practical drawing and music, with hardly an attempt to begin either the history and criticism of music and visual art forms, or the criticism of those forms of film, televised drama and jazz to which every child will go home. Even in English, despite the efforts of many fine teachers, most children will leave even grammar schools without ever having practised the critical reading of newspapers, magazines, propaganda, and advertisements, which will form the bulk of their actual adult reading. Meanwhile, in science, the vast and exciting *history* of scientific discovery will have been given quite inadequate attention.

Moreover I have tried to show that whereas at first sight community studies and the expressive arts seem highly disparate, in reality they are complementary, since one of the primary functions of some aspects of the expressive arts is the creation of solidarity within the community. This connection between community studies and the expressive arts could be greatly strengthened if the school gave many more public performances to its host community. Traditionally schools simply invite outsiders into the school for the school play; and most of that audience consists of parents. Too rarely does the school take its performances out to the wider community – a performance going 'on tour' if you like. There are, in fact, many groups of people, in old folks' homes, in day centres for the elderly, in hospitals and prisons, in works' canteens and Church halls, who would receive such performances with delight. It would be a form of community service, a concept which should not be reduced to visiting the elderly and tidying up their gardens. To do this, of course, a flexible approach to the school timetable would be essential.

Whilst a similar argument can be made for operas and music festivals of various sorts, one cannot be made for art, drawing and painting: an art exhibition at school does not engender much community spirit or offer much community service. Yet over many years I have noticed how in virtually all schools, and not least those with many 'behaviour problems' among pupils, art and craft lessons are very rarely subject to the disruption or boredom that is common in other lessons. Even to the casual visitor, the art (or craft) room is clearly a relaxed place, with a quiet hum of activity. The reason why pupils, even those with few talents in this domain, enjoy art lessons are several. Each pupil has a high degree of autonomy in a task which challenges one's creative powers. Each lesson tends to have a clear product as an end in itself; every picture is complete in itself, not just an isolated exercise as part of a complex syllabus which exists only in the teacher's mind. Moreover, there is no 'right answer' already known to the teacher; there is no absolute standard of what makes a good drawing or painting. In contrast to many conventional subjects, in art two utterly different pictures on the same theme can both be outstandingly good. The teacher can advise, guide, suggest and support; he rarely makes the dogmatic statements to pupils that are common in other lessons. Some English teachers have sought to model their own subject on such a pattern, but I suspect art lessons have their own special magic to many pupils.

Sports teams are traditionally seen as one of the most sacred forms through which group loyalty can be inculcated. My impression is that they are less strongly valued in many contemporary comprehensive schools. There are various reasons for this, but certainly the lack of a morning assembly for the whole school, in which the achievements of the school teams can be proclaimed to all, makes such activities less salient in the eyes of the school community. In many schools there is poor support at matches after school and at the weekends: a call of 'Up the school!' from the touch-line

157

today would have a quite different meaning to that of thirty or more years ago. As we saw earlier, support and loyalty for school sports' teams have tended to be deflected towards professional teams. Among progressive teachers there is sometimes a suspicion of team games for it is held that they emphasize competition rather than co-operation. There is some truth in this and no doubt a surfeit of competitiveness can be harmful. But competition between groups stimulates co-operation within the group. We cannot abolish competition, but we can use it constructively and channel it in positive ways. The energies which now flow to excess in 'soccer hooliganism' could in part be harnessed within the school. In good schools team games make a vital contribution to the life of the school and its solidarity. The vacuous demands of policemen and politicians, alarmed at the misconduct of a minority on football terraces, that schools should in some way (never specified, of course) train our young men to be 'good citizens' are probably best met by the skilful cultivation of the solidary aspects of team games in school. There will always be a stronger competitive element to sports than to musical or dramatic performances; but opposition to all forms of competition are ill-conceived since the fostering of both excellence and co-operation in part depends on a degree of competition.

Physical education and sporting activities have, fortunately, become considerably diversified in recent years; the concentration on football (or rugby) and cricket for boys, and hockey (or netball) and tennis for girls, has given way to a new variety of physical activities. Such diversification is important and needs to be extended further, since as many pupils with as varied talents as possible must be involved in these activities. Otherwise a small sporting elite soon excludes a majority who, as in the academic curriculum, lose interest when they feel they lack the requisite abilities, and the activities cease to give any intrinsic pleasure. There seems to be no good reason why schools should not introduce activities such as table tennis and darts as team games; too often these are left as non-serious lunch-time diversions.

Inter-school team games can thus become an important means of generating loyalty to the school and the experience of co-operation. In practice some pupils, and especially those from a working-class background, tend to be excluded because the activities take place in the evening and on Saturdays when some pupils have part-time jobs to provide pocket-money. If pupils are to be involved in large numbers, it is essential that these activities in drama, music and sport are no longer so heavily consigned to the voluntary extra-curriculum but are integrated within the formal curriculum and take place during normal school hours. This can only be achieved at the expense of some of the time now given to the academic curriculum. But I believe it would be worth it and a general increase in pupil loyalty and co-operation might stimulate a general rise in commitment to other aspects of schooling. I am convinced that it is the great richness of the extra-curriculum which gives many independent schools their advantage over some state schools. If this is to be transferred to the state comprehensive schools, it must become part of the compulsory formal curriculum. In no other way can it achieve the significance it merits and become a central part of the education of all pupils.

My final suggestion relates to holidays organized by the schools. In former years most schools planned various camping holidays for their pupils, especially in association with the popular youth movements, such as the Scouts and Guides and military organizations. In more recent times school holidays, following the general increase in family financial resources, have begun to specialize in trips to various European countries where the pupils live in student hostels or even hotel accommodation. No doubt a first-hand experience of foreign countries is of considerable educational benefit to pupils; my concern is that these holidays then become patterned on the ordinary family holiday abroad. The 'school camp' has some important virtues, apart from cheapness, for it provides a vivid experience of communal living in which the basic necessities of life, such as living quarters and feeding, have to be provided by the pupils themselves in co-operative work. This I believe to be of more profound educational value for it is an experience that cannot be obtained in the ordinary family-type holiday. I do not believe that such holiday ventures, so rich in solidary potential, have lost their appeal to pupils so much as they have to teachers, who have to work especially hard on these occasions. Some schools still offer them with considerable success. Here, as in many of the issues which I have been discussing, it is not that schools have intentionally repudiated such experiences for pupils, but rather that in the flurry of educational and social change they have simply fallen by the wayside. This is part of our educational heritage we cannot afford to forget and must recover with urgency.

The challenge for the contemporary comprehensive school is that of combining two kinds of reform: the first consists of re-vitalizing old ideas, which we dare not lose, into new forms which are appropriate to our age; the second consists of a continuation of what has always happened in our educational history, namely the process by which the curriculum is adjusted and expanded to include the range of knowledge, ability and skill which is needed in contemporary society.

6   A proposal and some objections

The comprehensive school had a difficult birth. It was always an unwanted child for some, who impatiently awaited an opportunity to commit a discreet infanticide. For others it was an infant prodigy which needed to be carefully nurtured and to be defended against envious enemies. It survived. We must now plan its future, for it will not grow and develop naturally without more care and thought and agreement from us. A clear and assured future for the comprehensive school, from the closing years of this century into the early decades of the next, can be provided only if we think out an agreed set of goals and purposes for it and take seriously the old questions: what kind of society do we want, and how is the education system going to help us to realize such a society? The best of our current achievements and aspirations must be retained. There can be no new eleven-plus, no return to premature selection. We shall need to continue the difficult struggle to make the education system more open and just.

We shall also have to eliminate some of the present system's least desirable features and prepare the young for an active role in adult society, where they understand the nation's problems and are willing to help to solve them. We can no longer afford an education system that for too many pupils is an unpleasant induction into the experience of failure and inferiority. Our traditional academic and cognitive-intellectual curriculum, which we inherited from the past and from the grammar schools, must, in the new comprehensive school, itself become more comprehensive and balanced. The school curriculum must endow all pupils with a sense of their own competencies; it must draw upon a wide range of knowledge,

161

skills and abilities, so that all children can derive from their education a realistic sense of their strengths and weaknesses; and this must be cultivated within a strong spirit of corporate solidarity. Only if the comprehensive school can achieve this can it justly claim to confer a genuine sense of dignity on all its pupils. We know that the school must help to invest young people with a creative capacity for the positive use of leisure, as the working week and working life become shorter. It is easy to produce empty slogans about the urgent need for the school to prepare young people for the creative use of increased leisure time. In practice we resist the harsh necessity of working out the implications of such worthy aims for the content of the secondary-school curriculum and for the personal and social qualities with which schools need to endow its pupils. An increasing number of pupils will continue to be prepared for higher education, but we must also prepare pupils for the new elite positions, such as trade union officials, local councillors and community leaders. We need men and women who will take greater responsibility for the vitality of the various communities, including the local residential communities, of which they will become members. These communities need to be more self-determining, more self-reliant and more democratically controlled. As communities become more solidary, members must learn how to recognize and further the interests of that community whilst carefully preserving the basic rights both of the individual person and of other communities. It is on that basis that a stronger national solidarity can be founded. We must all improve our skills in the resolution of conflict among the nation's sub-communities.

And all that, of course, is only too easy to say. The much more demanding task is the design of a scheme by which these high purposes might be achieved, a scheme which elaborates in some detail how the education system might play its own partial but nevertheless important and distinctive role in a huge social enterprise. We know from the past that such schemes tend to fall far short of the objectives they are intended to achieve; such is the way of all schemes. Some parts of the scheme are subsequently found to be totally inadequate to the task, and others have unforeseen and unintended problems and consequences. But knowledge that our schemes are inherently flawed does not remove the obligation to create them: the lesson of history is that we must see the schemes as provisional and as no more than a framework. It is in this spirit that I offer, on the basis of the earlier analysis, the following proposal.

All the sixteen-plus public examinations must be abolished. The comprehensive-school curriculum can then be reconstructed or revised. From the age of eleven to fifteen years all pupils will follow a core curriculum with two central elements. The first is an integrated course in community studies. This will be taught by teams of teachers with a variety of subject expertise, but as part of this course none of the traditional subjects need be taught in separate blocks with the traditional subject labels. The course will be taught in blocks of days and half-days. Pupils will sometimes move out into the community and at other times outsiders with relevant expertise would be brought into the school. The second part of the compulsory core curriculum will comprise the expressive arts, crafts and sport. Whilst there will be some conventional lessons here, there should also be multidisciplinary approaches to the critical study of the mass media. A major part must also be devoted to the production of plays and festivals of art and music. These will be offered for public performance in school but they will also be taken out to the community.

This core curriculum, which will incorporate all the traditional school subjects and introduce some new ones, will comprise about one half of pupil work in school. The remaining half will be given to two other essential activities. The first will consist of 'remedial' options. In many aspects of the core curriculum it will soon become apparent that some pupils lack the basic skills needed to undertake and complete the set tasks. Remedial options will offer special help in these areas, especially numeracy and literacy, where weakness is limiting the pupil's capacity to contribute to or profit from the core curriculum. Some remedial options may be relatively self-contained with few formal links to the core curriculum. Others will be more 'individualized', meeting the specific needs which pupils experience in their core-curriculum work and which pupils are most motivated to remedy. Some of this remedial work may be taken by highly gifted pupils – a

163

change in our conventional connotations to the term 're-medial' thus being involved – since some pupils will need a stronger and deeper disciplinary backing for their core-curriculum work.

The second element in the optional half of the curriculum will consist of particular fields of study where pupils show a special interest or talent. The purpose of these is not so much to respond to pupils' felt needs arising out of the core curriculum but rather to foster interest and talents for their own sake. It is possible that they might be offered under the conventional subject labels. But I suspect we could gain more by avoiding these labels and instead using more specific topics for a limited period of time. Thus instead of offering additional *English* as an option we might present this subject in much smaller and more precise units – 'contemporary science fiction', 'the Victorian novel', 'Romantic poetry', 'the portrayal of war in literature'. This can be done for all fields of study, for science and mathematics as well as for history and geography. If pupils then dislike an option, the course does not last for too long and the dislike becomes attached to the topic, not to the subject of which it is a part. It is one of the great advantages of a comprehensive school that the sheer size of staff permits the development of a wide range of flexible options, as some current practice has shown.

Among those options, many of which will have a strong academic flavour, there should be some multidisciplinary options, in which teachers with different subject backgrounds come together to offer joint courses. Multidisciplinary approaches should not be confined to the courses in community studies. Schools have much to learn from the Open University here; the fact that so many Open University graduates are in fact teachers could be of great help. These teachers know that multidisciplinary work does not necessarily lack discipline and rigour.

The purpose of this design for the curriculum is to cover as wide a range of knowledge, skills and abilities as possible and keep choices and interests as open as possible for as long as possible. All this curricular work and the organizational framework of the school must be permeated with a staff commitment to the creation of solidary sub-communities.

Through them will be created the solidarity of the school, an education in the acknowledgment of individual and group rights, and the discovery of means for the resolution for conflicts between the individual and the group or between different sub-communities.

After the age of fifteen the proposed secondary-school curriculum will cease. The present system has replaced the old eleven-plus with a new selective test – the thirteen-plus when pupils are allocated to the three bands of 'O'-level, CSE and non-examination groups. The abolition of the sixteen-plus examination puts an end to selection at thirteen-plus, but of course selection cannot itself be terminated. In this scheme the selective allocation takes place at fifteen-plus. Those pupils who now wish to move towards 'A' levels are allocated to the appropriate academic course, which now takes *three* years rather than the present two. Pupils who intend to leave school at sixteen to enter directly into work are allocated to more vocational courses. Some of these will be concerned with providing work experience and immediate vocational skills. Other courses will be more academic and will prepare pupils for examinations in vocationally related or relevant subjects. Some pupils will need more careers education and vocational guidance; and some, sadly, will need help in preparing for unemployment. The central focus of the last year at school will be direct preparation for the experience of leaving school.

The fifteen-plus allocation of pupils might take place within the comprehensive school. It would make more sense, probably, that the academic sixth-form 'A'-level work be done in the comprehensive school or at a sixth-form college, and the more vocational work and study be pursued in the colleges of further education, which in general have far more of the relevant knowledge and skills at their disposal than do the comprehensive schools. Better still all the pupils might be transferred at fifteen to a common tertiary college, which combines sixth-form 'A'-level work and vocational courses, whether academic or not, under the same roof. The distinction between academic and vocational orientations are never in practice so sharp as my comments, or our present institutional divisions, suggest.

165

The proposal requires some radical rethinking by teachers about the content of the curriculum and the organization of the school's teaching programme. The costs fall on the teachers, who need to be flexible and open-minded; no huge financial expenditures are involved. The effect of the abolition of the sixteen-plus examinations on the secondary schools is like the effect of the abolition of the eleven-plus on the primary schools: an exciting new opportunity for changes in the content and methods of teaching becomes available for those teachers with vision and commitment. Many of the elements in the proposal simply systematize and elaborate on some existing good practice in secondary schools especially during the first two or three years. We have to learn from that good practice and improve our methods of disseminating it. Lessons have to be learned from community schools, which have worked through many of the problems associated with strengthening ties between the school and the community. All the seeds of the proposed reform are already growing healthily somewhere in comprehensive and community schools.

No school, nor even one local educational authority, can adopt these proposals alone. The agreement about the abolition of the sixteen-plus examinations and the provision of a compulsory core curriculum focused on community studies and the expressive arts will have to be a national agreement. Before we consider how such a proposal might be implemented, we must consider some of the objections that can and should be made. I must act the role of sober critic to my own heady ideas.

1   *Your diagnosis of the ills of our society and of the education system are greatly exaggerated, and your proposal is too dramatic a change in the content of schooling.*

This book was never intended to be a balanced appraisal of all the strengths and weaknesses of the whole comprehensive-school system. Rather the aim was to highlight a set of particular problems of the complex relationship between education and society, especially as these relate to the secondary school. In that sense the diagnosis must be selective and partial. I have drawn on evidence where possible, but there is usually too little evidence and even that is open to more than one interpretation. The diagnosis rests on judgments and opinions more than on simple facts which are beyond dispute, so obviously some will disagree with it.

I suspect that the diagnosis is more likely to be shared by teachers in inner-city working-class schools than by those who teach in more middle-class schools in more favoured areas. The attention I have given to inner-city, working-class schools is intentional; they have the most severe problems which merit discussion and attention. The proposal for change would ·for some schools involve a fairly sharp and sudden change, and in general I am sympathetic to a rather slow, piecemeal process of reform which Popper has defended so eloquently.[1] But I fear that our present piecemeal reform is not guided in any systematic or rational way, but is rather a process of disorganized drift. In any case just how does one abolish the sixteen-plus examinations except in a sudden way? I remain unconvinced that the constraining power of public examinations at sixteen can be modified to any substantial degree by small adjustments here and there. Perhaps the more telling objection to the proposal is that it makes a curious combination of a 'radical' reform – the abolition of sixteen-plus examinations – with an apparently 'conservative' reform – the strengthening of social solidarity. That combination suggests the proposal as a whole will be acceptable to very few people. But then I have found that other proposals offered in recent years are too narrow or too partial – Illich's suggestions that we de-school society, or Bowles and Gintis's suggestion that teachers should fight for a more socialist society, and so on. There are radical ideas and conservative ideas, and both make telling judgments on the education system and society. I have come to the conclusion that the truth lies in both extremes. I am not looking for the middle-ground, some thin-blooded compromise position half-way between extremes. Instead I want to combine into a constructive whole elements taken from extreme positions which are generally taken to be incompatible. Our crude dichotomy of 'radical' and 'conservative' is dangerous because it over-simplifies and polarizes, as if the complexity of ideas involved in any discussion of education and society can be neatly subdivided into cowboys and Indians. Even worse, each extreme position develops or seizes an idea or insight and takes full possession of it; the other extreme then rejects or discounts the idea or insight which is held to be the tainted property of the opposition. On very rare occasions – the idea of educational vouchers is an example – an idea is taken up by the political left *and* right, to everyone's consternation. But for the rest of the time most of us want to be plain cops or robbers. I cannot really complain or be surprised if 'radicals' and 'conservatives' alike accuse me of theft and treachery.

2   *Your proposal assigns to the school a powerful role in the creation of social solidarity. By your own admission that aspect of educational institutions has been declining in recent years, so is it not foolhardy to attempt to restore it?*

That the social, solidary and – in Durkheim's sense – the moral functions of the school have in recent years been in sharp decline is beyond dispute. The problem is whether we try to recover those functions and express them in new forms appropriate to our age, as I have argued; or whether we believe that the present trend is essentially beneficial and should be encouraged or even accelerated. Frank Musgrove, in a book which interestingly has some common ground with this one on the matter of diagnosis, comes precisely to this conclusion. He energetically argues that the school should, in the Durkheimian sense, be rapidly 'de-moralized':[2]

> Both England and America in the late twentieth century are inheritors of a massive tradition of education as socialization: schools are first and foremost about shaping people and to only a subsidiary degree about the acquisition of skill, knowledge and understanding. In 1980 this is not only an irrelevance: it is a gigantic impertinence. The first judgement that I make is that schools should be systematically demoralized. . . . For Bereiter schools have no business concerning themselves with 'the whole child'. . . . In an impoverished and brutalized society schools properly and necessarily take on much wider tasks; to arrogate these wider tasks in highly sophisticated modern

societies is an effrontery. As I have argued elsewhere, in modern societies the teacher's job is expert, technical, restricted and professional in providing an efficient service for clients. . . . With the demoralization of schooling must go the death of the school as a community and on its grave must rise a fundamentally different kind of organization: voluntary in character, sensitive to the needs of clients and consumers, tolerant of diversity, unceremonious and indifferent to tradition, careful of the contractual rights of its members, consultative and participatory in its style of management. It probably will not have a football team; there may be neither school crest nor colours. It will be an association and not a community . . . there must be (in the schools of the future) more specialization (both within schools and between them) and not less, and there must be more selection (largely as a corollary of this) and not less. . . . It makes no sense in modern highly sophisticated societies to make all adolescents follow broad courses of study.

Musgrove's determination to de-moralize the school is a persuasive counter-argument to my proposal that we re-moralize the school.

Musgrove does not explicitly deny that people need community, solidarity, ceremony and ritual; his proposal is that the education system should dissociate itself from these notions. Presumably solidary experiences would have to be sought elsewhere. Unfortunately Musgrove does not consider any alternative sources, as did Durkheim, and perhaps wisely; for he would most likely have come to Durkheim's conclusions, that the family, religion and the local community have become too weak to meet man's social needs. The problem of generating greater social solidarity, of creating greater democratic participation and of finding means of resolving conflicts between groups, Musgrove blandly ignores. His position is one of extreme individualism in which the school offers strictly limited services to meet the instrumental needs of voluntary clients. Presumably the universities would model their new role on that of the colleges of further education. But I doubt very much whether this is really what most teachers, parents or pupils actually want from schools. Musgrove firmly shuns what we have come to define as 'education' in favour of a narrow, specialized and technical 'training'. Parents, by contrast, generally accept that the school, if it is a good one, has far more to offer than this: it furnishes a much broader experience than the family can supply on its own limited resources. Is this not one of the reasons why the public schools are so popular and why the most esteemed state schools cultivate a richness and breadth of conception that extends far beyond mere training? Schools which parents like are busy places after four o'clock, in the evenings, at the weekends, and in the holidays. Parents do not want the social experiences of their children to be restricted to informal peer and youth cultures, and nor, fortunately, do most teachers, who have far higher ideals and deeper commitments than their equivalents in France, where secondary education is closer to the Musgrove model. More important still, Musgrove's individualistic and technical conception of education would almost certainly increase the disadvantages of working-class pupils. And I remain convinced that unless we greatly increase the solidarities in the various communities that comprise democratic society and educate them to resolve their conflicts, then we shall create a political vacuum which would most easily be filled by an authoritarian regime of the extreme left or right.

3   *Under your proposals academic standards will fall and very able children will be held back.*

It is natural that comprehensive re-organization would arouse fears that academic standards would fall, and it is perfectly reasonable to demand that standards should be monitored with special care during periods of change in the structure of the education system. At present there is little evidence of a general decline in educational standards.[3] But my proposal goes much further in its curricular innovations than did comprehensive re-organization, so the objection is fully in order. In one sense *academic* standards *might* well be lower for sixteen-year olds than they are at present. After all, the curriculum under my proposal would be considerably broader than it is now, so standards in the academic, intellectual-cognitive domain might be lower in that pupils would not be able to reach the same level of achievement if they were entered for the present 'O'-level papers. At the same time standards in other areas – the aesthetic-artistic, the affective-emotional, the physical-manual and the personal-social – would probably rise, since much more time and effort is being devoted to their cultivation. One might therefore be lowering standards in one area but improving standards in other domains, so the general standards would remain constant. But there is no reason to believe that academic standards for eighteen-year-olds would fall, since the 'A'-level courses would take three years of preparation rather than the present two. One would hope also that the more balanced curriculum would lead to an improvement in levels of motivation. The vast majority of teachers will readily concede that the major problem in our secondary schools is not one of ability but of motivation: children have talent in plenty, but many lack both the interest and willingness to work hard that are needed for high achievement. My proposed curriculum is no panacea for motivation, but I do believe that it might prevent many children from turning against education in the early years of their secondary schooling.

I also see no reason why, under my proposals, general levels of achievement in numeracy and literacy should fall. Integrated studies have one useful side-effect: they tend to spread concern about pupils' literacy and numeracy among the whole range of teachers. It is one of the disadvantages of our present system that the responsibility for literacy and numeracy is too often seen to belong uniquely to English and mathematics teachers respectively. If all teachers assume this responsibility, there should be a general improvement in standards. But there is, of course, the danger that no-one would take the responsibility and that the problem would be diverted to the 'remedial' programmes in literacy and numeracy outside the common curriculum. For this reason among others I believe it would be essential that the proposal be closely monitored. We already have some appropriate machinery in the Assessment Performance Unit which has developed tests in some basic areas. If these tests were applied regularly and the results fed back to the school, then each school would know if and to what extent pupils were falling behind in the levels of basic literacy and numeracy that are agreed as appropriate for a particular age.

The issue of general educational standards (or of academic standards) must not be confused with the more specific one of the most able or so-called 'gifted' minority. Under this heading we might include pupils who possess a particular talent within one area, say music or mathematics, but are 'average' in other fields, and the rather different group who show a very high level of ability across a much wider range of academic subjects. It is perfectly possible for there to be a general improvement in educational standards which masks a fall in the levels achieved by this minority of exceptionally able pupils. It is right that we should be concerned about them and offer them at least as much attention as we do to the other extreme, those who show exceptional disability. Has this minority suffered as a result of comprehensive re-organization? In her excellent book *Clever Children in Comprehensive Schools* Auriol Stevens concludes that re-organization's:[4]

> massive and dramatic disruption has so far done nothing to raise academic attainment at the top levels but has coincided with growing measured attainment at the middle ability levels. . . . And my hypothesis, based on scrutiny of the figures and the general rhetoric, and on impressions of schools, is this: the cleverest group are no longer reaching the same level of detailed, disciplined *academic* work at the age they reached it before. At the same time, the middle range of children have gained self-confidence and certificated success in a whole range of courses, conventional and unconventional. [Italics added]

This is an honest and sensible appraisal which gives no grounds for complacency. We can rejoice at the improved achievement of the middle-ability pupils, but it is clear that there is a danger of neglecting the most able group. But one must add that the loss among the most gifted is in *academic* terms; it is perfectly possible that these able pupils have gained by an improved *general* education in comprehensive schools. My proposal would accept such a transfer of achievement from one area to another amongst the eleven-to-fifteen age-group, but would expect this short-term academic loss to be made up during the more academically intensive three-year 'A'-level course. One would have to ensure in addition that academically gifted children were given every opportunity to exercise their talents in the 'academic options' in the half of the curriculum time which remains outside the common-core curriculum. There is no good reason why most of the core curriculum could not be organized in terms of 'mixed-ability' groups; but much of the academic option work would almost certainly have to be streamed or setted by ability if the most able pupils are to be stretched. We might recall, too, that the 'remedial' groups I proposed in conjunction with the core curriculum would also include provision for pupils of high ability, for these children might often wish to pursue in depth topics which arise out of the community-studies course and the expressive arts but which could not be easily done in a mixed-ability setting.

Able children always need careful monitoring and the work which is now being undertaken to improve the provision for the identification and stimulation of very gifted children in comprehensive schools must be encouraged. For some, Auriol Stevens's conclusions will confirm their worries about comprehensive schools. But she herself does not call for a return to selective schools and a more academic education. She knows that such a step would be a retrograde one to an excessively academic educational system which is designed to serve the minority at the expense of the majority:

> It is of crucial national importance that as many young people as possible become productive, as few as possible become dependent. It is not a vast number more academics – or even a vast number more Nobel prizewinners, excellent as they are for national morale – that we need. We need versatile, practical people, capable of managing their lives, contributing to the lives of others, earning their living and enjoying their leisure. The answer is not, there-fore, to unpick the comprehensive system or even substantially to modify the principle, reverting to an older,

173

academic approach. Postponing selection and segregation seems to offer the best chance of achieving what is needed. . . . Between 20 to 25 per cent educated to a high level is no longer anything like enough, and academic skills alone are too narrow a basis on which to build a sound industrial nation.

The comprehensive school is capable of realizing this task without neglecting able pupils. As far as my own proposal is concerned, I must remain open-minded. If it could be shown that children with special gifts in particular areas could not, in fact, be catered for adequately in the comprehensive school, then we would have to take action. We already acknowledge the need for and value of special schools for those with outstanding talent at music or ballet, and the same principle might have to be applied to other fields such as mathematics or modern languages. Such special schools would recruit such a very tiny minority that the general comprehensive principle would not be threatened. However, this step should be taken only when it can be justified by evidence. We must never lose sight of the fact that all children, however gifted, have rights to and needs for a more general education than the purely academic, especially during their secondary schooling. As Dr Arnold of Rugby School used to remind his pupils:[5]

What I have often said before I repeat now: what we must look for here is, first, religious and moral principle; secondly, gentlemanly conduct; thirdly, intellectual ability.

It is the contention of this book that the first two purposes of education adduced by Arnold need some adaptation now that a century has passed since he uttered these wise words. But I am in complete agreement with him that the cultivation of intellectual ability should not be the cardinal aim of education in the secondary school.

4   *Why is there no mention of a foreign language in your proposal?*

The controversial position of modern languages in the secondary-school curriculum is neatly caught by the opposing position of two former professors of education at the University of York, one (Eric Hawkins) believing that a foreign language should be part of a compulsory core curriculum and the other (Harry Rée) equally convinced that it should not.[6] It is certainly a good example of the grammar-school curriculum now being imposed on all in the comprehensive school. Under the tripartite system grammar-school pupils were expected to learn a foreign language, not least to satisfy university entrance requirements. It was generally assumed that a foreign language was inappropriate for the education of the vast majority of secondary-modern school pupils. It is the emergence of the comprehensive school, and perhaps Britain's entry into the Common Market, which has provoked arguments that all children should at least learn the elements of a foreign language. Now it must be admitted that most pupils will in five years' compulsory learning of a language reach a very modest level of achievement, probably no more than a capacity to indulge in what Bantock has called 'the banalities of tourist conversation' – which might incidentally be learned just as easily by adults from the excellent radio and television language programmes. And if tourist conversation is the most tangible goal for most pupils, then it would be difficult to justify the ubiquitous emphasis on French, since pupils are far more likely to spend their holidays in Spain. I sometimes think that the main consequence of learning French is to give the British adult the competence to ask nervously 'Parlez-vous anglais?' the moment he sets foot on foreign soil. For 'O' level may give one a basic mastery to speak a foreign language, but as tourists discover to their horror it does not give one the competence to hear and understand the language as spoken by the natives. The main point of learning a foreign language is the understanding of its culture and the access to its literature; but this is beyond the powers and interest of most pupils. It is said that the British show an unwarranted aversion to modern languages. It is not really so. The fact that the Americans show the same aversion demonstrates that it is an English-speaking rather than British phenomenon. Because English

175

is an international language there is little incentive for most of us to learn a foreign language for purely communicative purposes on rare trips abroad. The Dutch and the Swedes are in a contrary position; they speak a minority language and so it is part of their culture to impress upon all the need to speak one or more of the international languages. It is unrealistic to try to implant that same impetus in modern Britain.

So I see no point in making a foreign language part of the core curriculum, partly because it is of no immediate or direct value to the study of the community or the expressive arts, and partly because I am not persuaded that all pupils should spend so much time in learning the rudiments of a language they will soon forget. It seems to me far more important that all children should increase their powers of communication in their own language, especially oral communication, which is so often disgracefully neglected. But a refusal to impose a foreign language on all is not to deny it to some. There will be children with the ability and interest to enjoy and succeed in learning foreign languages and the school should provide them with the opportunity. A subject can justifiably be made part of the compulsory curriculum only if it can be shown that it inculcates knowledge, abilities and skills which are essential to all. A good comprehensive school will offer opportunities for access to a very much wider range of knowledge, abilities and skills than can be considered essential to all. A comprehensive school which offers *no more than* what is considered essential to all pupils will maintain an atrophied curriculum; a comprehensive school which *insists* that all pupils should pursue a field which cannot be shown to be essential to all is just as misguidedly egalitarian. In my proposal, therefore, foreign languages should be available as one of the academic options available outside the core curriculum. Some pupils will no doubt lose interest after a while; but others will cover the elementary ground before entering a three-year 'A'-level course. In short, we must get away from the universal 'drip-feed process by which the language was fed in for four or five short periods a week' as Rée describes it and take seriously the fact that 'a language can be much better learned elsewhere than in a classroom, can be learned in a far shorter time, and to a far better standard, by spending two or three months in a foreign family, talking and hearing nothing but the foreign language'. One might add that the imposition of a foreign language on all pupils can only make the shortage of foreign-language teachers more acute, for there are few rewards for such teachers in spending so much of their time attempting to teach the basic elements to an uninterested set of pupils with few language skills.

5 *The universities will never permit the abolition of the sixteen-plus examinations.*
     In recent years the universities have considerably curtailed their once stringent demands for specified passes at 'O' level. General demands for, say, Latin or a modern language have now been withdrawn as have the more restricted demands such as 'O'-level German for intending chemists. I suspect this trend will continue and that the universities' interest in 'O' levels will fade away. As long as 'A' levels are not disturbed and as long as general standards at this level do not decline I can see no special grounds for university opposition to the abolition of sixteen-plus public examinations.

     There has for a long time been considerable controversy over the specialized versus general education provided by schools. The universities demand as high grades at 'A' level as they dare, but they also want to recruit students with a good general education and broad interests through which students will contribute to and benefit from a full university education. The tension has been acute in the sixth form: just how much 'general studies' should be required? Under our present system school pupils have to specialize at a very early age, often before 'O' level, in order to reach 'A' level and university entry standards in the time available. My proposal removes irrevocably early specialization in favour of a broad general education; the three-year 'A' level course permits greater specialization among older adolescents, who have often resented the 'general studies' programmes which distract them from their specialized interests. It must also be said that as our knowledge has expanded so rapidly in recent years, university degree courses have become fuller and more

177

demanding. One way in which this pressure has been reduced is by universities cramming more into the 'A'-level syllabus or even by expecting extra achievements during the 'third-year sixth' between 'A' level and university entry. It is time we dealt with this in the only proper way, by extending university degree courses from three to four years.

6 *Employers need and use the sixteen-plus examinations and so will oppose their abolition.*

Employers certainly use the sixteen-plus examinations as a selective device in their recruitment procedures, and I suggest that in many cases it is neither proper nor just for them to do so. It seems that employers often work on the general principle that they want the 'best' possible recruits. They want to exclude those with a poor school record, the allegedly 'under-qualified', and also those who seem to be too good for the job, the so-called 'over-qualified'. In the present phase of such very high unemployment among the young it is both these groups who become least likely to secure a job (though the latter group can sometimes suppress knowledge of their academic success from employers and in any case tend to be a smaller group than the former). Sixteen-plus examination results thus become 'qualifications' and a principal basis of occupational selection and recruitment. We live in an age of 'credentialism'. This is not a proper procedure because although sixteen-plus examinations are popularly called 'qualifications' they are not really so. Nobody can be simply 'qualified' *tout court*: one has to be qualified *for* something. Thus we say that medical examinations qualify doctors to practise medicine: the examinations are the prerequisite for a professional licence. But what do sixteen-plus examination results qualify young people for? Strictly speaking, the answer must be very little. 'O'-level results are not, in fact, very good predictors of achievement at 'A' level, even in the same subject; they are thus only a weak qualification for further work in the same field. In what sense, then, are these examination results legitimately to be treated as *occupational* qualifications? They are probably very poor predictors of how well a person will do his job, and probably only a small element of what is tested by these examinations is a necessary prerequisite of success in the job. They cannot then properly be referred to as qualifications when it is *occupational* qualifications that we really have in mind.

Once employers use these examination results as a convenient (if unwarranted) basis for recruitment, a social injustice is committed. By their practices employers create a correspondence between the academic hierarchy in school achievement and the hierarchy of job prestige. Social justice in the allocation of jobs prevails only if those persons who are genuinely qualified with the known prerequisites for, or known skills of, the job are recruited, or if those who can be shown to do the job best are offered employment. In a period of high youth unemployment employers' use of sixteen-plus examination results as a selective test thus constitutes a social injustice; and it is a social-class biased injustice, since it is known that some sections of the working class, and black immigrant youth, will tend to perform less well than their middle-class peers in tests of cognitive-intellectual achievement. It thus comes about that middle-class youth, and working-class youth with high academic qualifications, are actually displacing many less academic working-class and black youth from the jobs which they have traditionally entered and at which they may well be just as successful. And once sixteen-plus examination results become synonymous with occupational qualifications then the principal incentive for working hard at school is one of improving one's chances of obtaining employment; it is this fact which underlies the heavily extrinsic and instrumental attitudes of young people to their secondary-school education.

Some employers, especially the large organizations with personnel departments, know that the examination results can be poor predictors of job performance and job satisfaction. So they develop their own selective methods, which lead to increased worker satisfaction and meet managerial demands to reduce waste and inefficiency. Smaller firms cannot afford this expertise of personnel officers and industrial psychologists, so they tend to use the sixteen-plus examination record, sometimes supplemented by their own tests which are often out of date and of no known relevance to the jobs which are being filled.

In his book *The Diploma Disease*, Ronald Dore offers a sophisticated discussion and criticism of 'credentialism' and suggests a number of alternatives.[7] From Dore's work I want to draw out two proposals. Each of these would need to be given legislative force. First, it must be an offence for any employer to recruit an employee on the basis of the latter's possession of paper qualifications unless it can be demonstrated that these test qualities and skills which are necessary to doing the job successfully. The same rule must apply to any selective tests used by the employer as an alternative to public-examination results. Second, it will be an offence for an employer to promote an employee on the basis of paper qualifications unless it can be shown that these measure knowledge, abilities and skills needed in the new post. This is surely the most sensible way in which to achieve social justice in the allocation of jobs. It was found necessary to introduce legislation in support of our determination to stamp out discrimination on the basis of sex, race and religion. Occupational discrimination on the basis of education is surely in the same category. At the same time I would want to see greater co-operation between schools and employers so that the final year at school for those pupils who do not enrol on 'A'-level courses would in part be orientated to work experience and the acquisition of relevant skills and knowledge. Employers should be making much more effort to increase and improve, as some already do, the occupational education and training of their own employees. In James Callaghan's Great Education Debate the schools received a whipping from industry and commerce; they became a scapegoat for Britain's industrial ills. With luck this disgraceful episode will promote better communication and co-operation between teachers and employers, but unless there is a determined effort to end credentialism I do not think that schools will be able to get on with their proper function, that of *educating* the pupils in their charge. For this reason I believe that my curriculum proposals have little chance of implementation until we enact some legislation which will set the relation between examination results and employment on a proper footing. The abolition of the sixteen-plus examinations is no more than one part of this legislative package. We could then begin the serious task of improving and increasing – for some already exist – those examinations which assess work-related knowledge and skills and which constitute more genuine occupational qualifications.

7   If there are no examinations, standards will fall; pupils will have nothing to aim for and no incentive to work hard.

I have already dealt with the common confusion between and conflation of examination results and occupational qualifications. This new objection displays a confusion between assessment and public examinations. All teaching and learning requires some form of assessment. All education is deeply imbued with unceasing assessments by both teacher and taught. Pupils constantly assess the efforts they make and the accuracy or worth of the product of those efforts. Teachers make the same judgments about the pupil and also try to check the effectiveness of their teaching as one component of increasing pupil effort, interest and quality of product. But most of these assessments are highly informal. Assessment becomes more formal when teachers grade particular pieces of work and assign marks which may be recorded. Sometimes these assessments take the form of tests with the format of an unseen examination. All this is an essential part of an education. In Dore's words:[8]

> The prime function of achievement tests – the reason they seem to teachers indispensable – is their internal function as an aid to instruction. And that they *do* have these important internal functions is undeniable. Frequent informal achievement tests, even occasional grander, more ritualized, stressful tests can be useful to both teacher and pupil when they do no more than give the teacher information about how successful the teaching efforts have been, and give the pupil short-term objectives to ease his long haul up the slope towards mastery, offer him some measure of his progress from which he can take satisfaction and encouragement, or receive a salutary jolt to his complacency, whichever he needs most.

If all assessment and testing were abolished, or even minimized, standards would undoubtedly fall, since teaching and

181

learning would be severely damaged. It is thus profoundly mistaken to interpret proposals to abolish sixteen-plus public examinations as an attack on the principle of educational assessment.

It should now be crystal clear that my objection to the sixteen-plus examinations is not that they are assessments, but that they are in the main assessments of a rather narrow set of cognitive-intellectual abilities, skills and knowledge; that they exercise a narrowing influence on the education of young people; and that they have become occupational qualifications and thus an instrument of social injustice. I do not for one moment deny that they can act as a challenging incentive to teachers and pupils; but their abolition would not excise all incentive or assessment from the educational system. It is also true that they are a measure, and one which is external to the school, of the individual school's and national standards. But this important function could be taken over by the Assessment of Performance Unit and the work of Her Majesty's Inspectors of Schools.

There is one further point in favour of abolition which has not been mentioned so far, namely the sheer *cost* of the sixteen-plus examination system. It is now a vast industry. Many schools spend more money on the entry fees for these examinations than they do on the resources, such as books and equipment, needed in the preparation of pupils for the examinations. This is surely absurd and indefensible.

8   *Your proposals are not really egalitarian: there is nothing here to disturb the status quo; the elites with great power, with access to the most prestigious jobs, and with great wealth will survive unscathed; and the public schools will continue to provide a 'cycle of privilege' to those who are already advantaged at birth.*

In this book I have intentionally avoided the term 'egalitarian', a concept which is as slippery as it is popular. For some people it is a term of abuse to be hurled against those who seek any kind of reform or against those who see each and every human and social difference as examples of unwarranted privilege. For others it is a favoured word to characterize a better and more just society. The term has come to mean little in itself; to grasp its meaning one must know the identity of the speaker and the drift of his argument. When terms become so debased by slogans and rhetoric they need very careful analysis and scrupulous use, or they should be excluded from our vocabulary. I have chosen the latter course and so will concentrate on the more substantial and specific charges in the objection.

There are good grounds for thinking that in advanced industrial societies there will always be some individuals and groups who possess more than average power and wealth. It is quite a different matter to judge that our present distribution of power, occupations and wealth is equitable. I judge that it is not, and like most people believe that political and economic reform is needed to make our society more fair. It is patently absurd to think that a reformed education system could do this alone. But it does not follow from that position that education is largely irrelevant to social change, or that educational reform must be consequent upon more fundamental political and economic reform rather than being part and parcel of such reform. I have already suggested that some legislative change would be needed to implement my proposals. But the new education then offered in secondary schools would itself contribute to social change and to further legislative reform. The education system has a special function in the cultivation of human dignity. This is achieved in part by the cultivation of a much wider range of knowledge, abilities and skills and in part by the promotion of greater solidarity in the various communities of which pupils will become members. At the centre of my thinking is the belief that one of the most important and intractable problems of our society is the resolution of conflict between various groups and communities. We are not proving to be very successful at this task in the political arena; politicians dramatize and exaggerate what they can achieve through legislation. The resolution of conflict requires solidary communities throughout society, communities of men and women with dignity and a commitment to the basic rights of man. These seem to be to me the preconditions of the good sense and goodwill by which conflicts can be resolved, and secondary schools have a powerful role to play in realizing

183

those preconditions. The relation between education and society I see as a reciprocal one; each is needed to facilitate and enhance the achievements of the other. It is for this reason that I am sceptical that direct political action will solve our problems. An excellent case can be made, for example, for the further redistribution of wealth in our society and that would have to be taken by direct political action. But that reform would not automatically ensure a redistribution of dignity. Even if all men earned the same income, or believed that a certain distribution of wealth were an equitable one, they would not thereby also feel of equal worth. The abolition of economic inequalities does not automatically entail the abolition of other inequalities and injustices. Dignity cannot be bought so cheaply. Education has little to contribute directly to a more just distribution of wealth; the most we can hope is that, with appropriate legislation as suggested earlier, we can reduce the extent to which the educational system actually contributes to the maintenance of economic and occupational inequalities. But education can and should have a central role to play in the redistribution of dignity.

In his study of social mobility and class structure in Britain today, John Goldthorpe has rightly noted that there is still a strong collective base for the working class in the trade union movement, which is becoming an increasingly potent force in society. He concludes his discussion of contemporary inequalities with the proposition that:[9]

> if class inequalities are to be significantly modified, this can only be achieved through a process of conflict between classes: that is, through those who are chiefly disadvantaged by the inequalities that prevail compensating for their lack of social power as individuals by acting collectively, and being able, by virtue of their numbers, organization, and solidarity, to mount a successful challenge to the status quo. Whatever form such a challenge might take, in terms of its institutional – or extra-institutional – expression, the factor crucial to its success would be the forcefulness of the class-based action that could back it against the class-based opposition which it would inevitably meet.

184

This is not a very original conclusion – class conflict in which the working classes find their solidary base in the trade union movement. I am not persuaded that all inequalities should be so understood in exclusively class terms, and I think Goldthorpe underestimates the significance of conflicts of interest among groups which are all working-class. Leaving that aside, however, we learn very little about how solidarity is to be increased in underprivileged groups, how such solidarities must also be generated, as surely they must, outside the trade union movement, and how we shall find the mechanism by which conflicts of interest can be justly resolved. In my view Goldthorpe over-simplifies the problem of inequality by reducing it all ultimately to class terms and then proffers an over-simple 'solution' in the form of a recipe for more union-based class conflict.

The objection that my proposals do not disturb the status quo in society is sustained in the trivial and self-evident sense that education cannot directly and of itself produce an end to inequalities. But an acceptance of that proposition does not entail a denial that education could exercise an important and unique role in the process of social amelioration. With legislative support, and in concert with direct political and economic reforms, the education system could make that contribution. To that end we must refuse to confine secondary education to the culture of individualism and design a secondary education with more self-conscious social and political objectives. Otherwise the school will continue to act as a conservative force, reflecting and confirming the status quo rather than generating the will and the skill through which we can make a better society. Of course the riposte from my critic might be that the proposed legislation and reforms in secondary education could themselves only be a product of class-based social conflict. We shall return to this point later.

The objection against the public schools is a potent one. The evidence that a public-school education increases one's access to positions of power, to prestigious occupations, and to wealth is overwhelming. There is no space here to discuss this complex and vexed question in any detail. I am not persuaded that parents have an inalienable right to spend their money on their children's education in any way that they choose, though I am more concerned at the threat to our freedom of assembly that the enforced closure of the public schools might entail. The public schools have in our age begun to ape the state schools in some respects; they are much more obsessed with public examinations than they once were. Parents now do not blindly trust the public schools to give a good education to their children: they want high grades in public examinations as well. I would hope that the two systems might converge in other and more important ways. None of the schemes for integrating the two is likely to be successful, and some of the most recent proposals for their abolition (such as charging former public-school pupils the full cost of their higher education) will unjustly penalize children for their parents' earlier educational decisions on their behalf. Other schemes, such as the removal of the charitable status of the public schools, would make them more expensive, but almost certainly would not eliminate them completely.

I do not have the answer to the problem of the public schools and they are a thorn in my proposals as they are in any other suggested reform. However, I must concede that the public-school sector displays several virtues I would like to see within the state sector – diversity, choice, commitment and accountability. The public-school sector, though small, tends to contain within itself greater diversity of educational philosophy than does the state sector with its universal comprehensive school. One can find public schools that are 'conservative' and 'radical' in outlook, where most of the staff subscribe to an agreed school philosophy. In the state sector such agreements among the staff of a school are rare: comprehensive schools survive on an uneasy compromise among a staff with very different educational views. Comprehensive schools rarely sustain a highly distinctive educational philosophy, shared by all the staff who then put it into practice. It is much more common to find headteachers with strongly held views which are then presented to the public as the school's philosophy, but the dissent from and even attempted subversion of this philosophy by the school's staff is soon detected behind the headteacher's rhetorical mask. As a result there is substantially more choice for parents who can afford a public-school education for their children. In the state sector most parents have little choice but the local comprehensive, and even where choice is available the schools among which the choice can be exercised are often surprisingly similar. Because public schools are more likely to have agreed aims and methods, the commitment of teachers to the school is often greater than in the state sector. The commitment of parents is also sometimes much higher and the school can call upon them for help and support, including financial aid. Finally, public schools tend to be more accountable to their clients: parents pay, and so their views must be listened to.

I am sometimes tempted to think that state schools would be better if they could imitate the public schools in these ways. It would be possible if we decentralized the education system, and made the schools self-governing rather than so strongly under the control of central and local authorities. In other words, parents would be given educational vouchers to spend on their children's education as they thought fit. Schools would finance themselves on the basis of their income from these vouchers. Each school would develop its own philosophy and recruit an appropriate staff. If it failed to attract clients, it would become bankrupt and have to be taken over by another regime of teachers, a new 'educational company'. General control of education must inevitably remain in central hands: the DES would have to certify that the schools were 'efficient' by some agreed criteria and would inspect them regularly. But the schools would be essentially self-governing and highly accountable to parents.

There are many problems with such a proposal; it would take another book to elucidate them. I mention them here merely to make the point that the choice between eliminating the public schools or retaining them is not the only possibility. Our task is not even one of integrating them, which was the preferred conclusion of the tedious reports of the Public Schools Commission. Rather, we might adapt both sectors in the light of the virtues of each. If I might put the matter another way, I should like to see our education system evolve more nearly to the style and structure of the Church of England than to the Church of Rome. The former has always promoted a high degree of local autonomy for churches, which show great diversity in style of worship and doctrinal commitment, whilst all nevertheless subscribe to a few basic religious principles. The Church of Rome, by contrast, has always exercised a very strong central hand and is suspicious of local diversity in belief and practice. Our education system was once closer to the Anglican pattern, but the present state system of comprehensive schools seems premised on the Roman style. I wish it were not so. My own proposals for a core curriculum are offered in the spirit that this would constitute the equivalent of the Anglicans' 'few basic principles' and beyond that local autonomy, diversity, choice, accountability and commitment might flourish, without the encumbrance of a centralized and bureaucratized state education system. The public schools in their present form cannot be justified, but they have much to offer to education if they were less defensive and parochial in their self-centred fight for survival. If they had any sense, they would be showing how some of their virtues could be made more widely available in the state system. And the state system would see the public schools not as competitive enemies but as a source of ideas about how greater diversity, choice, commitment and accountability could, with some reform, be increased in the state sector. For there are many demands for these four features and our attempts to meet them may make the individual comprehensive school the unfortunate battle-ground for conflicting and irreconcilable forces – on the one hand, more direction and control from a powerful DES implementing government policy and, on the other hand, greater sensitivity and responsiveness to the expressed needs and idiosyncratic preferences of the pupils' parents and the local community. The problem of the public schools will not be best resolved if we persist in the neat either–or partisanship which has bedevilled so much educational and social reform in the past.[10]

Within the Labour Party there is a renewed determination to abolish the public schools. We should remember that even if the public schools were closed and their pupils redistributed through the comprehensive schools, the certain effect would be the enhancement of a small minority of schools within the maintained sector, namely those which serve middle-class residential communities. Residential segregation by social class is even now masking an educational segregation, as most middle-class parents – and their estate agents – already know. The closure of the public schools would merely increase the existing differences *between* comprehensive schools as middle-class parents transform their local schools into the kinds of institution they desire.

In the next few years the academic community will surely document in great detail how differentiation inside the comprehensive school allows the selection processes of the former tripartite system to continue almost unabated *within* the individual comprehensive school. In practice the comprehensive school may well prove to be failing to extend greater equality of opportunity to children from working-class homes; indeed, it is a tenable hypothesis, and one which must be put to the test, that the comprehensive school could reduce equality of opportunity and then to make matters worse, hide that fact from public recognition and scrutiny. Our continuing reliance on the sixteen-plus examinations of GCE 'O' level and CSE as occupational qualifications, combined with massive unemployment among young people, could deal a severe blow to those ideals which formed the foundation of the comprehensive system. I do not see how the ingenuity of the middle classes to make sophisticated and self-interested use of restricted occupational and educational opportunities can even begin to be eroded until we introduce the anti-credentialist legislation discussed earlier. Among the academic community, there is already considerable pessimism about the capacity of the educational system to promote greater social justice and a fairer distribution of power and wealth. The passionate belief that educational reform can improve social justice and national efficiency is still alive; but the comprehensive school is no longer seen as the principal mechanism by which such ideals can be realized. The popularity of neo-Marxist scholarship among many sociologists of education rests upon this tempered idealism. But, it must be said, these scholars have not as yet produced any very convincing designs for an educational system in the socialist society towards which they are striving. The evident skill of these scholars in making incisive diagnoses of the faults in our present systems, and in finding sound objections to the kinds of reform proposed in this book, has still to be matched by a clear and detailed specification both of their own vision for education in their future society and of the precise means by which we might create both.

9 *It may well be that many pupils, especially those who are working-class, will like a core curriculum of community studies and the expressive arts no more than they like the present school curriculum. If so, much of the point of the proposed reform will be lost.*

This is a telling objection; and there is no evidence by which it can be refuted. Many pupils see their present curriculum as dull and/or irrelevant, so my proposals naturally hope to make some improvement here. But that is a hope which would have to be put to the test. Interest and relevance are not, however, the key criteria by which a curriculum must be judged. All curricula find their ultimate justification in conceptions of what is good for individuals and for society, and my proposed curriculum is no exception. If it cannot be justified in these terms, then however interesting and relevant pupils found it to be, it would still be suspect. In education, consumer reaction is more relevant to teaching style and method than to the determination of content, and there is no such thing as a 'pupil-proof' curriculum. Pupils will always like some parts of the curriculum more than others and it will always be difficult to motivate a small minority in anything at all. My proposal offers a curriculum which covers as wide a range of knowledge, abilities and skills as possible in the hope that all children, whatever their talents and interests, will find at least some parts of the total curriculum attractive to them. Many working-class children will probably find the core curriculum of greater interest than the academic options, and this preference may reverse in the case of children with cognitive-intellectual abilities. So it should be. The object of the curriculum is the provision of greater choice and balance, and the belief that somehow all pupils can be persuaded to take the same interest in the whole curriculum diet is naive. It is, of course, important to interest pupils in the curriculum as far as one can. But I believe it is far more important that the structure and content of the curriculum transmits to *all* pupils a clear message that a lack of cognitive-intellectual abilities and skills does not make one a 'failure' or formal education an irrelevance.

10   Teachers will not like your proposals and would be highly resistant to their enactment.
This is a sound objection; however attractive a proposal for educational change, if the teachers cannot or will not implement it, then the proposal is worthless. Such a fundamental objection needs a chapter to itself. The questions we must ask are these: what is the current state of the teaching profession in secondary schools and how ready are teachers for the new role which the proposals envisage for them?

7 The culture of teaching

Most adults remember their teachers with great vividness as a motley collection of individuals. Idiosyncracies and eccentricities are recalled with laughter and horror, and particular incidents become part of a folklore which is often transmitted from one generation to another. Our teachers' peculiarities of appearance, speech and action, their praise and encouragement, their anger and punishments, all these retain a curious clarity and freshness in our memories of life at school. Every teacher brings to the exercise of his or her profession a unique personality and set of attitudes, skills and preferences. So it is with most jobs. Nobody wishes to be engulfed by work, to become an anonymous cog in a dehumanized occupational machine. Those of us in professional and highly skilled jobs are aware of our powers and privileges: we can to a degree adapt the job to the kind of person we are so that the job becomes an extension and expression of our unique individual identities.

It is also true that our work moulds and shapes us in many subtle ways. The relationship between identity and work is reciprocal: an occupation provides an opportunity for self-expression but the job in turn makes its own distinctive marks upon the man. For most of us entry to the world of work involves joining an occupational community. We work with others, colleagues and clients, and meet a host of people who have strong expectations about how we should behave. A novice has not merely to acquire the technical skills of his job; he also has to adapt to the social world of work. Most jobs, in other words, are located within an 'occupational culture' with which we must come to terms

- a set of beliefs, habits, traditions, ways of thinking and feeling and relating to others that are shared and understood by those already in the occupation. This occupational -culture, so obvious and taken for granted by the initiated members, is often obscure, mysterious and difficult to learn to the tiro. Yet it is in part through this culture that our occupational identities are transformed and stabilized.

Our interest is in what teaching does to teachers, for teachers as well as pupils are changed and shaped by the process of schooling. Some of these adaptations made by teachers are unique to this profession; others are shared with other jobs. Most teachers at some time experience the shock of discovering how they are seen by pupils and this can make explicit the ambivalences teachers feel towards their work and the way it makes an unwanted impact on them. Here is one case:[1]

> I was talking recently with a group of fourth-year boys – the girls were at a talk on sex education. The boys were bemoaning that they were not there, too. 'Trouble is, Miss,' said one of the boys, 'school doesn't teach us anything we really want to know.' Pursuing the notion of building sex education into the curriculum, I asked whether they would not be embarrrassed to talk about sex with a teacher they saw around all the time. 'Well, yes, maybe,' said the same boy, 'but perhaps we need not have a teacher – perhaps we could have a proper person.' I am beginning to believe that it is almost impossible to be both teacher and a 'proper person'. It has taken me twelve years to be as sure as I am now, and it might take a few more to be absolutely sure. However, given the choice, if that is a choice, there is no question as to which I would rather be. That is why I think I shall probably give up teaching in two or three years. I shall not really want to.

To understand the occupational diseases and the occupational culture of teaching, we must look closely at the central interests, concerns and problems of teaching. This is no easy task. Because teachers are so very different, there are few generalizations one can make with confidence about teachers that go beyond the self-evident or platitudinous. So I want to draw a caricature of our secondary-school teachers. A caricature is not a portrait; it does not intend to be very detailed or accurate. A caricature is distortive and partial, sacrificing all to a few bold strokes which capture something of the essence of the subject. But a caricature must remain recognizable; it selects and highlights, and makes more of blemishes and warts and unfavourable profile than is strictly warranted. The subject of a caricature is often hurt; but we should laugh too. My caricature of teachers is not intended to wound, but I hope it will give food for thought and an occasion for laughter. After all, books on education by academics are more often lightweight than lighthearted. I take three themes as the dominant features of my caricature: teachers' concerns with their status, their competence, and their social relationships.

In a survey conducted in 1974 secondary-school teachers reported that their most important dissatisfaction was with the status of the profession in society.[2] For well over a century teachers have been worried about their standing in society: are they a profession or not? If teaching is a profession, then teachers might legitimately expect both the high levels of remuneration and high degree of self-management already enjoyed by the established professions of medicine and law. They must also, of course, conform to appropriate standards of conduct expected of the professions. On this, teachers are divided. Some teachers see teaching merely as a job and are happy to use the conventional union channels to fight for better pay and conditions of service, including, if necessary, strike action. Other teachers are unhappy about unionization and believe it quite improper ('unprofessional') for teachers to go on strike. The first group is more concerned with pay than prestige; the second group insists that respect is more important than remuneration.

Teachers know very well that professional standing rests on the possession of *expertise*. They do not need the sociologist Everett Hughes to tell them that their claim to be a profession cannot be sustained unless they can show that they possess:[3]

194

esoteric knowledge systematically formulated and applied
to the problems of a client. The nature of the knowledge,
substantive or theoretical, on which advice and action are
based is not always clear; it is often a mixture of several
kinds of practical and theoretical knowledge. But it is part
of the professional complex, and of the professional claim,
that the practice should rest upon some branch of knowledge to which professionals are privy by virtue and long
study and by initiation and apprenticeship under masters
already members of the profession.

What is this 'esoteric knowledge' from which teachers might
derive a professional mandate? In the secondary school this
usually takes the form of expertise in a traditional *subject* of
academic respectability obtained in a university degree. On
this view pedagogical skills are of secondary importance;
they can be picked up 'naturally' in the early years of teaching or during a post-graduate year of professional training in
a university department of education. It is the degree, not the
teacher training, which establishes one's credentials as a
teacher and as a professional. The teacher's authority ultimately rests in the authority of his subject. For such a teacher
his subject expertise is absolutely central to his identity. He
thinks of himself not as a teacher, but as a mathematics
teacher, or a history teacher and so on. He dislikes the
burden of teaching other subjects, as he is sometimes asked
to; and he is happiest when he is teaching his subject in the
sixth form where his life style is closely akin to that of the
university don. His aim, at least in the short term, is to be
head of department in his subject.

Many schoolteachers – indeed the majority of the former
secondary-modern schoolteachers – entered teaching via the
colleges of education rather than the universities. They had
no degree, and often no one subject of special expertise.
Inevitably therefore their professional identity was organized
around pedagogical rather than subject expertise: these
teachers claimed to be teachers of pupils, not subjects. It is
true that they often felt somewhat inferior to their graduate
colleagues, and they certainly earned less pay. What they
lacked in formal qualifications was compensated by their

practical professional skills. They revelled in stories of the brilliant graduate with the first-class degree who was a complete failure in the classroom.

This graduate versus non-graduate distinction has deep roots. Its origins lie in the nineteenth century with its divided teaching profession: graduates for the public and grammar schools, certificated teachers from much shorter training-college courses for the elementary schools provided for the working classes. But times changed. It was generally thought that the quality of teachers ought to be improved as educational standards rose, and the creation of the comprehensive school was to unite this divided teaching profession under a common roof. Teacher unions realized that their claim to professional standing would be enhanced by an all-graduate teaching force. The answer, of course, was the BEd degree, offered by the new colleges of education after a longer course of study (three or four years rather than two), and validated by the universities. But the colleges were not to offer conventional university degrees in academic subjects. After all, most of the college staff were not themselves qualified to become university lecturers. So the new BEd degree was to have a strong 'professional studies' component which would give continuity with the past and yet provide a more substantial academic base through the study of the disciplines of education – psychology, sociology, philosophy, history. The old 'principles and practice of education' courses were displaced by the academic social sciences which would legitimate the new degree. Here was the major answer to a new 'esoteric knowledge' for teachers that could match the traditional university subjects. Jean Piaget (in child development and psychology), Basil Bernstein (in sociology) and Richard Peters (in philosophy) acquired a new eminence and a new following. Parents would always know their children more intimately than the teachers did; but only the teachers, armed with the new esoteric knowledge of their education courses, knew how the children *ought* to be growing and developing and the pedagogical imperatives that flow from such knowledge. The BEd graduate could now match his old university-graduate rival, and those certificated teachers, who had become teachers before the institution of the BEd degree, could follow such a course on a part-time or in-service basis at the university or the education courses in the Open University, where at one stage teachers formed nearly 40 per cent of the students.

In practice, back in the schools, this unified all-graduate teaching profession was not so easily realized. The traditional graduates still tended to feel superior to their BEd colleagues, who often felt that their degree was a second-class one. And whilst educational psychology often seemed helpful to the primary schoolteacher, not least in the apparent relationship between Piaget's work and progressive philosophies of education, there was a problem. Piaget had little to say about children after the age of twelve or so. There was little new specialized and esoteric knowledge about the adolescent in the secondary school, and the university graduates knew it.

The thesis that the BEd degree would confer special pedagogical expertise was doomed from the very beginning. It was designed by lecturers in teacher-training institutions, not by practising teachers. It is thus that the proposals never came to confront the basic fact that most teachers believe teaching to be an *intuitive* activity, one in which the skills defy easy analysis and explanation and thus cannot readily be transmitted to the novice. The skills of teaching are, it is commonly held, conferred by nature ('the born teacher') or acquired slowly and patiently by real experience in class-rooms. As Jackson points out:[4]

> One of the most notable features of teacher talk is the absence of a technical vocabulary. Unlike professional encounters between doctors, lawyers, garage mechanics, and astrophysicists, when teachers talk together almost any reasonably intelligent adult can listen in and comprehend what is being said. Occasionally familiar words are used in a special sense, and the uninitiated listener may be momentarily puzzled by the mention of 'units', or 'projects', or 'curriculum guides', or 'word attack skills', but it is unlikely that he will encounter many words that he has never heard before or even those with a specialized meaning. . . . The absence of technical terms is related to another characteristic of teachers' talk: its conceptual

197

simplicity. Not only do teachers avoid elaborate words, they also seem to shun elaborate ideas.

The lack of sophistication in teacher talk about pedagogy is a direct consequence of their intuitive conceptions of teaching. The social sciences studied during training have entirely failed to provide teachers with a new working vocabulary. Because it is seen to be of little direct help to teaching, that knowledge and vocabulary is abandoned and left at the college gates as soon as the BEd examinations are over. I sometimes think that the principal function of professional training in education is to inoculate teachers against books on education. For as far as education books are concerned, most teachers are illiterate; they even read *The Times Educational Supplement* more for the job advertisements than for the articles.

It soon became obvious, too, that the heads of department in the new comprehensive schools were being recruited from the grammar-school staff, from conventional university graduates. And it seemed likely that such positions would continue to be filled in the same way. Indeed, the abolition of the secondary-modern schools was now to make it much more difficult for those who had been heads of department in those schools to reach the same position in the comprehensive schools. There might be a more unified graduate teaching profession in a common secondary school, but career paths and opportunities were to become more divergent. Fortunately for the former secondary-modern schoolteachers, there was a strong public fear that the much larger comprehensive schools would be impersonal and alienating for pupils. In response, the comprehensive schools developed new systems of 'pastoral care' and there had to be formal positions – heads of house, heads of year, etc. – to operate these new systems. Here was a happy answer to the initial loss of a career ladder for the secondary-modern teachers and the BEd graduates: there could be two parallel but alternative career routes for teachers. The graduate can still aspire to teaching pupils on public-examination courses, to a heavy quota of sixth-form work, to an occupational destination as at least a head of department or 'faculty'. The former secondary-modern teachers and those with a BEd degree are less likely to have sixth-form,

'A'-level and even 'O'-level work; they have a disproportionate amount of non-examination work, of 'junior' (first–third year) classes, of pastoral-type duties. There are exceptions, of course, but the broad patterns remain. Ambitious young teachers must be sensitive to these patterns. Falling rolls and reduced educational resources are causing the profession to stagnate suddenly; the opportunities for early and rapid promotion (except in shortage fields, such as mathematics and physics), which were widespread when the education system was expanding, have now been terminated. The motto for the young teacher must now be 'Where there's death there's hope'. And young teachers must get into the right queue; they must choose one of the alternative routes and prepare and 'qualify' themselves (by the appropriate in-service courses) for those whose shoes they hope to fill.

One consequence of this allocation and specialization of different kinds of teacher within the comprehensive school is in the reinforcement of grammar-school hierarchies and stratifications, which have particularly strong effects on the curriculum. The academic subjects retain their grammar-school dominance; the expressive arts, music, art and craft, drama, as well as media studies, religious, moral and political education, community studies, all have low status, and a relatively lower status in many cases than they had in the secondary-modern schools. The secondary-modern tradition of breadth and integration between subjects does not die, but it flourishes best where the former secondary-modern teachers are most strongly represented – in the junior years, among non-examination courses and in CSE courses. This work is not disvalued, for the former grammar-school and university graduates have no strong desire to teach such pupils; the secondary-modern tradition can survive as long as it does not threaten the public examinations – the 'bright' children who are in the top sets, preparing for 'O' level and the sixth form. And, as we have seen, in this they are encouraged by headteachers who act as if public-examination success rates are the key criterion of the comprehensive school's effectiveness. Power is in the hands of the grammar-school tradition, which shapes the general direction of the school. Formally speaking, power seems to be shared. The now common 'senior-management team', which is used by the headteacher to steer the school, contains the heads of houses and heads of years as well as the academic heads of department, but in curriculum matters power remains in the hands of those teachers who are committed to the academic domain and the teaching of the single-subject grammar-school tradition. It is all achieved with great subtlety, but beneath a smooth surface in many schools lie the half-articulated troubles and resentments of those who espouse the secondary-modern tradition.

A similar interplay between status concerns and subject expertise recurs when we move from relations between teachers to relations between teachers and pupils. One of the most striking characteristics of teachers is their addiction to didactic talk. Teachers are qualified in their subjects; they *know*; and they are not satisfied until they have told their pupils what they know. In the jargon of the educationists this is the 'transmission' model of teaching: the function of the teacher is to impart knowledge to (in this respect) ignorant pupils, and the most obvious way in which to achieve this is by telling. It is the model of the university lecture. The popularity of this conception of teaching is shown in the near-universal structure of teacher–pupil interaction in classrooms. There are three steps: first, the teacher asks a 'closed' question, that is, one to which he already knows the answer; the pupil answers, and the answer will be right or wrong; then, as the third step, the teacher evaluates the answer, and moves on to the next question. The format by which the teacher lectures to, then questions, the whole class has proved highly resistant to change. It appears to vanish in some 'progressive' classrooms, but the appearances can be deceptive. Some teachers no longer address the whole class as frequently as they once did; now they say the same thing thirty times to each child individually.

Didactic talk marks teachers for ever. An interesting game to play on holiday is 'Spot the teacher', in museums, art galleries and historic buildings. The English schoolmaster is soon recognized on a hot summer day in the Vatican museums, not merely by his Harris-tweed jacket, but by the fact that, armed with his guidebook of authoritative knowledge, he will be haranguing his spouse and children just as if they were 3B out on a school visit. The thirst for knowledge is admirable; the determination to pass it on verbally less so. It breeds a constant and obsessive desire to be expert, to be omniscient. Teachers do not enjoy admitting 'I don't know'; they condemn those words from the mouths of pupils too often to feel comfort in the same confession.

Teachers think of themselves as teachers, and so lose their capacity to be learners too. Many years ago Willard Waller drew attention to:[5]

> that peculiar blight which affects the teacher's mind, which creeps over it gradually, and, possessing it bit by bit, devours its creative resources. Some there are who escape this disease endemic in the profession, but the wonder is they are so few. That the plague is real, and that it strikes many teachers, the kindest critic cannot deny. Those who have known young teachers well, and have observed the course of their personal development as they become set in the teaching pattern, have often been grieved by the progressive deterioration in their gradual adaptability. And hardly a college teacher who has taught a summer school has failed to lament that lack of supple comprehension and willingness to follow the ball of discussion which characterizes the teacher in class. Teachers make a sad and serious business of learning.

The truth of Waller's words were brought home to me when, after just one year as a teacher, I took driving lessons. After the fourteenth lesson, and very little progress on my part, the instructor stopped me in desperation and sighed, 'You must be a teacher.' I was amazed at his perspicacity and asked how he had guessed. 'It's quite simple', he replied. 'You just won't let me teach you – you want to teach yourself.' Once teachers are deeply entrenched in their expert status and didactic style, the loss in the capacity to learn makes teachers afraid of learning. They become insecure in school contexts where they have no expertise that can be transmitted. They hardly notice that pupils often have something to teach them; such role-reversals are uncomfortable.

In consequence teachers become bad listeners as well as learners. Pupil contributions to lessons are really little more than oral tests: pupil comments are right or wrong answers to teacher questions. And pupils are given very little time to respond. If the answer is not slotted into place within a second or two, the teacher will pass on to another pupil for an answer. Teachers have a very low tolerance for the silences and periods of thought that punctuate more normal conversations on difficult topics. With this goes a generally neurotic attitude to time. Silence is dangerous because it threatens to waste valuable time. And this attitude soon spreads. One needs more lesson time for one's subject; pupils cannot afford to miss a lesson or they will fall behind; and finally, in what is the ultimate expression of the attitude, if pupils are not exposed to this or that field of knowledge then they will never learn it -- even though in reality most of them will leave school with some four-fifths of their lives still to come.

But silences are dangerous also because they expose gaps in the busyness of school, which may be filled with irrelevancies, distractions and indiscipline. Pupils are a constant threat to teacher's authority and control; it needs hard and constant work to sustain both. Because there is an ever-present underlying challenge to order and control, teachers must learn the three Rs of classroom management – rules, regulations and routines. It is these which generate a stability and predictability which is difficult to disturb. But a price has to be paid; teachers risk becoming petty and parochial.

Once teachers have mastered the basic arts of teaching, knowing how to teach one's subject and how to control a class, then teaching can become too predictable. The challenges and stresses of the early years of teaching may fade, but they are replaced by a new boredom. After ten years of teaching the same subject to the same age range, teachers naturally find it difficult not to be bored by their constant repetition of the same predictable lessons.

For most teachers today teaching is not easy. Children have become more overt in their boredom and criticism, more difficult to manage and control. This, when combined with the teacher's own boredom, breeds a particular kind of exhaustion which seems to be quite unique to teachers and hardly understood outside the profession. When I became a don I found myself working very much longer hours than when I had been a school teacher, but I did not experience at the end of the day that curious sense of numbness, of being emotionally drained and empty, which can overwhelm the teacher. Professionals get tired; teachers become exhausted. It is no wonder that sometimes in the evening they feel able to do little more than sit in front of their television screens, watching trivial programmes with a blank gaze. Their pupils, of course, are often doing the same.

Some teachers go out or work in the evenings. But there is a curious masochism in teachers by which they subject themselves in the evening to more of what exhausted them during the day. Outside the home they teach in evening classes and run youth clubs. At home, they mark exercise books. Some years ago it was shown that one of the best predictors for success in teaching was the possession of a wide range of cultural knowledge and interests. The explanation, I suspect, is that sensible teachers indulge their cultural interests as fully as they can in their spare time. The best inoculation against the diseases of teaching is a busy cultural life: it removes the tensions of teaching and keeps the mind alert. Yet many teachers claim that their marking, their evening classes, and their youth clubs, give them no time for cultural pursuits. It is a devotion to teaching which becomes truly self-sacrificial: the best teachers have more sense. It is a similar reason which explains why women teachers seem to succumb less frequently than men to the stresses of teaching. Women cannot be just teachers: most of them have domestic roles as wives and mothers with all the work that that entails. It makes life hard for the woman teacher, but it also serves a protective function. The women are simply too busy to take teaching too seriously. It is the men who have the leisure in which to have crises over their occupational identities.

Teachers tend to be curiously modest about their achievements and skills as teachers and they rarely boast how good they are at their job. The reason is simple: it is very difficult to judge the professional competence of teachers. Lawyers win and lose cases; doctors cure patients and bury their mistakes. There are no such unambiguous outcomes for the teacher. Certainly there are good teachers and bad teachers, but there are very different ways in which one can be good or bad and there are few universally agreed criteria by which teaching can be judged to be good or bad. Teaching is thus replete with 'endemic uncertainties' about competence:[6] most of the time one is not really very sure about how well one is doing, whether pupils succeed because of the teacher or in spite of him, whether the pupils' failure is to be attributed to them or to the teacher. Teachers are, in other words, short of clear feedback. Moreover schools are busy places which give teachers little time to think or take stock. This fact, when taken into consideration with the lack of an agreed analytical language, makes it difficult for teachers to do a regular or systematic post-mortem on their work. So teachers have to rely on whatever feedback becomes available, and this tends to take several forms. First, there is the short-term feedback on the pupils' response to lessons. When pupils show obvious interest and involvement, when they moan as the bell signals the end of the lesson and they reluctantly put their work away, this is the moment when teachers take a special pleasure in their work and feel that they are succeeding. But for most teachers it is difficult to teach more than one or two lessons a day which yield such joy. So teachers tend to rely on the long-term feedback of the cumulative achievements of pupils, and this is most readily provided by examination results. Agricultural metaphors are popular among the profession: teaching is a matter of sowing seeds which will bear fruit in mysterious ways in the future. The examinations are the harvest time. If the pupils do well, this is a sign that the teaching has been good. Many a teacher, when waiting for the 'O'-level results, is anxious for his pupils; but he is always anxious for himself too, since if they fail, he is failing also. The teacher's second response to seeing the examination results is to compare the percentage of passes or good grades in his subject with the equivalent percentages achieved in other subjects, for success is a relative concept. To be a good teacher one must obtain from one's pupils better results than one's colleagues can muster from the same pupil material. Public examinations thus provide an important means of reducing teachers' competence anxieties.

The judgments are objective, external to the school and free from bias, and they are publicly available for all to see. It is a source of feedback teachers would be reluctant to relinquish. There is also the special gratification of praise from former students. It is a treasured consolation when old pupils return to thank teachers for having made the pupil work harder than he would otherwise have done, or when a pupil distinguishes himself in later life. Educational harvests may be long in coming, but teachers can be patient in waiting for their rewards.

Teachers naturally make judgments on the professional competencies of their colleagues, but they are rarely discussed openly. In schools neither teacher success nor teacher failure is ever flaunted. Teachers may get little public praise, but then neither do they get much public criticism. Of course every teacher has a reputation, a place in the pecking order of competence. Reputations are common knowledge, but they are transmitted *sotto voce* in the channels of staff gossip. They never become formal and official evaluations, except in the headteacher's confidential references. Each teacher has to judge himself as best he can.

This leads to our third theme, teachers' social relationships. Teachers are the most incestuous of all the professions: they have a strong penchant for marrying one another, and this has notable consequences on their domestic lives. When two teachers arrive home from school, exhausted and yet with the story of the day to tell, their conversation has a Pinteresque quality. Each has much to grumble about – for the capacity to grumble is a mark of the experienced teacher – but neither is much interested in the grumbles of the other. The conversation appears to be normal, each party taking synchronized turns, but in fact each indulges in a long grumbling monologue. And when a group of teachers meets in a pub or for a dinner-party, the grumbling continues. Teachers cannot stop talking shop. It is one of the reasons why other professional groups find teachers so boring. It is well known, except by teachers, that the best way to kill a party is to invite a lot of schoolteachers.

Relations between colleagues in school, are, as we have seen, characterized by sensitivities in matters of competence, but these are but one expression of a much deeper value, the commitment of teachers to *autonomy*. Although teachers are strongly constrained in what they teach, by syllabuses agreed within the school or subject department or predetermined by public-examination boards, they have in this country considerable freedom over how that content is taught. Teaching methods and styles are left to individual teacher choice. A similar freedom is enjoyed in most matters of classroom management and control. In effect this autonomy means that the teacher is king of his own classroom where he reigns supreme with virtually no interference. Teachers guard this autonomy jealously; they do not like colleagues or other adults in the classroom. Secondary-school teachers, much more than their colleagues in primary schools or universities, do not like being observed. For them, teaching is like sexual activity: it is a highly intimate act, best conducted in private, and to be watched by intruders is to inhibit one's performance. The root of this sensitivity is to be found in competence anxieties. Observers are likely to make judgments on one's teaching abilities and so their presence lays one open to potential criticism. Observation will be evaluative, and implicit and unspoken judgments by witnesses are threatening. Autonomy, then, is the polite word used to mask teacher's evaluative apprehension and to serve as the rationale for excluding observers.

Such insulation of teachers in their classrooms shows that the culture of individualism is not confined to pupils but permeates the social relations between teachers. The isolated teacher must teach himself the art of teaching – and if he fails to do so, then he fails on his own. Insulation from observation protects the teacher from criticism, but it also precludes him from obtaining support and help. Headteachers and senior staff often encourage the young and inexperienced teachers to come for help if they have problems, but if the new teacher follows this advice, he immediately exposes his weaknesses and incompetence to his superiors. The staffroom may not be a source of help either. Young teachers soon learn that the staffroom is a forum for grumbling rather than for the serious discussion of classroom problems. One must grumble about the pupils that everyone else finds to be a problem too; such grumbling consoles each teacher that the problems are shared.[7] To grumble about problems that are unique to oneself is merely to display one's incompetence.

Many attempted innovations flounder on this addiction to autonomy. Team-teaching soon becomes turn-teaching: the teachers do not work simultaneously in the same classroom, but take the whole class in turn. In 'open plan' spaces, book-cases and screens of various sorts soon appear to reconstitute the walls which guard classroom privacy. Most secondary-school teachers lack the skills needed to work together with pupils. They have a defective sense of classroom co-operation. They can co-ordinate with one another, certainly, but in matters of collaboration, the strong form of co-operaton, they must be judged remedial.

The caricature of what teaching does to teachers has now been sketched. Partial it may be, but the features which have been highlighted suggest that our present system of secondary-school education can have damaging effects on teachers as well as on pupils. It is surprising in some ways that more immediate action is not taken by teachers to relieve some of their problems. The hierarchical structure of teaching, for example, offers a career ladder with rising levels of pay and responsibility. But some teachers have reached the upper rungs at an early age and have little to look forward to in terms of new challenges and promotion. An obvious solution to this frustration and boredom would be to allow a temporary *sideways* movement by which teachers would exchange responsibilities at the same status and pay levels as, for example a head of an academic department becoming a head of house for a period. Such a circulation of responsibility could maintain interest and commitment as well as providing a much broader base for promotion to deputy headships and headships.[8] We could also implement Harry Rée's ideas on 'planned demotion'. Once teachers have reached their highest point in the status and pay hierarchy, they remain there until retirement, in order to preserve their pension, whether they want to or not, and whether or not they are carrying out their duties as energetically as they might. If the level of pension were to be fixed on the basis of the best, rather than last, three years of service, many senior teachers with major administrative responsibilities might well 'demote' themselves into less demanding duties, which would help them as they move towards retirement and give younger teachers an earlier and more frequent opportunity for work at the highest level.

I am similarly puzzled that many secondary schools do not let more parents and other adult community-members into the private world of classrooms. They have important knowledge and skills to contribute to secondary education which would more than offset the loss of job-protection. Even letting parents into classrooms as observers would in the long term greatly help teachers, as primary-school teachers have found. Some parents are difficult and hostile to teachers to be sure; but a parent who witnesses the problems with which teachers have to contend, and then sympathetically spreads the message into the wide community, is worth a thousand talks from the headteacher on Open Days and a thousand letters sent to parents from school.

But if teachers are reluctant to experiment with modest reforms such as these, and ones which are directly designed to ease their lot, what hope is there for the more fundamental changes in the proposals I have offered in this book? It is probably true that teacher caution is a product of the many demands made upon them in recent years and the cavalier way in which comprehensive re-organization was hastily implemented without taking into account the stress this would impose on some teachers. If teachers are really caught in a defensive battle for day-to-day survival, then surely this is an ill-chosen time to propose yet further reforms?

Yet not all teachers suffer from all the occupational diseases of teaching. A few escape most of them permanently, as if they have some in-built resistance. Others catch the full gamut of diseases almost at once; they are so susceptible that they become, as it were, terminal cases after no more than a year in the profession. Most catch some of the diseases, which in any event are of different kinds; some are slow, incurable cancers and others, like the influenza virus, come and go. It is when teachers are partially infected that they show the ambivalence towards teaching displayed by the teacher I quoted at the beginning of the chapter: one wants to leave teaching to save oneself, but one also wants to stay for the special joys and satisfactions that teaching can bring. As far as I can tell, this ambivalence is very strong in teachers in the 25–35 year age-group. They have been long enough in the profession to lose a romantic naivety of the probationer and to have mastered the art of teaching; they have not been teachers long enough to be utterly demoralized and cynical. My caricature is a depressing and pessimistic sketch, but it leaves out of account those teachers who are fighting a vigorous campaign against the occupational diseases for their own sakes as well as those of the pupils. Almost all schools contain at least one or two of these teachers, and some schools have many more. It is they who tend to be the pioneers of community schools and community studies; team-teaching and integrated studies; dialogical pedagogies and broad curricula. There is nothing in the curricular proposals I commended earlier which is not already being practised somewhere with enthusiasm and success.

That successful practice, however, cannot be easily coordinated and disseminated through the secondary-school system. The reason is simple: in general those who share the major ideas of this book are in positions of relatively low formal power and status. The majority of those teachers who are least attuned to the occupational culture – those who are least concerned with an occupational identity founded in subject expertise, those who are dissatisfied with didactic talk as the basis of pedagogy, those who are most sceptical about the central role of the cognitive-intellectual domain and the constraining influence of public examinations, those who take a wider view of the school curriculum and social organization, those who seek collaborative relationships with colleagues and community adults who are drawn into the school – tend to find themselves in positions that are peripheral in the centres of power and influence, both within the school and in those wider political spheres in which teachers can and do operate. And because their powers are so limited, they lack the capacity to institutionalize reforms on a wider basis. There are some exceptions, of course. I know of headteachers whose views are quite close to those outlined in this book. But in many cases they obtained their headship during comprehensive re-organization from their experience as headteacher of a secondary-modern school. Such headteachers brought to the comprehensive school the broad ideals and the vision of the best of the secondary-modern tradition. But even they have been constrained by those forces which have driven comprehensive schools to model themselves on grammar schools and they cannot afford to ignore the pressures to public accountability through examination performances. An even greater cause of concern is that such teachers are now increasingly less likely to be appointed to headships. Many of the present ex-secondary-modern heads obtained their jobs in the musical chairs of re-organization; future headteachers will probably be more closely aligned to the grammar-school than to the secondary-modern tradition. In short, I fear it is becoming more difficult and more rare for the teacher who espouses an educational philosophy consonant with the proposals of this book to be appointed to a position of power and influence.

Yet, it seems, it is on that relatively powerless minority that I must pin my hopes. History gives me grounds for optimism. A hundred years ago the warm, caring relationships between teachers and pupils which are common now-asays were unusual or even revolutionary; and many of the subjects on our contemporary school curriculum would have been ridiculed a century ago – and until very much more recently in our public schools. It is in the nature of educational pioneering that present practices and assumptions are transcended; in the process of educational evolution the rare becomes typical. Many recent reforms have been in the interests of pupils, or in the pursuit of important and commendable ideals such as greater social justice, but rarely have the costs incurred by a heavily burdened teaching force been taken into account. It is quite reasonable to consider the occupational culture of teaching as a potential agent of resistance to the changes I have proposed. It is even more important to show that the occupational culture of teaching can serve to reduce the potential rewards and pleasures of teaching. Teachers who are now working in line with the proposals of this book are eager to claim that they are striving to provide a better education for the pupils in their charge; they have been much less effective in showing that such teaching brings enormous benefits to teachers, as well as hard work and inevitable problems. Indeed, it is because they find their work so rewarding that these teachers often step off the conventional career ladder that leads to positions of power. I do not for a moment underestimate the changes required of teachers, if my proposals were to be implemented, but I am confident, simply from my observation of practising teachers, that these changes would help to make teaching a much more satisfying job than it usually is. But we are still left with a fundamental problem: how can the proposals be implemented if those who espouse them are lacking in power?

8 Teachers and the future

A teacher once asked me to recommend to her the most challenging, persuasive and original book known to me which might help her to understand our educational history and provide her with a vision for the future of the comprehensive school. Without hesitation I suggested Raymond Williams's *The Long Revolution*, first published in 1961, and especially the chapter on education and British society.[1] This book not only laid the foundations for what is today, among many historians and sociologists, a relatively conventional perspective on our educational past; it also provided a radical reappraisal of the secondary-school curriculum. Williams understood that reform could not be limited to making the grammar-school curriculum available to all, for that narrow academic curriculum was an inadequate means of initiating pupils into the creative and expressive arts. He observed, too, that modern man needs to understand his environment, yet social and community studies are rarely part of the curriculum, and even then tend to be assigned a peripheral position and to be taught as yet another academic subject called 'civics'. By nearly two decades Williams anticipated our contemporary concern to design for the comprehensive school a 'core curriculum' (which he referred to as educational 'essentials'), and outlined a highly imaginative programme which, surprisingly, has been neglected in recent curriculum debates. In parts Williams's proposal seems uncontentious, as in his emphasis upon the natural sciences, and the language, history and arts of at least one other culture. Other aspects were more novel: a knowledge of ourselves, our environment and our society, to be achieved not directly through the teaching of

212

the usual academic disciplines (history and geography), though drawing freely upon them, but also through other disciplines not normally used in schools (law, politics, psychology, sociology); the history and criticism of the visual arts, music, drama and architecture, as well as of literature; extensive practice in democratic procedures; a critical understanding of the mass media. All this, of course, has much in common with the ideas of this book. And this is not surprising, for Williams was consciously searching for a new and more comprehensive curriculum for a changing education system in a changing society.

Williams denied that his proposals were utopian. For him they were more a matter of common sense, provided that one recognized that the education system must adapt to changing society and that the change was directed towards the creation of an educated democracy. Among educationists Raymond Williams's work is often treated as 'seminal' - the polite term academics use to describe a pioneering contribution which the academic community finally applauds, but which has little effect in changing the world. Why has Williams's work suffered this relative neglect and why have we failed to adopt his proposals? It is surely because, as Quintin Hoare suggests, the reform is rather naively presented as if it would naturally and inevitably be accepted and implemented by enlightened men and women who acknowledged the good sense of the ideas. If we assent to the proposals, then surely there will be no problem in translating them into practice within the emerging comprehensive school? In fact, however, it is the gap between the new idea and existing educational practice which is a central problem. As Quintin Hoare so uncomfortably points out:[2]

> There is no discussion of who could impose it and who would oppose it, and no reference to the concrete politico-cultural structure of Britain or the existing social composition and outlook of teachers. Williams' fundamental mode of presentation is the rational appeal to men of good will. ... Williams' whole scheme in effect hangs in the air, suspended in a kind of atemporal void. There is a basic failure to ground the proposed programme in any actual

213

historical situation. Above all he completely overlooks the fundamental fact that a reform of the educational system involves a reform of the educators as well, and that this is a *political* task, which immediately ricochets back to the question of transforming consciousness and ideology throughout society. As they stand, Williams' proposals remain purely 'institutional', exhibiting a detachment from actual political reality.

The criticism is as telling as it is trenchant. Many more modest schemes for curriculum reform have foundered for just the same reasons. In the last chapter I have tried to show that the ideas of this book (and so also those of Raymond Williams) are not at all consonant with the 'existing social composition and outlook of teachers', or at least the majority of them. The unhappy fate of Williams's proposals reinforces my conviction that we must look very closely at the means by which reform might be implemented.

Once it is conceded that reform is a political task, it is natural that we should look, at least initially, towards those agencies which possess power and influence and which are located in relatively central positions within the political process. The first obvious candidate is the Secretary of State for Education.[3] Here, surely, is the most powerful single person in the field of education, and if the occupant of that high office can be persuaded of the validity of the proposals, then the reforms can be implemented. And this could perhaps be achieved even against the will and outlook of the teaching profession. After all, the majority of teachers were opposed both to the raising of the school-leaving age and to comprehensive re-organization, but both reforms were nevertheless introduced. Anthony Crosland's famous 10/65 circular about comprehensive re-organization is, on this view, the precedent for yet further reforms about the now generally established comprehensive school. Undoubtedly there is some merit in this view. If the minister were indeed convinced by the proposals, implementation would be greatly facilitated. But, as far as I know, the minister is not so convinced. In any case we are in danger of overestimating the power of the minister. In the field of education central powers are severely circumscribed, especially in matters of the curriculum, where local authorities and schools jealously guard their own autonomy. It is much easier for the minister to exercise power and influence in the field of school organization and finance than of the curriculum. Whilst it is true that the sixteen-plus examinations could not be abolished without action on the part of the minister, such action could not be taken unless there were other powerful groups to support the minister in the enterprise. The minister may, from time to time, act against the will of the teachers, but he or she can do so only when other powerful groups – the local authorities, party political, backbench opinion, public opinion – can legitimate action in defiance of the teachers. The minister takes account of many points of view, and very often these are in conflict. Ministerial intervention is constrained, so even if (a daring hypothesis) he believed in the reforms proposed in this book, implementation could not be effected until a number of powerful groups had been persuaded to offer their support. There is no evidence that I know of to suggest that any of these groups are at present committed to these reforms. It seems more reasonable, therefore, to move towards reform by influencing these other groups, rather than the minister directly. And we should remember that the Secretary of State for Education does not in any case always have the status in Cabinet commensurate with the Department's spending power, and any individual minister's tenure of office may be quite short.

Because the responsibilities of the Department of Education and Science are immense, the minister has to rely very heavily upon the advice of senior civil servants. Perhaps, then, it is the Whitehall 'mandarins' who should be a target for influence if the reforms are to be implemented. Inevitably civil servants are a difficult group to influence. Officially speaking, they are not open to influence, since their function is to execute ministerial policy, though everyone recognizes that in practice they must influence policy through the advice they tender to the minister. In practice, also, civil servants are open to influence from those within the education service, yet they remain relatively invisible persons and the influence exerted upon them is hidden and subtle, rather than overt and explicit. Civil servants naturally tend in some matters (not all, of course) to have a relatively conservative

view, for they have responsibility for continuities that have
to be maintained in spite of changes of minister and government, and they know from experience that reforms are
easy to implement in theory but in practice demand a long-
term attention to difficult detail which is easily overlooked
by reformers. Even if we bear these reservations in mind, we
cannot ignore the evidence that the Department seems
remarkably closed to outside influences and is highly self-
protective in denying to outsiders access to the bases of
policies and proposals that emanate from the Department.
An OECD document on the Department of Education and
Science notes the significance of the Department in determining the direction and tempo of educational development,
whilst recognizing that the formal powers are limited:[4]

> A permanent officialdom possessing such external protec-
> tions and internal disciplines becomes a power in its own
> right. A British department composed of professional civil
> servants who have watched ministers come and go is an
> entity that only an extremely foolish or powerful politi-
> cian will persistently challenge or ignore. The prestige,
> acquaintanceships, and natural authority of leading civil
> servants give them a standing in the civil forum often
> superior to that of their *de jure* political superiors. They
> are, in the continental phrase, *notables*, whose opinion
> must be given special weight, whether or not votes in the
> next election will be affected.

The document goes on to note that:

> the United Kingdom offers an example of educational
> planning in which the structures for ensuring public
> participation are limited. This has at least two consequen-
> ces. One is that in certain cases policy is less likely to be
> understood and therefore less likely to be wholeheartedly
> accepted when the processes which lead up to its formula-
> tion are guarded as arcane secrets. The second is that goals
> and priorities, once established, may go on being taken
> for granted and hence escape regular scrutiny which may
> be necessary for an appropriate realignment of policy.

216

This latter consequence is discernible in the White Paper's posture of acquiescence towards existing goals. The method of planning it evinces, as it sets forth its programme for the allocation of resources, directed towards effecting incremental improvements within existing structures, derives from the assumption that the basic directions of educational development are largely foreclosed; determined, one infers, by historical circumstances, demographic trends, and changes in public attitudes.

The White Paper under discussion is *A Framework for Expansion* (1972). The document notes the tendency of the White Paper to ignore several important areas, such as the 16-19 age-group. The decision to exclude an area for discussion is, of course, an important exercise of power, and one which can effectively inhibit discussion of areas of educational reform. By restricting itself to projections and proposals for resource allocation, the White Paper implicitly accepts the existing institutional framework and thus discourages the raising of fundamental questions about the purpose or content of secondary education:

> Departmental perspectives, the self-interpretation of
> any role of civil servants as apolitical, or in any case
> neutral, servants of the state, and the views of the content
> of education as a matter for local self-government, that
> is for teachers and local authorities, seem to preclude
> the possibility of interpreting the role of education as
> an agent for innovation and social progress.

In other words, by an apparent acknowledgment of its restricted powers over the school curriculum, the DES can actively inhibit discussion about the purposes of the comprehensive school and the need for a curriculum to realize such purposes. The concluding summary of the document is unsparing:

> The White Paper, as critically reviewed in this section,
> reflects an active bureaucracy, largely in a position to
> determine itself the framework and nature of its activity.

Within this definition of its role, the organization and articulation of this bureaucracy are particularly effective, especially in diffusing the location of planning work within the sectors which carry substantive responsibility for the implementation of decisions. The chief features of the bases for its policy seem to be characterized by attempts to: minimize the degree of controversiality in the planning process and its results; reduce possible alternatives to matters of choice of resources allocation; limit the planning process to those parts of the educational services and functions strictly controlled by the DES; exploit as fully as possible the powers, prerogatives and responsibilities given to the DES under the 1944 Education Act; understate as much as possible the full role of government in the determination of the future course of educational policy and even minimize it in the eyes of the general public.

This OECD report makes it clear that the official DES view of itself, namely that:

> The Department does not plan education itself; curricula, pedagogical and professional matters are, by a long tradition in this country, matters which the central Government does not control

is an absurdly naive one which does not reflect practice with any real accuracy.

Since these events, as far as one can judge, matters have deteriorated rather than improved. When Prime Minister James Callaghan initiated the Great Education Debate in 1976, here surely was a unique opportunity to examine the basic purposes and curriculum of the comprehensive school. But the agenda for the debate was in the hands of the DES and not surprisingly it again used its power to inhibit discussion of these questions. Moreover the DES had the additional power of controlling the membership of the regional conferences which contributed to the debate. More than one commentator has concluded that the debate was a carefully controlled charade, a half-hearted attempt to create public participation and discussion which masked the fact that most of the answers to the agenda questions had in reality already been largely predetermined:[5]

> What seems to have happened is that pre-conceived proposals, such as those for a [traditionally conceived] 'core curriculum' and for testing of basic competencies, were aired to see what kind of support or opposition they met and whether it would be politically wise to modify them in some way, or whether clarification of one kind or another would be helpful in getting support for them.

To be fair to the DES officials, it might well be argued that they worked in the interests of their political masters, for the Education Debate had unquestionably been initiated by James Callaghan to allay growing public alarm that the comprehensive schools were responsible for a decline in educational standards. The original political initiative, then, itself ensured a conservative focus within the Debate, for it now had to be shown that by the most conventional criteria the comprehensive schools were effective, or could be made to be effective. The issues of the purposes of the comprehensive school and the relevance or appropriateness of its curriculum and examinations had thereby to be excluded. Because the Prime Minister was cast in a defensive mode, so too were the Ministers of Education and the DES, and the status quo had to be reaffirmed. The lost opportunity to discuss and debate the nature and future of the comprehensive school should, in the light of these matters, be seen as the direct responsibility of the Prime Minister, not of the DES.

Yet even if one takes this charitable view, I remain quite unconvinced that the DES wishes to see any fundamental debate about the comprehensive school and its curriculum. It is difficult not to believe that the DES would like to gain more control over the curriculum and to exercise that control conservatively. The discussion of the 'core curriculum' has tended to reinforce traditional conceptions of the secondary-school curriculum and the proposal to have a common examination at sixteen-plus in place of the present dual system of the GCE 'O' level and the CSE, whilst sensible on several grounds, will surely have the effect of bending the examination to the rather more traditional, academic GCE forms, at the expense of the broader syllabuses and more flexible types of assessment (for example, Mode 3) of the CSE. And the discussion of the 'rationalization' of the various examination boards to five or six regional boards will act as a further pressure towards a uniformity of approach which is closer to the GCE forms. In such a situation the DES could exercise greater influence upon the examination boards, and since the boards are the most powerful single constraint on the curriculum and its assessment for children in the 14–16 age-group, the DES can thereby exercise an enormous, if indirect, influence upon the secondary-school curriculum, and upon the accountability of schools through public examinations. Accountability is a fashionable concept and the DES has everything to gain from such an imprecise, complex and nebulous term. Accountability to the parents of children in school is not ignored, but it is difficult to achieve in practice. It is patently obvious that there is a deep contradiction in accountability to parents and the local authority, on the one hand, and central planning and co-ordination of education through the DES, on the other. It must be an irresistible temptation for ministers and DES officials to strengthen their own hand by arrogating to themselves the right to interpret what 'public opinion' is demanding in terms of the accountability of schools and teachers and then to set the grounds and the means by which schools are to be held accountable. It is easy to slide into an excessively conspiratorial view of the DES and its intentions and workings; but it would be recklessly naive for any reformer who seeks to change some of the basic assumptions of the status quo to think that the DES is likely to be a supportive ally. The events of the last decade or so suggest quite clearly that an aspirant reformer must, at the very least, be capable of enlisting the committed and voluble support of those influential groups who in the final analysis constitute the 'public opinion' to which ministers and civil servants may then be responsive.

Among such influential groups can be listed school inspectors, educationists, parents, local education authorities, employers and headteachers. None of these groups is at present likely to be a natural spearhead to the kinds of reform that I have proposed. Her Majesty's Inspectors are without question one of the most able and experienced groups of men and women in the whole field of education. Some of them would be in sympathy with many of the ideas in this book. But they are a divided group and it is not part of their traditional role to make a fundamental reappraisal of a whole educational sector, such as secondary education. Their recent publications have tended to be cautious and fairly conventional, though there are hints of more radical views here and there. They, too, are constrained by the political climate of the times and seem to enjoy relatively little power and prestige within the DES, unless their findings and recommendations are in line with established policies and priorities. In any event there are signs that the Inspectors are returning, perhaps rightly, to an inspectorial rather than advisory role. Local chief education officers constitute a second group of able and powerful people, but they also are limited in the degree to which they can engineer fundamental changes. They are constrained, on the one hand, by local party politicians who are usually, but by no means always, in line with national party politics and, on the other hand, by the broader national setting in which the local authority is embedded. On their own, chief education officers can do nothing of consequence to change the secondary-school curriculum or sixteen-plus examinations.

Academic educationists and those involved in teacher education, that substantial body of lecturers in colleges and university departments of education, are well known for views which are, relative to those of the teaching profession, distinctly radical. (We should not forget, though, that the most radical ideas and criticisms have come from figures such as Raymond Williams and Ivan Illich rather than from education lecturers.) Indeed, it is precisely on these grounds of excessive radicalism that the teachers have objected to the educationists. The common complaint of teachers that the educationists are recruited from among failed teachers is, in my experience, almost always ill-founded. Colleges and universities would hardly be so very foolish. It is true, however, that education lecturers had often become rather bored with school-teaching and chose teacher education because it is one of the very few fields with interesting and challenging work to which an experienced teacher can aspire. It is also true that the lecturers were often critical of school whilst they were full-time schoolteachers – that was part of their dissatisfaction with the job – and once in a college or university that critical appetite is readily fed. The charge I would bring against educationists is much more serious than any of those that are commonly voiced. It is that they have failed to feed their critical insights and enthusiasm for reform back to experienced teachers. Instead, they have relied heavily on a short-term strategy of converting each new generation of student teachers to their views on the assumption that in the longer term this would influence the whole teaching profession. It has, of course, been a mis- guided philosophy. Its effect has often been to alienate many ordinary teachers who have come to see educationists as ivory-tower figures who are 'out of touch' with the realities of schools; and since student teachers must, in order to survive, adapt to schools as they are during the first full-time teaching post, they too tend to become disenchanted with the views of their former tutors. If educationists continue to address most of their reforming efforts – and most of their books – to an audience of student teachers, they cannot hope to influence the teaching profession in any depth or with any speed.

Many employers have little interest in the education system and are sometimes surprisingly ignorant about it. In recent years some have snatched at every opportunity to attack teachers for failing to produce pupils who are ready for the world of work. There is some substance to this claim, and certainly in many comprehensive schools the concept of vocational education has fallen into disrepute. Some of the criticisms, however, are ill-founded and one- sided. Charges about declining educational standards do not bear much weight when it is known that some employers assess young candidates for jobs on the basis of extremely old-fashioned tests which simply do not reflect current teaching in schools and, more to the point, the very skills which will be needed at work. Schools are a convenient scapegoat on which to unload the contemporary ills of British industry, but the fact remains that too few employers show any genuine anxiety to take very much responsibility for the education and job training of the young worker. In a period of educational expansion the employers slid into 'credentialism' by using sixteen-plus examination results as the selective device for recruiting young employees. Today there are still many employers who, when trying to fill a vacancy of any description for a young school-leaver, will eliminate all candidates who do not possess at least five 'O' levels. As I pointed out earlier, many large companies are now realizing the fatuity of this recruitment technique. As such employers learn that more careful selection, using more broadly based and less academic criteria, creates better predictors of job satisfaction and successful job performance, they naturally become much more disenchanted with sixteen-plus examination results. Once these facts become more widely known, and once young people and their parents learn that employers are not so impressed as they used to be by public-examination results, parents can begin to question the purposes of school-work and public examinations as they relate to the world of work. The employers, then, may make an important if indirect contribution to the debate about the relation between education and society and at the same time perhaps even initiate a more fruitful dialogue between education and industry.

Parents are potentially a most powerful group, at least if we take the optimistic view that they might create public opinion directly rather than merely reflecting it as a consequence of the impact of influential opinion-makers. The more pessimistic view that parents would need to be persuaded is surely more realistic, for the simple reason that fundamental reform would be seen by most individual parents as threatening to the interests of their children. Many parents have real insight into the rat-race for the so-called qualifications of examination results but naturally feel locked into a situation that is not of their making and in which they must fight for the best they can for their child in the struggle for entry into an occupation or higher education. Many are nervous about broadening the curriculum. And there are always enough parents for whom 'examinations as qualifications' is so effective an appeal to make them fear change, and among these the more vocal middle classes appear in disproportionate numbers.

Finally we come to the headteachers. Collectively they represent a large and powerful group. Yet they are deeply divided among themselves. It is quite natural that many of them should approve of the status quo, for a degree of conformity to it was perhaps necessarily involved in their promotion to a headship in the first place. It would be very odd if it were not so. Although I have met many individual headteachers with very deep reservations about the directions in which comprehensive schools and the examination system are moving, there are many reasons why it would be unrealistic to expect radical reform from headteachers. They cannot, of course, opt for a 'go-it-alone' strategy. Any single headteacher who ruthlessly adopted the proposals in this book by broadening the curriculum and by refusing to enter pupils for public examinations (for that is all he could do alone) would rightly be subject to the sharpest censure, for his action would do much to penalize his pupils and do nothing to reform the wider system. We noted earlier that Her Majesty's Inspectors have been critical of the undue emphasis that some secondary schools place upon public examinations, but it must be said in the defence of headteachers that this emphasis is often a direct reflection of parental demands, which are difficult to resist. Many headteachers are only too conscious of the narrowing effect of public examinations, but feel powerless to propose any alternative. Headteachers have in any case learned the lesson of the Risinghill and Tyndale 'scandals': it is extremely dangerous for a single school to be too different. Moreover in recent years headteachers have had to cope with the enormous problems of re-organization, and more recently with falling rolls and reduced resources. In many of the larger comprehensive schools they have also faced the unenviable task of creating a relatively smooth bureaucratic functioning of the school. Headteachers might perhaps *follow* a move towards more fundamental reform, but they are not likely as a group to lead it. Indeed, it can be argued that headteachers' collective powers and potential have been considerably reduced in recent years. As schools become more accountable, they tend to be compared with one another, for example in examination results' league tables. This must inevitably engender a competitive relationship between headteachers as each one fights to defend himself or herself and the school for which he or she is responsible, and the competitive struggle is exacerbated where schools have been affected by falling rolls and greater parental choice of school. This is hardly a climate in which one can expect headteachers to work towards becoming a corporate pressure group, though there are a few signs that some headteachers are beginning to see that if they are divided they will be ruled by others. It is surely only by collective action that headteachers can today exercise any deep or lasting influence. All the great individual headteachers are dead. They could exist in the public schools of the last century for then both the central and local controls and constraints were weak. Today there are too many constraints to permit the emergence of an innovator such as Arnold. The tragedy is that now the embryonic innovative headteachers have never been greater in number, but never have they been more effectively stifled.

And so we come back full circle to the secondary-school teachers themselves. Apart from the parents, they are by far the largest group I have considered. Yet their outlook and occupational culture is not conducive to the reforms I have outlined. Moreover, their collective capacities are distressingly weak. I have already noted the weakness among teachers at collaboration within the school. The culture of individualism is by no means confined to pupils; there is a parallel culture of individualism among teachers. At the school level this is often actively encouraged by the headteacher, for it strengthens his powers and weakens conflict and opposition. On this view it is the headteacher's job to determine general school policy (in consultation with the school governors); it is the teachers' job to come into line with that policy but to enjoy a high degree of professional autonomy in the classroom. If a teacher dissents, he or she must do so without active disruption or must leave. Clearly if teachers in a school had well-developed corporate capacities, their opposition would gain in power and be highly threatening to the head-teacher who sometimes defines his role as the ultimate policy-maker. Yet many teachers are by no means discontent with the traditional allocation of roles. Such teachers are satisfied with classroom autonomy in exchange for the head taking full responsibility, the praise as well as blame, for school policy. In its ultimate expression, this culture of individualism among teachers produces a teacher who restricts his role very sharply to what he does within the privacy of the classroom. The general direction and determination of educational policy, both within the school and in society, is someone else's business: he is simply a teacher doing his job. 'Who am I,' he will say, 'to determine what kind of society we should have and what kind of education should be created to realize that society?' Such an attitude is, of course, a denial of professional responsibility. It is a self-defence which neutralizes the inherently political nature of education. At first sight the teacher might be humbly refusing to arrogate to himself the rights to determine the shape of education and society. In reality it is a refusal to recognize that in his present work he is inevitably contributing to a certain kind of society and to an educational system which helps to create and sustain it. If only the political aspects of education could be so readily disavowed, how much easier the lot of the teacher would be. In reality the attempt to hide behind this apolitical mask is a fraud. By depoliticizing their work, the teachers make their task more, not less, difficult for they are thus prevented from developing an explicit philosophy of the relation between education and society.

Yet the teachers do have a collective voice – in their unions and professional associations. In the middle of the last century the architects of mass schooling were a small elite who had to design a teaching force as well as schools and a curriculum. It was widely feared that the new elementary-school teachers would develop professional aspirations and seek to rise above the lowly station in life which had been planned for them. These fears have proved to be well-founded. It has been part of my thesis that a hundred years after the introduction of mass schooling we face a new crisis in the relation between education and society. The nineteenth-century education designs were in many respects very effective. Elementary schools were made to provide basic literacy and numeracy for the working classes, who also had to be rescued from the 'immorality' of industrial towns and cities packed with the 'indisciplined' immigrants from rural communities. In the 1860s the Clarendon and Taunton Commissions extended this bold social engineering to the public schools and grammar schools and their organization and curricula. In designing new plans to face the new challenges upon the comprehensive school and its curriculum, the teaching profession can no longer be so easily ignored or be treated by powerful elites as a necessary group who are part of someone else's design. The teachers are now a large body of some half million men and women and they represent a substantial section of the most highly educated members of society. The teachers will continue to be part of any future plans, of course, but now they must participate in the designing as well as the execution of such plans. The teachers' unions seem the most obvious agency for such a role. Indeed, it can be argued that, in default of leadership from other groups, it is the teachers themselves who must play the principal role. A superficial analysis of the teachers' unions suggests, however, that the profession is far from ready to adopt such a significant and demanding role. The vast majority of teachers show little interest in and have no more than minimal commitment to their unions. It must be conceded at once that most teachers join a union for cynical and self-centred motives: in the first place to obtain insurance and in the second in the hope that union activities will improve teachers' pay and conditions of service. This reaction to the unions stems in part from teachers' ambivalence about their professional status. Many teacher union members remain overtly hostile to unionization and in particular to the use of industrial action. In part it is also a reflection of the 'culture of individualism' among teachers which breeds a suspicion of collective action. As long as so many teachers think of themselves as autonomous classroom prima donnas, the capacity of the unions to reach common agreements and to act as the collective voice of the profession will remain undeveloped.

The hand of history lies heavily upon the teachers'

unions and explains why there is not a single union for all schoolteachers. The sex of the teacher has traditionally been one of the most divisive forces, though today it is less strong than in the past. We had separate unions for the Assistant Masters and the Assistant Mistresses, and when the National Union of Teachers (NUT) was opposed to equal pay, the National Union of Women Teachers formed a new splinter group. As soon as the NUT accepted the principle of equal pay, the most reactionary men formed the new union of the National Association of Schoolmasters. Division by status and social class has been common. Headteachers have tended to form their own union (the National Association of Headteachers, the Secondary Heads Association), and the 'Joint Four' (significantly calling themselves associations rather than unions) represented the more middle-class grammar-school tradition, while the NUT has had a stronger working-class link with the elementary schools and the secondary-modern schools. There are even divisions by educational sector, with the NUT covering most primary-school teachers, the Joint Four the secondary schools, and yet further groups (Association of Teachers in Technical Institutions, the National Association of Teachers in Further and Higher Educations, the Association of University Teachers) to represent teachers in further and higher education. Even 'outside' unions, such as ASTMS, have from time to time recruited members from among teachers. One group, the Professional Association of Teachers, has a strong conservative 'anti-union' orientation and perhaps constitutes a reaction against the overtly left-wing philosophy of the 'Rank and File' group within the NUT.

The NUT, with some quarter of a million members, is the numerical leader among the unions. It is clearly ambitious to become the single union to represent teachers and seems to have adopted the strategy of realizing those ambitions by acting as if it really were the only teacher union. In so doing, it arouses the hostility of the other, smaller unions, who feel threatened by what they see as the arrogance of the NUT. It is thus not uncommon to find officials of the NUT engaging with the officials of other unions in pettily abusive and mutually recriminating letters in the correspondence columns of the national newspapers. The effect, of course, is to confirm teachers in their cynical attitudes to the unions and to convince the public that teachers are the small-minded dogmatists of the popular stereotype. The NUT faces a further problem. As it grows in size, its members become more heterogeneous, making it more difficult for the union to represent and consolidate different sectional interests and highly divergent attitudes. The natural tendency is therefore to avoid the most controversial issues, even when they are of central significance for the future of education. Caution and compromise become the mark of union attitudes to many of the issues raised in this book; the union tends to become known (and this is not by any means a very accurate picture of the union's work) for its stance on the one issue on which almost all teachers agree – the need for increased resources (including teacher pay) for education. It is argued by some that a General Council for teachers would transcend these problems. There may be merits in such a proposal, but it is ridiculous to think that in some magical way the problems currently faced by the NUT would thereby vanish overnight.

The teacher unions, then, are potentially capable of considerable leadership in educational reform, and some of their activities reflect that potential. Yet the active participation of teachers is at a rather low level. Perhaps we should rely on smaller pressure groups among teachers.[6] Many of these, such as the National Association of Teachers of English, or the Science Teachers Association, are far too closely tied to particular subjects to be able to exert pressure for more general reform, and the same limitation applies to some other pressure groups, such as CASE or STOP, which may have been very successful in their own terms but are restricted to a particular reform, such as the abolition of physical punishment in schools. One very promising pressure group, PRISE, has frankly been too small to exercise influence on the appropriate scale. Other groups have taken highly explicit party political positions and they immediately alienate the majority of teachers who prefer to keep party politics out of education and/or who themselves lack party political affiliations and commitments. Indeed, one of the major problems of expecting teachers to take a lead in educational reform is that the task *is* a political one, and reformers need to politicize the 'middle ground' among teachers who eschew party politics.

The teaching profession is no more likely than the other groups we have considered to fight for the educational reforms that I have proposed. Those who now believe in the value and necessity of the reforms are small; it would be difficult for them to convince other teachers; and there are many obstacles in the way of mobilizing the profession as a whole to exert pressure on those other agencies who are essential to the implementation of reform. It is hard to avoid reaching the pessimistic conclusion that the prospects of teacher-led reform are distinctly gloomy and that our recent history of drift, that is of piecemeal reform of a limited and often inconsistent and short-sighted kind initiated by central government and the DES in partial response to what is taken to be politically expedient and to what is held to be public opinion, is likely to continue for the foreseeable future. If that happens more and more contradictory demands will be made upon the teaching professions as the politicians move from crisis to crisis. The teachers who are already in a highly demoralized condition will be subjected to yet more criticism and to higher expectations.

It is from this 'scenario' that I draw a little comfort and see a glimmer of hope. Teachers are aware that the many changes made in secondary education over the last two decades, when combined with the effects of profound social changes in society, have made the job of teaching much more difficult and onerous than it used to be. Yet teachers are also aware that the work of many other groups has during the same period become easier and more satisfying. Part of the reason for this is that so many of the educational reforms have been made in the *pupils'* interests, which in itself is a most commendable element of educational reform and change. But very little account has been taken of the costs of these changes on teachers; and these costs have often been very heavy. Teachers do not normally expect to receive much gratitude or acclaim for having shouldered these additional burdens and among the teachers I know there is still a strong sense of self-sacrifice and vocational duty to young people. At the same time it is intolerable that on those rare occasions when an educational reform is designed to be of direct benefit to the teachers themselves, as when the James Report recommended that teachers should have a contractual right to regular sabbatical leave, the reform is very quickly 'shelved'.[7] After the upheavals of the last twenty years many teachers would dearly like a quiet period of consolidation, but most know only too well that this will not be provided. On the contrary, yet more changes are likely to come, and many of these – such as the effects of increasing youth unemployment, the need for more education for leisure, the demands for greater accountability from schools – will bring yet further problems and burdens for teachers.

This is the major crisis for the teaching profession. Are they to remain the relatively passive and acquiescent body of men and women on whom yet further challenges and problems are to be unloaded? Or must they now take a stronger initiative in participating in the design of future reform from motives of self-protection? I detect signs of this second response and it may well be led by those who already espouse many of the ideas contained in this book. I must emphasize that it is this group which is most determined to make the experience of schooling a more rewarding one for teachers as well as pupils. They believe in community schools and the presence of adults in classrooms because by that means many of the traditional and increasing 'discipline' problems might be alleviated. When the teacher is not the only adult in the classroom, when some of the 'pupils' are highly motivated adults, then the classroom climate can be transformed. They are willing to experiment with team-teaching because this approach permits teachers to give up the pretence that every single teacher is a 'superman' who is highly skilled at everything a teacher is called upon to do, and instead teachers can develop and exercise their particular strengths without having to worry too much about their weaknesses because they are complemented by different strengths and weaknesses of other members of the teaching team. They enjoy integrated studies because then they do not have to be expert teachers of subjects all the time but can instead become learners who profit from the expertise of colleagues and the pupils. They promote a broader curriculum with more community studies and the expressive arts at the centre because they, like their pupils, need more community skills and a better preparation for leisure, for they, like many other groups, will have an increasingly shorter working life. It is these teachers who know that it is meaningless to talk of 'education for unemployment'; that concept can have meaning only if the basic curriculum is generally orientated to a general provision, for all pupils, all adults, and the teachers themselves, of ways in which increased leisure and reduced working time can be creatively used to enhance everyone's quality of life. If the teaching profession can come to believe that the educational reforms are needed in everyone's interests, and that their nature must from now on be determined by their capacity to enhance both the pupils' *and* the teachers' lives, then there is a real chance that the teaching profession will take a more active role in determining the shape of the relationship between education and society as we move towards the unpredictable twenty-first century.

It will be no easy task. Almost certainly it will have to be achieved through the teacher unions. This means that sectional differences, grounded in the complex history of the profession, must be overcome to permit the co-ordination of teachers into a single union, the NUT. Teacher participation in the union will need to increase dramatically, not merely because the leaders of the smaller unions may be the most resistant to unification, but because great pressure and concerted action will be required to drive the necessary reforms to the centre of union policy and activity. And the increased participation must be at both national and local levels. It also means that teachers will have to acquire a set of skills which the vast majority of them now lack – political skills. They will have to educate and persuade 'public opinion' and this will entail a new relationship with parents. Traditionally teachers look at their relations with parents in terms of enlisting their support and co-operation so that the child will become a more responsive pupil in school. Now they will need to explain in detail the problems experienced by teachers, the need for the new educational reforms in the interests of all children, and the means by which parents can help to generate reform. Teachers will also have to learn to use the mass media – television, radio, newspapers and magazines – to propagate their ideas. This seems to be a very romantic aim until we remember the success with which a single teacher, Dr Rhodes Boyson, has used the media to broadcast his concerns and ideas. Many teachers do not agree with his views, but they should admire (and emulate) the skill with which he has influenced public opinion, and through that, political policy-making.

It also means that teachers will have to form effective pressure groups to exert influence directly on politicians at the national and local levels. This is an arena in which the vast majority of teachers have no experience, and they must learn quickly. (Experienced union officials will have much to teach them here.) Most teachers, I suspect, will not view this task of winning friends and influencing people with any enthusiasm. Unless it is a sophisticated 'pincer' strategy directed at parents and politicians, there is little hope of success. But, if they refuse this role, then the alternative is quite clear: they will continue to be told what to do, the message will be critical and contradictory, and they will be forced back yet further into a defensive and burdensome position. If that happens, the growth and development of the comprehensive school will be stunted. The 1980s ought to be a period in which the comprehensive school passes beyond the 're-organization' or administrative and structural phase and so embarks upon the difficult task of creating a comprehensive curriculum which is consonant with the earliest ideals of comprehensive education: the provision of an education which meets the full range of needs and talents of all children and the needs of the twenty-first century in which they will become mature adults. The teaching profession does have the power to influence the changing relationship between education and society and to do so through the secondary-school curriculum. Many forces will be marshalled against the teachers. Whether or not their potential powers are exercised with courage and conviction depends upon the teachers themselves. The challenge for the comprehensive school is the challenge for the teachers and it is the critical test of their professionalism.

Notes

General note

As suggested in the preface, this book is directed towards a general rather than the conventional academic readership, so I have tried to avoid cluttering the main text with references. Some of the ideas dealt with in this book I have already presented to a more academic audience and the following papers often contain more detailed academic references for my argument.

'The two curricula and the community', *Westminster Studies in Education*, vol. 1, 1978, pp.31–41.
'What teaching does to teachers', *New Society*, vol.43, no.805, March 1978, pp.540–2.
'Power and the paracurriculum' in C. Richards (ed.), *Power and the Curriculum*, Nafferton Books, 1978.
'Durkheim, deviance and education' in L. Barton and R. Meighan (eds), *Schools, Pupils and Deviance*, Nafferton Books, 1979.
'The occupational culture of teachers' in P. Woods (ed.), *Teacher Strategies*, Croom Helm, 1980.
'A sociological critique of individualism', *British Journal of Educational Studies*, vol.28, no.3, 1980, pp.187–98.
'Social class, the curriculum and the low achiever' in E.C. Raybould, B. Roberts and K. Wedell (eds), *Helping the Low Achiever in the Secondary School*, Educational Review Occasional Publications no.7, 1980, pp.29–40.

1   The two curricula of schooling

1   J. Common, *Kiddar's Luck*, Turnstile Press, 1951.
2   K. Fogelman (ed.), *Britain's Sixteen-Year-Olds*, National Children's Bureau, 1978.
3   This and the following extract are taken from J. Holt, *How Children Fail*, Penguin, 1964.

4   School of Barbiana, *Letter to a Teacher*, Penguin, 1970.
5   This and the following extract are taken from J. Henry, *Culture against Man*, Penguin, 1963.
6   I. Illich, *Deschooling Society*, Penguin, 1971.
7   See, for example: T.B. Bottomore, *Classes in Modern Society*, Allen & Unwin, 1965; A. Giddens, *The Class Structure of the Advanced Societies*, Hutchinson, 1973; R. Dahrendorf, *Class and Class Conflict in Industrial Society*, Routledge & Kegan Paul, 1959; I.C. Jarvie, *Concepts and Society*, Routledge & Kegan Paul, 1972; E.P. Thompson, *The Making of the English Working Class*, Penguin, 1963; and for a rather different view, A. Marwick, *Class: Image and Reality*, Collins, 1980.
8   W. Waller, *The Sociology of Teaching*, Wiley, 1932.
9   This and the following extracts are taken from S. Bowles and H. Gintis, *Schooling in Capitalist America*, Routledge & Kegan Paul, 1976.
10 D.H. Hargreaves, *Social Relations in a Secondary School*, Routledge & Kegan Paul, 1967.
11 R. Sennett and J. Cobb, *The Hidden Injuries of Class*, Cambridge University Press, 1972.
12 P. Willis, *Learning to Labour*, Saxon House, 1977.
13 W.B. Miller, 'Lower class culture as a generating milieu of gang delinquency', *Journal of Social Issues*, vol.14, 1968, pp.5–19.

2   The decline of community

1   P. Cohen, 'Subcultural conflict and working class community', *Working Papers in Cultural Studies*, vol.2, 1972, pp.5–51 (published by the Centre for Contemporary Cultural Studies, University of Birmingham); reprinted in part in M. Hammersley and P. Woods (eds), *The Process of Schooling*, Routledge & Kegan Paul, 1976.
2   R. Roberts, *The Classic Slum*, Penguin, 1971; and *A Ragged Schooling*, Fontana, 1976.
3   Quoted in the *Observer* Colour Supplement, 11 March 1979.
4   This and the following extracts are taken from Cohen, op. cit.
5   Roberts, *The Classic Slum*.
6   P. Willis, *Learning to Labour*, Saxon House, 1977.
7   This and the following extracts are taken from H. Beynon, *Working for Ford*, E. P. Publishing, 1973.

3   Examinations and the curriculum

1   J. Henry, *Culture against Man*, Penguin, 1963.
2   S. Bowles and H. Gintis, *Schooling in Capitalist America*, Routledge & Kegan Paul, 1976.

3   In this section I am clearly working on the themes developed by the so-called 'new' sociology of education; see especially M.F.D. Young, *Knowledge and Control*, Collier-Macmillan, 1971.

4   R. Barker, *Education and Politics, 1900–1951*, Oxford University Press, 1972. See also M. Parkinson, *The Labour Party and the Organization of Secondary Education*, Routledge & Kegan Paul, 1970; and D. Rubenstein and B. Simon, *The Evolution of the Comprehensive School*, Routledge & Kegan Paul, 1969.

5   *Aspects of Secondary Education in England: a Survey by HM Inspectors of Schools*, HMSO, 1979.

6   *15 to 18* (the Crowther Report), HMSO, 1977.

7   G. Vulliamy, Culture clash and school music: a sociological analysis', in L. Barton and R. Meighan (eds), *Sociological Interpretations of Schooling and Classrooms: A Reappraisal*, Nafferton Books, 1978; and 'What counts as school music?' in G. Whitty and M.F.D. Young (eds), *Explorations in the Politics of School Knowledge*, Nafferton Books, 1976.

8   DES Statistical Bulletin, 6/80, 'The secondary school staffing survey', 1980.

9   W.B. Miller, 'Lower class culture as a generating milieu of gang delinquency', *Journal of Social Issues*, vol. 14, 1968, pp. 5–19.

10 H. Blumer, *Symbolic Interactionism: Perspective and Method*, Prentice-Hall, 1969.

11 D.V. Donnison, 'Education and opinion', *New Society*, vol.10, no.265, October 1967, pp.583–8.

12 See P. Woods, *The Divided School*, Routledge & Kegan Paul, 1979, ch.2; and 'The myth of subject choice', *British Journal of Sociology*, vol.27, 1976, pp.130–49.

13 For a useful discussion see J. Ford, *Social Class and the Comprehensive School*, Routledge & Kegan Paul, 1969.

14 For discussion and information on the proportion of working-class pupils in grammar schools, see F. Musgrove, *School and the Social Order*, Wiley, 1980; and A.H. Halsey, A.F. Heath and J.M. Ridge, *Origins and Destinations: Family Class and Education in Modern Britain*, Oxford University Press, 1980.

15 See Halsey, Heath and Ridge, op. cit.; and J.H. Goldthorpe, *Social Mobility and Class Structure in Modern Britain*, Oxford University Press, 1980.

16 P. Bourdieu, 'The school as a conservative force: scholastic and cultural inequalities' in J. Eggleston (ed.), *Contemporary Research in the Sociology of Education*, Methuen, 1974; and R. Dale *et al.* (eds), *Schooling and Capitalism*, Routledge & Kegan Paul, 1976.

17 It must be noted that Bourdieu's concept of cultural capital cannot be simply reduced to the cognitive-intellectual domain.

18 Bourdieu, op. cit.

19 Halsey, Heath and Ridge, op. cit.

20 P. Wilby, 'Towards a comprehensive curriculum' in H. Pluckrose and P. Wilby (eds), *The Condition of English Schooling*, Penguin,

1979. As will become clear in the main text, Wilby and I are in substantial agreement about the need for, and structure of, a comprehensive curriculum in the comprehensive school.

21 J. Common, *Kiddar's Luck*, Turnstile Press, 1951.

4 **The culture of individualism**

1 *Curriculum 11–16: working papers by HM Inspectorate: a contribution to current debate*, HMSO, 1977.

2 *The Times Educational Supplement*, 23 June 1978, p.6. Much the same sorts of criticism can be levelled against the later document, *A Framework for the School Curriculum*, DES, January 1980. I find myself in strong agreement with the withering comments of Max Morris (*The Times Educational Supplement*, 8 February 1980, pp.19–20) whose views are in a number of respects consonant with the ideas of this book.

3 Some recent work, M. Galton, B. Simon and P. Croll, *Inside the Primary Classroom*, Routledge & Kegan Paul, 1980, suggests that the Plowden Report had much less effect on classroom practice than has been commonly assumed.

4 I am not making a blanket condemnation of pastoral care, of course. For a useful account of some important achievements, see R. Best, C. Jarvis and P. Ribbins, *Perspectives on Pastoral Care*, Heinemann, 1980.

5 I find some empirical support for my argument in M. Rutter, B. Maughan, P. Mortimore, and J. Ousten, *Fifteen Thousand Hours*, Open Books, 1979.

6 An eloquent plea for a revitalization of the concept of fraternity is made in A.H. Halsey, *Change in British Society*, Oxford University Press, 1978. However, Halsey does not spell our the educational implications of Durkheim's emphasis on the corporate.

7 R. Morton-Williams and S. Finsh, *Schools Council Enquiry I: Young School Leavers*, HMSO, 1968.

8 Supportive evidence has been provided by C.J. Trees, 'Teachers' perceptions of their role in a comprehensive school', unpublished MEd dissertation, University of Manchester, 1979.

9 Some of the best writing on this theme has come from philosophers rather than sociologists. See, for example, M. Warnock, *Schools of Thought*, Faber, 1977; and J.P. White, 'Teacher accountability and school autonomy', *Proceedings of the Philosophy of Education Society in Great Britain*, vol.10, 1976.

10 D. Rubenstein and C. Stoneman, *Education for Democracy*, Penguin, 1970.

11 For a most interesting discussion on this and related themes, see G. Grace, *Teachers, Ideology and Control*, Routledge & Kegan Paul, 1978.

12 P.L. Berger, B. Berger and H. Kellner, *The Homeless Mind*, Penguin, 1973.
13 R. Roberts, *The Classic Slum*, Penguin, 1971.
14 Berger, Berger and Kellner, op. cit.
15 E. Durkheim, *Suicide*, Routledge & Kegan Paul, 1952.
16 P. Marsh, E. Rosser and R. Harré, *The Rules of Disorder*, Routledge & Kegan Paul, 1978; and R. Ingham *et al.*, *Football Hooliganism*, Inter-Action Inprint, 1978.
17 Reported in *Guardian*, 14 June 1980, p.3.
18 E. Durkheim, op. cit.
19 E. Durkheim, *The Division of Labour in Society*, Collier-Macmillan, 1933.
20 E. Durkheim, *Moral Education*, Free Press, 1961.
21 Ibid.
22 E. Durkheim, 'Individualism and the intellectuals' (trans. S. Lukes), *Political Studies*, vol.17, 1969, pp.14–33.
23 E. Durkheim, *Moral Education*, op. cit.

5 The curriculum and the community

1 There is a very extensive literature on this theme. Among the best-known sources are C. Fletcher and N. Thompson (eds), *Issues in Community Education*, Falmer Press, 1979; C. Poster, *The School and the Community*, Macmillan, 1971; E. Midwinter, *Education and the Community*, Allen & Unwin, 1975; J. Boyd, *Community Education and Urban Schools*, Longman, 1977, E. Midwinter, *Patterns of Community Education*, Ward Lock, 1973; P. Jones, *Community Education in Practice – A Review*, Social Evaluation Unit, Oxford, 1978; G. Smith, *Community Schools*, Inspectorate Bulletin Occasional Paper no. 4, DES, 1974; J.K.P. Watson, 'Community education – prospects for the 1980s', *New Era*, vol.61, 1980; A.N. Fairbairn, *The Leicestershire Plan*, Heinemann, 1980. There are various sources for ideas on community studies in the curriculum, both in books (for example, C. and M. Ball, *Education for a Change: Community Action and the School*, Penguin, 1973; R. White and D. Brockington, *In and Out of School: The ROSLA Community Education Project*, Routledge & Kegan Paul, 1978; R. White, *Absent with Cause: Lessons of Truancy*, Routledge & Kegan Paul, 1980) and in articles in the popular educational press (for example, R. Housden, 'Adventures in the neighbourhood', *The Times Educational Supplement*, 6 June 1980).
2 H. Rée, *Educator Extraordinary: The Life and Achievement of Henry Morris, 1889–1961*, Longman, 1973.
3 *A New Partnership for our Schools* (the Taylor Report), HMSO, 1977.
4 E. Midwinter, *Education and the Community*.

5   P. Woods, *The Divided School*, Routledge & Kegan Paul, 1979.

6   G.H. Bantock, 'Towards a theory of popular education', *The Times Educational Supplement*, 12 and 19 March 1971, and reprinted in R. Hooper (ed.), *The Curriculum: Context, Design and Development*, Oliver & Boyd, 1971.

7   A.H. Halsey (ed.), *Educational Priority*, vol.1, HMSO, 1972.

8   J. Watts (ed.), *The Countesthorpe Experience*, Allen & Unwin, 1977.

9   H. Judge, *School is Not Yet Dead*, Longman, 1974. Mr Robert Aitken, the Chief Education Officer for Coventry, has also called for the abolition of sixteen-plus examinations to break the academic stranglehold on the secondary-school curriculum. *The Times Educational Supplement*, 4 July 1980.

10   G.H. Bantock, *Dilemmas of the Curriculum*, Martin Robertson, 1980. An excellent antidote to Bantock is D. Lawton, *Class, Culture and the Curriculum*, Routledge & Kegan Paul, 1975.

11   Quoted in Rée, op. cit.

12   E. Burke, *Reflections on the Revolution in France*, Penguin, 1969.

13   J. Dewey, *Democracy and Education*, Free Press, 1916.

14   Ibid.

15   'Education in the unions', *Radical Education*, vol.11, 1978, pp.22-3.

16   J. Seabrook, *What Went Wrong?* Gollancz, 1978.

17   For an incisive, if one-sided, account of the abuse of the concept of 'the national interest' see, 'Sir, writing by candle-light . . . ' in E.P. Thompson,*Writing by candlelight*, Merlin, 1980.

18   G. Barnfield, *Creative Drama in Schools*, Macmillan, 1968.

19   D. Self, *A Practical Guide to Drama in the Secondary School*, Ward Lock, 1975.

20   B. Way, *Development through Drama*, Longman, 1967.

21   This and the following quotation are taken from the DES, *Drama: Education Survey no.2*, HMSO, 1968.

22   R. Williams, *The Long Revolution*, Penguin, 1961.

6   **A proposal and some objections**

1   K.R. Popper, *The Open Society and its Enemies*, vol.1, Routledge & Kegan Paul, 1945.

2   F. Musgrove, *School and the Social Order*, Wiley, 1980.

3   For an excellent review of the *Black Paper* attacks and claims in this and other respects, see N. Wright, *Progress in Education: A Review of Schooling in England and Wales*, Croom Helm, 1977.

4   This and the following quotation are taken from A. Stevens, *Clever Children in Comprehensive Schools*, Penguin, 1980.

5   Quoted in L. Strachey, *Eminent Victorians*, Penguin, 1918.

6   H. Rée, *The Times Educational Supplement*, 11 January 1980, pp.17-18. Note also a completely different view expressed on

another page in the same issue by Professor E. Hawkins.

7 R. Dore, *The Diploma Disease: Education. Qualification and Development*, Allen & Unwin, 1976.

8 Ibid. Dore's stimulating work might today be read in conjunction with some interesting experiments taking place in Australia. See Peter Newell, 'Going the non-competitive way', *The Times Educational Supplement*, 7 March 1980, pp. 22-3.

9 J.H. Goldthorpe, *Social Mobility and Class Structure in Modern Britain*, Oxford University Press, 1980.

10 See also some related ideas in A.H. Halsey, 'Democracy for education?' *New Society*, 24 April 1981.

7 The culture of teaching

1 P. Blackie, 'Not quite proper', *The Times Educational Supplement*, 25 November 1977.

2 S. Hilsum and K.B. Start, *Promotion and Careers in Teaching*, NFER, 1974.

3 E.C. Hughes, *The Sociological Eye: Collected Papers*, Aldine, 1965.

4 P.W. Jackson, *Life in Classrooms*, Holt, Rinehart & Winston, 1968.

5 W. Waller, *The Sociology of Teaching*, Wiley, 1932.

6 D.C. Lortie, *Schoolteacher*, University of Chicago Press, 1975.

7 P. Woods, *The Divided School*, Routledge & Kegan Paul, 1979. Chapter 9 gives an excellent account of the consolatory functions of humour in the staffroom.

8 A few local education authorities are now offering teachers opportunities for 'horizontal mobility', that is moving to a different school at the same salary and status level. This should be encouraged between authorities too, since in this case a teacher who seeks to change job without promotion is usually regarded with great suspicion.

8 Teachers and the future

1 R. Williams, *The Long Revolution*, Penguin, 1961.

2 Q. Hoare, 'Education: programmes or men', *New Left Review*, vol.32, 1967 and reprinted in J. Beck, C. Jenks, N. Keddie and M.F.D. Young (eds), *Worlds Apart*, Collier-Macmillan, 1976.

3 See M. Kogan's *The Politics of Education*, Penguin, 1971. Some further books relevant to this section are M. Kogan, *The Politics of Educational Change*, Fontana, 1978; T. Becher and S. Maclure, *The Politics of Curriculum Change*, Hutchinson, 1978; R.A. Manzer, *Teachers and Politics: The Role of the NUT in the Making of National Educational Policy in England and Wales since 1944*, Manchester University Press, 1970; and T.D. Coates,

Teachers' Unions and Interest Group Politics, Cambridge University Press, 1972.

4   This OECD report was first published in *The Times Higher Educational Supplement*, 9 May 1976 and is reprinted in P. Raggatt and M. Evans (eds), *Urban Education 3: The Political Context*, Ward Lock, 1977. For two further strongly critical views of the DES see M. Morris, 'Ruling classes', *Guardian*, 1 July 1980, p.13; and D. Lawton, *The Politics of the School Curriculum*, Routledge & Kegan Paul, 1980. This is one of those rare occasions when Max Morris and a sociologist of education are found to be in close agreement. Some interesting observations on, and conceptualization of, these issues are to be found in R. Dale, 'The politicisation of school deviance: reactions to William Tyndale' in L. Barton and R. Meighan (eds), *Schools, Pupils and Deviance*, Nafferton, 1979.

5   W.A. Reid, *Thinking about the Curriculum*, Routledge & Kegan Paul, 1978.

6   On educational pressure groups, and some other issues raised in this chapter, see M. Locke, *Power and Politics in the School System: A Guidebook*, Routledge & Kegan Paul, 1974. See also note 3 above.

7   *Teacher Education and Training* (the James Report), HMSO, 1972.

Index